SAME PLANET,
DIFFERENT WORLDS

SAME PLANET, DIFFERENT WORLDS

UNMIK and the Ministry of Defence Police Chief Constables

JOHN DUNCANSON

MENIN HOUSE

Menin House is an imprint of
Tommies Guides Military Book Specialists

Gemini House
136-140 Old Shoreham Road
Brighton
BN3 7BD

www.tommiesguides.co.uk

First published in Great Britain by
Menin House Publishers 2015

ISBN 978-1-908336-75-0

Cover design by Vivian Foster@Bookscribe
Typeset by Vivian Foster@Bookscribe

Printed and bound in Great Britain

*This book is for the Ministry of Defence Police
constables whose professionalism, dedication and
commitment was tested and proven beyond doubt,
whilst seconded to the United Nations Interim
Administration Mission in Kosovo.*

JOHN DUNCANSON

Contents

"Morale is the capacity of a group of people to pull together persistently and consistently in pursuit of a common purpose."

Alexander H. Leighton

Acknowledgements

I OWE AN enormous debt of gratitude to the many people without whom I could not have contemplated the idea of writing this, my first and most probably my last, book.

My former MDP friends and colleagues have been a tremendous help in assisting me and reminding me of dates, people, places and situations; I'm exceedingly grateful to you.

I also want to thank my former MDP colleagues who made contributions to the book by supplying me with details of their own endeavours while working, at times, in a very arduous and hostile environment.

Alasdair (AJ) Stewart, Alex Robertson, Allan Barr, Alun Ferguson, the late great Billy Boyle, Calvin Tonks, Christian Linetty, Dave White, David McLean, Davy Rodden, Frank Granger, Geoff Heal, Glyn Wilson, Greig Henderson, Ian Barwick, Ian Drummond, Ian Gibson, Jim Gillen, Jim Moore, John Pearson, Jonathan Tyndall, Mark Cunningham, Martin Walsh, Reyburn Logie, Pat Kearney and Rob Foster.

I'd like to thank former UNMIK colleagues, KPS officers and close friends who gave me their support, guidance and assistance (during my three UN missions), especially during periods of time when I was under extreme pressure.

Alan Phillips, Aleksandar Markovic, Alice Holmes , Arsim Krasniqi, Amod Kumar, Andrey Yudin, Armin Muth, Biljana Djuric, Chuck Pagliuca, Daniel Chira, Dave King, David Carter, Davie Hutton, Ed Cottrell, Enriko Waldmann, Fehim Pantina, Felix Okediji, Flavius Crisan, Frank Becker, Gary Smith, Gene Ray, Guenter Rundel, Horst Decker, James Fern, Jan Ravnholt, Jocken Kehl, John Foreman MBE, John Powell, Kaiwan (Kevin) Abbassi, Larry Miller, Lebzo Mohammad, Lidija Vasic, Mark Hansingo, Marius Cristea, Mariyan Dimitrov, Mary Beth Lovett, Miljan (Kani) Radivojevic, Nils Brauer, Olga Stefanovic, Paul Okruhlik, Pavel Dergaiev, Ralf Ossarek, Randy Darty, Raymond Guthy, Roger Phillips, Sanjay Yenpure, Sakher Alfarah, Scott Brown, Serkan Serin, Stan Osterhoudt, Spyridon Varsamas, Stefanos (Steve) Michailidis, Sury Pras Niraula, Suzie Foreman, Thomas Owens, Thomas Wilfong, Van Williams, William Darko, Zoran Kurz.

Thanks to David Keefe, Jim Mcginley, Mariyan Dimitrov, The Kosovo Police and Someone's Sons for allowing me to use your photographs.

I'd specially like to thank retired colleague Sergeant Ray Tidswell (Ministry of Defence Police) who supplied me with invaluable information regarding the MDP and its history. At one point Ray was hospitalised; however, from his hospital bed Ray continued to assist me in my research.

Finally thank you to retired MDP Superintendent, good friend (and former UK2 Contingent Commander) Andy Kirkwood who, when others wanted to hang me out to dry, made the decision not to send me home after I fell foul of the MDP disciplinary code during my second mission. Andy, thank you for that second chance. You turned my life around.

If I missed you out, I'm sorry, I just forgot.

"Peacekeeping has proven to be one of the most effective tools available to the UN to assist host countries navigate the difficult path from conflict to peace.

Peacekeeping has unique strengths including legitimacy, burden sharing, and an ability to deploy and sustain troops and police from around the globe, integrating them with civilian peacekeepers to advance multi-dimensional mandates.

UN Peacekeepers provide security and the political and peace building support to help countries make the difficult, early transition from conflict to peace.

UN Peacekeeping is guided by three basic principles:

* *Consent of the parties*
* *Impartiality*
* *Non-use of force except in self-defence and defence of the mandate*

Peacekeeping is flexible and over the past two decades has been deployed in many configurations. There are currently 16 UN peace operations deployed on four continents.

Today's multidimensional peacekeeping operations are called upon not only to maintain peace and security, but also to facilitate the political process, protect civilians, assist in the disarmament, demobilization and reintegration of former combatants; support the organization of elections, protect and promote human rights and assist in restoring the rule of law.

Success is never guaranteed, because UN Peacekeeping almost by definition goes to the most physically and politically difficult environments. However, we have built up a demonstrable record of success over our 60 years of existence, including winning the Nobel Peace Prize."

George Clooney – Actor and United Nations Messenger of Peace

Introduction

THE MINISTRY OF Defence Police (MDP) is currently deployed at numerous defence locations around the United Kingdom. These include military establishments, defence housing estates, military training areas, the Atomic Weapons Establishment and the Royal dockyards.

I joined the MDP in April 1990 and was posted to the Royal Naval Armament Depot (RNAD) Coulport (in Argyll, Scotland); a storage and loading facility for the UK's stock of nuclear warheads.

After years of relative boredom and the humdrum repetitive role of plodding behind Coulport's protective security fences, an opportunity arose for its officers to temporarily rid themselves of the adopted tag 'glorified security guards' when volunteers were sought for a United Nations overseas peacekeeping deployment.

On 6 June 2000, after months of speculation and deliberation, the MDP incredibly deployed somewhere in the region of fifty-five officers to the United Nation Interim Administration Mission in Kosovo (UNMIK). The UN English speaking and non-ranking mission which required an armed international police presence, was the first of many of the MDP's overseas Kosovo secondments.

Kosovo was a former autonomous province within the Republic of Serbia, which itself is a former Socialist Federal Republic of Yugoslavia.

My initial thoughts on the deployment were of excitement then fear. The thought of having an opportunity to escape from Coulport's big cage to work (with the United Nations) in the outside world and in a foreign territory was immediately appealing. However, my excitement quickly turned to fear and apprehension.

In 1999 Kosovo had been at war, thousands of innocent people were killed and in 2000 people were still being killed and seriously injured. Angry mobs were fighting against UN military peacekeepers, the recently formed local police and the United Nations international police. Although I seriously thought about it, I decided not to volunteer for that first MDP deployment.

Gradually my curiosity got the better of me and I started to think again, and at times for pretty ridiculous reasons – no one would be around to tell me 'make sure you tidy up, and make the bed', or 'don't think you're going to the pub tonight', and 'that T-shirt needs ironing.'

After months of discussions, then arguments, my wife reluctantly succumbed to my persistent antagonistic outbursts; my sons, Jamie (17) and Stephen (13) did not get involved.

One year to the day after the first deployment and after completing three weeks intensive pre-deployment training I was on a plane with the second MDP UK2 contingent bound for Pristina International Airport, Kosovo. I would become an UNMIK international (civilian) police officer (CIVPOL), seconded by the UN to uphold law and order in the violent and dangerous post-war and ethnically divided territory of Kosovo. That mission was a gigantic step for the MDP and an enormous challenge, especially for its police constables and specifically those serving at RNAD Coulport; one nuclear guarding establishment which is certainly not known for its high crime statistics.

I was one of around fifty MDP officers (of various ranks) who travelled out to the south-eastern Balkan peninsular to relieve the first MDP contingent that deployed the previous year. At that time, secondments usually lasted twelve months, however, six month extensions were normally granted.

Police colleagues from the Royal Ulster Constabulary (RUC), today called Police Service Northern Ireland (PSNI), were already present in Kosovo (since 1999); although, by 2002 all but a few had returned home, ending the RUC's official commitment to Kosovo. I spent eight years working between Coulport and Kosovo and of those eight years, I spent a total of just under five (covering three UN missions) as a CIVPOL officer.

The process of governing Kosovo derived from the mandate of UNMIK International Police in accordance with the Security Council Resolution 1244 (1999). The mandate called for UNMIK to maintain civil law and order in Kosovo with executive police powers.

Armed police personnel from over fifty nations were deployed outside their own home authority to re-establish and uphold the law in Kosovo whilst training the new Kosovo Police Service (KPS). From the start of the UN mission (1999) the quantity of CIVPOL officers outweighed the quality, and the supervision and correcting of the less qualified officer exhausted the confidence and enthusiasm of other CIVPOL. And, disappointingly, small groups of CIVPOL seemed more interested in making large amounts of money than being part of UNMIK and mentors to the KPS.

On the other hand, the PSNI, MDP and the majority of other UNMIK police were held in very high regard as they displayed dedication, enthusiasm and commitment towards UNMIK and the KPS. One senior German officer said of the MDP, 'One MDP *constable* is worth multiple other CIVPOL.' A great compliment indeed.

Before long the MDP's devotion, professional knowledge and eagerness to contribute to the mission, collectively, proved to be a big asset.

It didn't take long before myself and many other MDP constables became managers, responsible for the supervision, welfare and administration of large and diverse groups of CIVPOL, including police officers of a much higher rank than those MDP constables. Some of those higher ranks found those circumstances a little unmerited and difficult to come to terms with. Other CIVPOL officers took mission life as an opportunity to do very little work and at times were a little uncooperative when working alongside the more conscientious *British Bobby* and his enthusiastic approach to his daily chores.

As police authority was gradually handed over to the KPS, many of those MDP constables (CIVPOL) became less involved in managing other CIVPOL and KPS when they became monitors, mentors and advisors to the KPS patrol officers, mid-level management and more senior ranks.

This book is about my ups and downs as a UN police officer, or CIVPOL, and along the way you will meet other MDP officers, also CIVPOL, who made large contributions to UNMIK and the training and monitoring of a very young and new Kosovo Police Service.

Incredibly, one MDP constable, through his position as Mitrovica Regional Commander (a region's highest position) featured in a top ITV police series presented by ex-footballer and actor Vinnie Jones.

The pressure of working away from home was enormous and to relieve tension the international community regularly frequented the busy and lively café bars and clubs dotted all over Kosovo. During social evenings new friendships were formed and several MDP officers formed new relationships which eventually led to marriage. I know of MDP officers who married UN Language Assistants and also Kosovo police officers.

Where I felt the need, and in order to protect a number of people's identity, I have changed a few names and altered a number of dates and locations.

Today Kosovo continues to be a volatile territory, ethnically divided and disputed by its ethnic Albanian majority (mainly) living in the south and its ethnic Serbian minority (mainly) living in the north. Although the ethnic Serbians living in Kosovo are a minority group, the majority live in the north of Kosovo.

The Background

I HAVE OPENED the book with relevant information, which without it may have you lost and confused. This information basically lays a foundation for my journey and helps you understand a very complicated situation.

I have included a reasonably short history of the Ministry of Defence Police, followed by a very short history of former Yugoslavia and its break up. I have also included facts and circumstances surrounding NATO's intervention in the Kosovo war and its reasons for bombing Yugoslavia.

Finally I have explained why it was necessary for the United Nations to create the United Nations Mission in Kosovo and how it contributed to the creation of a new Kosovo Police Service.

The original name for the 'Kosovo Police Service' (KPS), was chosen by UNMIK police commissioner, Sven Frederiksen and throughout most of the book I have used either the titles Kosovo Police Service or KPS. However, on 20 February 2008, not long after Kosovo declared independence, the Kosovo Police Service became officially known as the 'Kosovo Police'.

Throughout the book, and depending on the situation or circumstances, you will find Kosovo's population, my friends, colleagues and associates referred to by ethnicity or name. I have also used the common English alphabet to spell out Kosovo's towns and cities.

At times I have mentioned senior UK police officers by their rank. Other times I have used the terms cop and coppers as collective words for all police ranks. When specifically referring to the lowest UK police rank I have used the term police constable, PC or simply constable.

The Ministry of Defence Police

THE MINISTRY OF Defence Police is a civilian police force which is part of the United Kingdom's Ministry of Defence. The MDP are not Military Police and should not be confused with the Royal Military Police or any other Service Police. The MDP are based at numerous defence locations across the United Kingdom.

The force was originally formed in 1971 by the merger of three separate service constabularies: the Air Force Department Constabulary, the Army Department Constabulary and the Admiralty Constabulary. The force, which consists of two divisions, is headquartered at MDP HQ Wethersfield, Essex.

Although outwardly similar to other UK police forces, the MDP is significantly different in role, function and accountability. The MDP's primary responsibilities are to provide armed security and to counter terrorism, as well as uniformed policing and investigative services to Ministry of Defence property, personnel, and installations throughout the United Kingdom. MDP officers are attested as constables under the Ministry of Defence Police Act 1987 and are trained in the use of various weapon systems.

The force has a number of specialised departments and also provides officers for international policing secondments; including the active policing of conflict areas overseas and training of resident police forces in these areas.

FUNCTION
The MDP's primary responsibility is policing the Defence Estate throughout the UK, including armed front-line security at high security sites; it deals with both military personnel and civilians. The MDP's activities fall into five key areas:

- Armed security and counter-terrorism
- Uniformed policing
- Investigation of crime
- Defence community policing
- International policing

DEPLOYMENT

The MDP is currently deployed at numerous defence locations around the United Kingdom. These include military establishments, defence housing estates, military training areas, the royal dockyards and the Atomic Weapons Establishment. Since January 2008, the MDP has also taken on the role of providing armed security at four gas terminals in the UK, part of the Critical National Infrastructure.

THE ROYAL DOCKYARDS

The Royal Dockyards are:

- Rosyth Dockyard
- HMNB Devonport
- HMNB Portsmouth
- HMNB Clyde

HMNB Clyde encompasses Faslane Naval Base and RNAD Coulport.

JURISDICTION

MDP officers are attested as constables in one of the three jurisdictions of the UK: England and Wales, Northern Ireland and Scotland, but can exercise their powers on Ministry of Defence estates throughout the United Kingdom. MDP officers' jurisdiction relates to subject rather than geographic area. Officers are based throughout the UK and exercise their jurisdiction over matters relating to the Defence Estate; there is no requirement for them to be on Ministry of Defence land when doing so.

The MDP is classified as a special police force. This gives it conditional allowance to exercise the powers available to a constable of a territorial police force; if an offence or incident is encountered outside their natural jurisdiction. Additionally the MDP is able to provide officers and specialist units to territorial police forces on a mutual assistance basis.

MDP officers are also able to take on the powers of constables of territorial police forces or other special police forces (such as British Transport Police) in certain situations, as set out in the MDP Act. Whenever MDP officers exercise police powers under this 'extended jurisdiction', the MDP Chief Constable has a responsibility to ensure the local Chief Constable is notified as soon as possible.

UNIFORM

MDP officers are often employed on firearms duties and wear black jackets and trousers, or black polo-type shirts. Headdress depends on role, and is either the standard UK police chequered flat cap or police baseball cap. Ballistic body armour and a black Kevlar ballistic helmet can also be worn.

Officers on unarmed general police duties wear a uniform similar to that of territorial police forces. The tunic dress uniform worn by MDP officers is almost identical to that of the Metropolitan Police Service apart from the insignia. All officers are issued with personal body armour, PAVA incapacitation spray, baton and Hiatt Speedcuffs.

ARMAMENT

All MDP officers are trained to use firearms. Most officers are armed with the force weapon, the Heckler and Kock MP7. Some specialised units do use other weapon systems including Heckler and Kock MP5 and the less lethal weapons, Taser and Baton launcher.

VEHICLES

The MDP uses a variety of vehicles, from general patrol cars to specialised escort vehicles, police launches and off-road vehicles. In 2006 the force adopted the Battenburg system of retro-reflective markings for its new vehicles. This brings the MDP's fleet appearance in line with most other UK police forces.

SPECIAL CAPABILITIES

The MDP has a number of specialist units, including: Marine, Chemical, Biological, Radiological or Nuclear Response, Dog Sections, Special Escort Group, Criminal Investigation Department, Central Support Groups, Operational Support, Tactical Support and Defence Community police officers.

INTERNATIONAL POLICING

The MDP carries out a number of international policing activities, including the active policing of conflict areas overseas and training of resident police forces in these areas. In recent years the MDP have provided officers to police contingents in many locations around the world, including Bosnia, Kosovo, Iraq, Afghanistan, Sudan and Sierra Leone. The MDP also provided policing for the Pitcairn Islands from around 2000 until 2007.

POLICE PROTOCOLS WITH OTHER FORCES

Local agreements with territorial police forces are made under the overarching general protocols agreed between the MDP Chief Constable and other Chief Constables. These set out the agreed working relationship between the MDP and other police forces; outlining, where necessary, areas of responsibility and accountability. The Protocols make provision for consultation and co-operation between the forces, with the aim of delivering the best policing on the ground. The *Police and Fire Reform (Scotland) Act 2012*, created a merger with the original eight regional Scottish police forces, including Strathclyde police. During the 1990s, relationships between Strathclyde police and the MDP were a little strained to say the least.

Yugoslavia

THE NAME YUGOSLAVIA is familiar to many of us older generation; however, maybe some of you couldn't point to it on an old world map or name its former republics and provinces. It's also possible that people who were born after the Kosovo war in 1999 have no knowledge of former Yugoslavia.

So, although Yugoslavia was a net importer of raw materials – fuels, iron and steel products – I remember it more for its football team… yes indeed. I first heard of the country when the national football team played against Scotland in the 1974 FIFA World Cup finals. The match ended in a 1–1 draw and also ended Scotland's progress in the tournament. Yugoslavia was eventually eliminated in round two.

In 1992 Scotland and Yugoslavia both qualified for the UEFA European championships; however, due to the ongoing Yugoslav wars, the country was suspended from international competition as part of a United Nations sanction. That suspension paved the way for Denmark to enter the competition. Ironically the Danish team, who originally failed to qualify from Yugoslavia's qualifying group, went on to win that Championship. Yugoslavia had also been drawn as the top seeds in Group 5 of the European zone for the 1994 World Cup qualifying stages, and again they were barred from competing in a football tournament.

Yugoslavia formed a strip of land on the east coast of the Adriatic Sea that stretched southward and took up much of south-eastern Europe. It was a socialist state and a federation made up of six socialist republics: Bosnia and Herzegovina, Croatia, Macedonia, Montenegro, Serbia and Slovenia.

Serbia, in addition, included two autonomous provinces, Vojvodina and Kosovo, which after 1974 were largely equal to the other members of the federation.

The map on page 21 depicts the Socialist Federal Republic of Yugoslavia, its republics and two autonomous provinces, before its breakup. The smaller insert shows the rest of Europe with Yugoslavia highlighted.

The disintegration of Yugoslavia, a region with a history of ethnic conflict, occurred as a result of a series of political upheavals and conflicts during the early 1990s.

Wars in the former Yugoslavia, with the exception of Macedonia, were fought in the 1990s between the republics (that sought sovereignty) and the government in the capital Belgrade which wanted either to prevent the republic's independence or keep large parts of that territory under its control. Macedonia declared independence on 8 September 1991 without any protest or intervention from the Belgrade authorities.

The wars are generally considered to be a series of largely separate, but related, military conflicts which occurred during the dissolution of Yugoslavia and affected most of the former Yugoslav republics.

The wars between the republics and the Yugoslav government ended in various stages and mostly resulted in full international recognition of new sovereign territories, however, with massive economic disruption to the successor states:

>Croatian war (1991–1995)
>
>Slovenian war (1991–1991)
>
>Bosnian war (1992–1995)

Croatia and Slovenia gained independence in 1991, with Bosnia and Herzegovina following in 1992.

Serbia and Montenegro became one country, created from the two remaining republics of Yugoslavia. Together they established a federation in 1992, known as the Federal Republic of Yugoslavia.

In 2003, the Yugoslav federation was replaced in favour of a more decentralised state union named Serbia and Montenegro.

On 3 June 2006, the Montenegrin Parliament declared the independence of Montenegro, formally confirming the result of a referendum. Serbia did not object to the declaration.

This map depicts the countries (including the disputed Republic of Kosovo) of the ex-Republic of Yugoslavia after they declared independence.

THE KOSOVO WAR

The Kosovo War was an armed conflict in Kosovo that lasted from 28 February 1998 until 11 June 1999. The battle was fought by the forces (military and police) of the Federal Republic of Yugoslavia, the Kosovo Liberation Army (KLA) an ethnic Albanian paramilitary organisation, and the North Atlantic Treaty Organisation (NATO).

In the late Middle Ages, the Kosovo region stood at the heart of the Serbian empire, however, they lost to the Ottoman Turks in 1389 following Serbia's defeat in the Battle of Kosovo. By the time Serbia regained control of Kosovo from Turkey in 1913, there were few ethnic Serbians left in a region now led by ethnic Albanians.

In 1918, Kosovo officially became a province of Serbia, and it continued as such after communist leader and Yugoslav Prime Minister Josip Broz Tito established the Federal People's Republic of Yugoslavia in 1945.

Tito finally gave in to Kosovo's demands for greater autonomy, and after 1974, Kosovo existed as an independent state in all but name.

Serbians came to begrudge Kosovo's self-sufficiency, which allowed it to act against Serbian interests, and in 1987, Slobodan Milosevic, elected leader of Serbia's Communist Party, promised to restore Serbian rule to Kosovo.

In 1989 Mr Milosevic became President of Serbia and moved quickly to overpower Kosovo, stripping its autonomy, and in 1990 sent troops to break up its government. Serbian nationalism led to the disintegration of the Yugoslavian federation in 1991; in 1992, the Balkan crisis deteriorated into civil war.

A new Yugoslav state was created consisting only of Serbia and the state of Montenegro, and Kosovo began four years of non-aggressive resistance to Serbian rule.

In 1996, the KLA began violent attacks in Kosovo against Serbian police. That was the early stages of the Kosovo war.

With weapons obtained in Albania, the KLA stepped up its attacks in 1997 prompting a sweeping offensive by Serbian troops against the Albanian insurgent organisation. Enlistment in the KLA increased dramatically after allegations of civilian deaths.

As large numbers of Albanians had fled Kosovo to avoid military service (and many persecuted for doing so), foreign volunteers from Sweden, Italy, Belgium, the UK, Germany, Albania, the US and France joined the KLA's ranks. Volunteers from the Croatian Forces International Volunteers Association also participated in training the KLA troops.

For two years the KLA put up armed resistance to Serbian and Yugoslav security forces which resulted in the death of many people, including civilians. During those battles, thousands of local citizens fled Kosovo into neighbouring countries with many more displaced within Kosovo.

The Yugoslav forces' strength and superior firepower began to overwhelm the KLA and in the summer of 1998 the KLA were being overpowered. Despite having the upper hand, the Yugoslav forces failed to destroy the KLA.

As in the previous Yugoslav conflicts the United Nations High Commissioner for Refugees (UNHCR) would later report that human rights abuse was widespread on both sides; however, both media coverage and the United States focused their criticism on the Serbian government.

News reports claimed the Serbian government was using its police and military, not only to do battle with the KLA, but to forcibly expel thousands of Albanian civilians (ethnic cleansing) from their homes before looting and burning their homes. Reports also claimed many Albanian civilians were being murdered.

These allegations of humanitarian catastrophes tipped international opinion of Yugoslavia over the edge and NATO edged itself closer to entering the conflict.

MORAL COMBAT – NATO AT WAR

A BBC documentary *Moral Combat – NATO at War* from 2000 helped me understand why NATO became involved in the Kosovo war and I hope this explanation helps you too. I have quoted from a number of those people interviewed in the documentary which featured some very powerful individuals.

By the middle of 1998 the United States Secretary of State, Madeleine Albright was eager to confront President Milosevic and pressed US President Bill Clinton to bomb Yugoslavia.

She is reported to have said: 'If you've got all the military power why not use it. If you can bomb and force people to do what you want them to do. Why spend months of delicate diplomatic negotiations?'

Instead Clinton sent US Envoy Richard Holbrook to meet with President Milosevic and leaders of the KLA. Richard Holbrook is best known as the architect of the Dayton Peace Accords which ended the war in Bosnia in 1995, and for which he was nominated for a Nobel Peace Prize.

Because of his reputation for confronting the warring leaders in the Balkans to get them to the negotiating table, Mr. Holbrooke was called 'the Bulldozer' or sometimes 'Raging Bull' in the region.

On 6 October 1998, during one of the meetings with President Milosevic, Mr Holbrook delivered a threat to the President saying, 'If the Yugoslav forces did not return to their barracks a bombing campaign against Yugoslavia would begin.'

Planes were on standby in Italy and the intended targets were already picked. The President agreed with Mr Holbrook's demands and a demilitarisation agreement was reached. In Kosovo the Organisation for Security and Co-operation in Europe (OSCE) was assigned to monitor the agreement.

An OSCE spokesperson later said: 'We now had the opportunity to work and to monitor and to seek a rational, logical civil solution to the problems and grievances within Kosovo. Kosovo was a political problem that could not be solved by NATO bombs, bombing from 23,000 feet. This had to be solved through negotiations and diplomacy.'

Washington's intervention was making Kosovo a global crisis and during October 1998 senior American diplomat, General William Walker, was sent to Kosovo by the US state department to meet President Milosevic. One of his tasks was to make sure President Milosevic's forces complied with the ceasefire agreement; which they did.

Ambassador Walker was selected by Madeleine Albright to set up the headquarters of the OSCE 'Kosovo Verification Mission' (KVM) in Pristina, conceived as an independent international body. Walker was not just working for the OSCE, he was part of the American diplomatic policy which vilified Slobodan Milosevic, demonised the Serbian administration and was providing diplomatic support to the KLA.

The agreed ceasefire had one fatal flaw: it was one-sided and required nothing verifiable from the KLA. One of the leaders of the KLA announced the ceasefire was very useful, it enabled the KLA to get organised, to consolidate and to grow. Their aim was to spread their units over as much of the territory as possible.

Major General John Drewienkiewicz, Ambassador Walker's deputy, watched as the KLA carried out this tactic and said he did not have the means of discouraging or stopping it. The Serbians asked the KVM to get the KLA to withdraw from their positions, but it couldn't.

During a briefing with the North Atlantic Council or NAC (NATO's governing body) Ambassador Walker is alleged to have said that the majority of violations were caused by the KLA.

After the war, during an interview with the BBC, the ambassador couldn't remember making such a statement. He said that most of his briefings given to the NAC were that, 'Both sides were in non-compliance. Both sides were doing things that were prerogative.' Walker also said it was easier to point at the government.

The KLA filled the positions the Serbians had vacated, a pattern that was repeated across the province. There was no clear mechanism to punish the KLA if they failed to behave in a reasonable way, however, Madeleine Albright said the punishment was that they would lose completely the backing of the USA.

With US backing for the KLA now barely concealed, President Milosevic sent the army back into action against the KLA. The march to war against NATO had begun.

The KLA continued to smuggle arms over the border from Albania to Serbia and during one such operation they walked into a Serbian ambush; thirty-one Albanian men were killed in that legitimate military exchange.

A short time later an apparent attack of revenge took place when a group of hooded men, later reported to be KLA gangsters, entered a bar in Peja/Pec. They opened fire with machine guns killing six young Serbians; five were teenagers.

Ambassador Walker condemned both massacres with an equal balance. On the Peja/Pec massacre he said, 'We really didn't know what had happened in Pec. Yes the government was saying it was KLA gangsters who had come in and sprayed this bar. When you don't know what has happened it's a lot more difficult to sort of pronounce yourself.' A short while later Ambassador Walker was to break this rule.

He pronounced himself when he described a massacre that took place in Racak, a village in central Kosovo.

In January 1999 the KLA moved into Racak and most of the villagers fled. They claimed the KLA's presence put them under threat.

An Albanian politician was reported to have stated, 'With Racak and lots of other villages, the Serbians played into KLA hands. The KLA would initiate battles from inside civilian villages then blame the Serbians for retaliating against the villagers.'

In the case of Racak, and from camouflage positions around the village, the KLA launched hit and run strikes against the Serbian forces and when four Serbian policemen were killed on the morning of 15 January 1999, retaliatory strikes were launched.

International observers watched from safe high ground as Serbian forces eventually took control of the near empty village; the KLA had retreated and moved out of Racak. Serbian forces reported they killed fifteen KLA members; in the afternoon they too moved out of the village. The International monitors entered the village and reported nothing unusual.

The Serbian retaliation was reported to Ambassador Walker and on 16 January 1999 he visited Racak where he was met by KLA members who had retaken control of the village. Where the day before nothing unusual was reported, the Ambassador was shown a number of dead bodies and later held a press conference in Pristina.

During that press conference Ambassador Walker said, 'The facts as verified by KVM include evidence of arbitrary detentions, extrajudicial killings and the mutilations of unarmed civilians of Albanian ethnic origin in the village of Racak by the MUP and VJ.' He was blaming the Serbian police and the Yugoslavian army. The ambassador was supposed to be a diplomatic, independent, international official.

He further said, 'Without calling on any of my capitals I told what I thought I'd seen, which was the end of a massacre.'

Richard Holbrooke and General Wesley Clark (Supreme Allied Commander Europe) remember that day's events a little differently. Mr Holbrooke claims Ambassador Walker called him from Racak. General Clark makes the same claim and said, 'I got a call from Bill Walker, he said, "There's a massacre, I'm standing here, I can see the bodies."' General Clark also said, 'Clearly after Racak extraordinary measures had to be taken.'

The Ambassador's comments gave the US the green light for entering the Kosovo war; the KLA succeeded in bringing in its ally.

Madeleine Albright said of the massacre, 'It clearly is a galvanizing event and the President really felt that we could then move forward, make clear that the US was going to be a part of an implementing force.'

Ms Albright insisted there could be no more diplomacy without the credible threat of force; the Europeans agreed. There would be one last diplomatic effort.

In February 1999 peace talks were held in Rambouillet, France, however, delegations from the Federal Republic of Yugoslavia and a delegation representing the Albanian majority population of Kosovo, could not achieve an agreement on a draft produced by NATO.

Members of the Serbian delegation refused to sign the agreement because part of it called for a NATO Peace Implementation Force in Serbia. This would give NATO unlimited rights of movement and deployment, which the Serbians said was little short of occupation.

One member of the Albanian delegation, Hashim Thaci also refused to sign the agreement because the offer did not include a referendum on Kosovo's independence. James Rubin, US Assistant Secretary of State said, 'Obviously, publically we had to make it clear we were seeking an agreement, but privately we knew the chances of the Serbians agreeing were quite small.'

On 14 February Madeleine Albright was summoned to Rambouillet and after three weeks of talks with Mr Thaci the Albanians signed the agreement; the Serbians refused. An Albanian political leader alleged Madeleine Albright told Mr Thaci, if you sign and the Serbians don't, we bomb.

The agreement became what is known as the 'Rambouillet Accord'. The accords called for:

- NATO's administration of Kosovo as an autonomous province within Yugoslavia;

- A force of 30,000 NATO troops to maintain order in Kosovo;

- An unhindered rite of passage for NATO troops on Yugoslav territory, including Kosovo and immunity for NATO and its agents to Yugoslav law.

Serbian forces continued with their offensive in Kosovo. On 24 March 1999 NATO initiated air strikes against Yugoslavia. NATO's reason for the air strikes was to stop a 'humanitarian catastrophe' which they said was taking place. The operation was not authorised by the United Nations and was the first time that NATO used military force without the approval of the UN Security Council and against a sovereign nation that did not pose a threat to members of the alliance.

Throughout the Kosovo war news reports suggested that a programme of ethnic cleansing (by the Serbians) was taking place which made intervention by NATO necessary.

The NATO strikes focused primarily on military targets in Kosovo and Serbia, but extended to a wide range of other facilities.

They also missed a lot of intended targets, which resulted in the death of many civilians. The bombing continued and like those who had already fled, thousands of Kosovo civilians were basically forced to take refuge in camps or neighbouring countries.

On 10 June 1999, the NATO bombardment ended when President Milosevic agreed to a peace agreement (The Kumanovo Treaty) proposed by Finnish President and United Nations diplomat and mediator Martti Ahtisaari and Viktor Chernomyrdin, a special representative of Russia in Yugoslavia.

The peace agreement called for the withdrawal of Serbian forces, including the police from Kosovo and their replacement by NATO peacekeeping troops. It also offered a UN mandate, something that was not offered during negotiations with NATO.

The mandate, United Nations Security Council Resolution 1244, authorised an international civil and military presence in Kosovo and established the United Nations Interim Administration Mission in Kosovo (UNMIK). Under the NATO occupation, Kosovo's autonomy was re-established; however, the province remained officially part of Serbia.

On 12 June 1999 NATO forces, also known as 'KFOR' (Kosovo Force), moved into Kosovo from Macedonia. The same day Russian troops arrived in the Kosovo capital of Pristina and forced NATO into agreeing to a joint occupation.

The Yugoslavian army and the Serbian security forces began their withdrawal from the province which was completed by 20 June 1999. On 21 June 1999, the KLA signed an undertaking on demilitarisation, received by KFOR, which established the methods and the schedule for the demilitarisation and transformation of the KLA. A compromise was reached and on 21 September 1999 the Kosovo Protection Corps (KPC) was created. The KPC had no role in defence, law enforcement, riot control, internal security or any other law and order duties. Their main tasks were to provide a disaster response capability to fight fires and industrial accidents, conduct search and rescue, provide humanitarian help, assist in de-mining and make a contribution to rebuilding communities and infrastructure.

President Milosevic was indicted by the UN's International Criminal Tribunal for the Former Yugoslavia for crimes against humanity in Kosovo. Charges of violating the laws or customs of war, grave breaches of the Geneva Convention in Croatia and Bosnia, and genocide in Bosnia were added later.

On 11 March 2006, President Milosevic was found dead in his cell in the UN war crimes tribunal's detention centre. Autopsies later established he died of a heart attack.

On 17 February 2008 (non-Serbian) representatives of the people of Kosovo declared independence establishing the Republic of Kosovo.

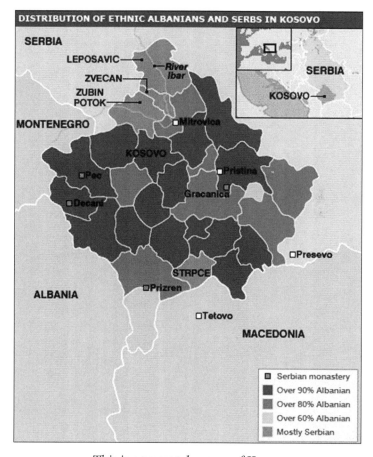

This is a present day map of Kosovo

29

In March 2008, KFOR and the KPC started preparations for the formation of the Kosovo Security Force (KSF), a new professional, multi-ethnic, lightly armed and uniformed Security Force that would be subject to democratic, civilian control and also carry out similar tasks to the KPC.

On 21 January 2009, the KSF was officially launched, however, it didn't replace the KPC which was disbanded several months later. On 5 March 2014, Kosovo Prime Minister, Hashim Thaqi, announced the Kosovo government had decided to establish a Defence Ministry and anticipated by 2019 the KSF would have transformed into an army which will have met all the standards of NATO.

The Kosovo Police Service

THE DEPARTURE OF the Serbian forces from Kosovo created a policing vacuum in a society with obvious deep ethnic divisions. Crime and looting was widespread, and criminal gangs took control in lawless parts of the territory.

Serbian police officers had vastly outnumbered Albanians in Kosovo's police service and had taken their direction from Belgrade. As many Serbians fled and others refused to cooperate with the Kosovo authorities, Kosovo lost its trained police and police infrastructure.

To fill the void, the UN assumed executive authority over the territory. Together with other international groups, the UN mission worked to establish and maintain law and order while organising and training the new Kosovo Police Service to assume gradual control.

On 15 July 1999, pursuant to Security Council Resolution 1244, UN Secretary General Kofi Annan nominated Bernard Kouchner, a French politician and doctor, as the first UN Special Representative and Head of UNMIK.

International organisations, led by UNMIK and the OSCE, held a mandate with two objectives: Establish law and order in the short term, and develop a homegrown Kosovo police service that could help restore the rule of law.

Sven Frederiksen, a Danish police officer (with regional experience in Croatia and Bosnia and Herzegovina), took command in Kosovo as the UN Police Commissioner and, along with Steve Bennett (a retired United States marine officer and a police officer), led the efforts.

The mandate's two objectives would be achievable in three phases:

First: the NATO-led forces would maintain order and ensure safety while UNMIK prepared to assume responsibility.

Second: UNMIK would take over policing responsibilities and would also recruit, select, train and deploy the KPS.

Third: UNMIK would transfer policing responsibilities to the KPS, a shift that would require the creation of effective monitoring institutions.

Shortly after his appointment as the UN Special Representative, Bernard

Kouchner initially requested over 3,000 UN police; a few months later, he increased the request by 1,500, which the UN approved.

The UN resolution assigned the OSCE the task of institution building, including the police, under the authority of UNMIK; however, the two organisations would share some responsibilities. For instance, UNMIK would handle the recruitment process and the OSCE would vet all applicants.

Whilst the OSCE would establish and direct all training conducted at the (Kosovo) police-training school, the UN would deploy police throughout Kosovo then conduct subsequent field training for probationary officers. Although the OSCE lobbied to develop the curricular for field training in order to create natural progression to classroom training, UNMIK insisted on managing all field training matters.

Though an effective international police force was necessary to secure law and order in the short-term, the development and growth of the KPS was the primary long-term goal and one that presented many challenges.

The first was harmonisation with several international institutions, such as NATO, the European Union (EU) and the OSCE. The institutions had overlapping security directives and responsibilities, and a need to adopt a comprehensible approach for the development of the KPS.

A key requirement for the UN force was to train Kosovo citizens in democratic policing, with an emphasis on protecting civilians. This was a significant departure from the Yugoslavian model, aimed to protect the state from its citizens. The requirement, selection and training of the KPS posed additional encounters.

Though UNMIK wanted to include ethnic minorities in the recruitment process, minority applicants were limited in the wake of the conflict. Kosovo lacked qualified police trainers, training facilities, materials and equipment.

Hundreds of ethnic Albanians had experience in the Yugoslavian police prior to 1999, but UNMIK initially refrained from recruiting them for the new service, fearing that Yugoslavian training could weaken the goal of creating a new force that focused on protecting the community rather than the state.

Building trust in the police was another significant challenge, influenced by a history of police abuse under the Yugoslavian system and the spate of post-conflict ethnic violence; Kosovo citizens didn't view the police as competent problem solvers. As a result, citizens often failed to report crimes, especially in Serbian enclaves.

On 6 September 1999, UNMIK began to build the KPS, selecting approximately 200 Kosovo citizens from tens of thousands of applicants to form the first class of police cadets. The OSCE prepared (training) modules with assistance of the International Criminal Investigation Training and Assistance (ICITA) even before the NATO military campaign had concluded. That pre-planning was the key to the success of the recruiting process.

Steve Bennett was appointed Director for Police Education and Development and became responsible for organising and overseeing the training of the KPS on behalf of the OSCE mission, installing the first class of recruits, just weeks after the fighting ended. Of the original class, and according to records, 173 officers, including 39 women and 17 minorities, graduated six weeks later. 'The Kosovo police will be the protector of human rights and will fight against any type of crime or corruption,' the class leader, Nuredin Ibishi, a former KLA officer, told the 173 graduates in the ceremony, a symbol of international attempts to bring normality to Kosovo.

Development of both internal and external police monitoring structures would follow and include increasing levels of participation from the budding KPS until it achieved institutional autonomy with Kosovo's Unilateral Declaration of Independence on 17 February 2008.

UNMIK independently established a detailed recruitment and selection process in 1999 that remained unchanged to 2009 despite its transfer to Kosovo control in 2003. UNMIK recruited cadets by using multilingual public radio broadcasts and newspaper advertisements.

Kosovo had a high unemployment rate and attracting well-qualified and educated applicants was relatively easy, initial salaries were low; however, they were higher than those offered to workers in the medical profession and education departments.

In addition to identifying recruitment goals for former KLA fighters, the UN mission set high goals for the inclusion of women and ethnic groups. The target was around 16 per cent female representation in the police service, which was extremely high compared to other European countries. The 16 per cent standard aimed to make Kosovo one of the Continent's leaders in female police representation.

The UN mission also sought to maintain minority representation at levels that exceeded those in the general population, with careful attention paid to include ethnic Serbians. UNMIK refrained from recruiting ethnic Albanians from the former Yugoslavian police. Concerns were their Yugoslavian training might be conflictive with the community-orientated philosophy of the new Kosovo police.

This policy was abandoned in March 2000 when an initial UN police shortfall warranted recruitment of experienced officers. With those former police having experience working in a multi-ethnic police service in the former Yugoslavia, many adapted quickly to the training and development programme, advancing to mid-level and senior management positions. Regardless of previous experience, however, all cadets undertook training by the OSCE and UNMIK.

After completing the application form and fingerprinting, the recruits underwent an arduous review process that involved a written exam followed by an oral interview, a physical fitness test that was the same for both men and women, a medical exam followed by a psychological exam.

By 2003 the KPS had assumed responsibility and published its first formal set of procedural policies for recruitment and selection. The formal process called for the police service to announce vacancies in three languages (English, Albanian and Serbian) for twenty-one days while confirming the established recruitment ratio.

The policy notice specified that the written test consisted of one hundred questions focusing on general knowledge, maths and verbal skills. The interview, medical examination, physical test and psychological test remained unchanged.

The recruitment and selection process did, however, suffer from three problems according to a senior programme officer. By the time they got around to adding together all of the ratios, there was almost no room in the force left for regular male Albanians, or ordinary people.

Unfortunately, ordinary men produced the highest levels of education and physical fitness and yet, most were excluded for the first couple of years of the programme by the ratio system.

The second problem was the lack of records after the war, which made it difficult to determine who may have committed atrocities and other serious crimes, especially among former military personnel. Although the OSCE compensated by publicising the names of recruits and interviewing neighbours in an attempt to uncover information that applicants might have withheld, the efforts had limited success in keeping out unwelcome recruits.

During some classes at the KPS training school, students would point at other students and say, 'That person killed my brother' or 'That man was in a group that destroyed our village.'

The third problem was some recruits forged education documents to meet the OSCE's standards. Most of the officers expelled from the KPS between 2002 and 2003 produced forged degree certificates.

Given the relatively small size of Kosovo and lack of complete records, the

OSCE had limited options; many Kosovo and international offices acknowledged the processes' shortcomings.

In 2006, police recruitment and basic training stopped when the service reached 7,335 officers, in addition to 1,600 civilian support staff and 600 guards to secure government properties and installation. UNMIK determined the number based on an international standard ratio of the population to police.

A sustained and comprehensive effort by the international community reinforced UNMIK's success in building an efficient, trusted KPS. As UNMIK and the OSCE began to build the Kosovo police during the next several years, ethnic and political tensions continued to ebb and flow.

The continued presence of thousands of UN police as late as 2008 provided time for the Kosovo police to receive proper training and experience. With continued UNMIK monitoring, mentoring, advising and assistance the Kosovo police gradually assumed command positions.

In August 2008, representatives of the UN and EU in Kosovo signed a memorandum aimed to regulate the transfer of power from the UN to the EU mission in Kosovo. In 2015, the UN, NATO and the OSCE all remained active in the territory.

In comparison to the standard UK police rank structure, the KPS is quite different:

UK police ranks

- Police Officer
- Sergeant
- Inspector
- Chief Inspector
- Superintendent
- Chief Superintendent
- Assisant Chief Constable
- Deputy Chief Constable
- Chief Constable

Kosovo police ranks

- Police Officer
- Sergeant
- Lieutenant
- Captain
- Major
- Lieutenant Colonel
- Colonel
- Assistant General Director
- Deputy General Director
- General Director of Police.

This is a list of the police regions of Kosovo, their municipalities and the number of police stations, including KPS RHQ and Regional Traffic.

- Prishtina/Pristina region/6 municipalities and 10 police stations
- Mitrovice/Mitrovica region/7 municipalities and 7 police stations
- Peja/Pec Region/5 municipalities and 11 police stations
- Prizren Region/5 municipalities and 9 police stations
- Gjilan/Gnjilane region/4 municipalities and 7 police stations
- Ferizaj/Urosevac region/4 municipalities and 7 police stations

THE KOSOVO POLICE 2015

KP bike unit

KP officers after graduating

KP patrols

PART ONE
THE FORCE WITH A DIFFERENCE

During the 1990s the MDP was some way off from being a respected police force like their territorial counterparts. I really had no idea of the difference between the MDP and the territorial police; however, when I arrived at Coulport I soon learned there was a vast difference.

From when I joined the force in 1990 until 1995, RNAD Coulport was under reconstruction and the unfamiliar and dire working conditions (for a police officer) greatly affected officer performance and morale. MOD staff and territorial police forces never took the MDP seriously and saw its officers as 'glorified security guards'; a derogatory tag which, to some extent, continues to exist today.

CHAPTER ONE
Her Majesty's Naval Base Clyde

WHEN I WAS growing up in my home town, Drumchapel, near Glasgow, Strathclyde police officers patrolled their beat on foot or by travelling in a blue and white (Panda) Ford Anglia car. In the wee Panda would be two big police officers. One, usually the driver, would be the angelic, mild mannered, father-like figure, whilst his typically bad-tempered partner, with his slashed peaked police cap worn like a Regimental Sergeant Major, would not tolerate the slightest hint of disrespect. A slap round the back of the head or a kick up the backside was the usual punishment for back-chatting PC Angry. Fortunately for me, I was never on the receiving end. When a good police officer paid a visit to my primary school to talk about road traffic safety, I remember thinking 'I want to be a policeman.'

In the 1960s Drumchapel, also known as 'The Drum,' was a well-known hot spot for violent clashes between rival gangs and the *polis* were often kept busy. I can remember, late at night, looking out my front room window and watching street fights take place across the road. Eventually the *Black Maria* police van would appear loaded with those bad police who, before making any arrests, would wade in and knock the living daylights out of those battling foes. My parents did a great job of raising my only brother and me and we managed to keep out of trouble. And I was never put off joining the police.

My family moved away from Drumchapel in 1974 and settled in Garscadden, another district of Glasgow. Today my mother (83) still lives in Garscadden; my father died suddenly in 1997, age 69, after a very short battle with liver cancer and my brother, Jim, moved to Aquitaine in France.

The thought of joining the police stayed with me throughout most of my teenage years; nevertheless, in 1975, when I was sixteen, and in spite of mixed emotions, I started my first day of work on the Glasgow Clydeside; I eventually became a shipyard (electric arc) welder.

I met my first serious girlfriend just after finishing my apprenticeship in 1979 and we married in 1982. We set up home in Clydebank, near Glasgow and in

1984 our first son Jamie was born. I gave up welding in 1983 and after training with the British School of Motoring, I qualified as a Department of Transport Approved Driving Instructor (ADI). Four years later our second son, Stephen, was born.

I was reasonably happy being a driving instructor until I was distracted (1989) by an article in a national newspaper promoting the police; however, not the territorial police but the (armed) Ministry of Defence Police. Despite having no knowledge of the MDP I wasn't deterred and decided to renew my interest in a police career. After a lengthy process, including physical tests, a medical examination and three interviews I began to realise the MDP are in fact considerably different to the 'other' police. After my fourth and final interview and, after being asked the question again, 'Are you afraid of guns?' my answer was still the same, 'I don't think so, I've never used one.'

My reply must have been an acceptable answer. The interviewer, a Police Superintendent, told me my application was successful and I would receive confirmation in the post, along with the details of where I'd be offered a position.

Two weeks later, sometime around early March 1990, I received my offer of employment and the terms and conditions. I was offered a position at RNAD Coulport which is one of two MOD bases encompassing Her Majesty's Naval Base Clyde. The other base, and Coulport's close neighbour, is Faslane Naval Base. Both those MOD establishments lie on the eastern shore of the Gare Loch in Argyll and Bute, Scotland (close to the seaside town of Helensburgh) and are about thirty miles from where I lived in Clydebank.

Her Majesty's Naval Base Clyde is one of three operating bases in the UK for the Royal Navy (the others being HMNB Devonport and HMNB Portsmouth). It is the service's headquarters in Scotland and is best known as the home of Britain's strategic nuclear deterrent, in the form of Polaris nuclear submarines. In recent years the Polaris submarines were replaced by Trident nuclear submarines armed with Trident missiles.

During the selection process and interviews I was told RNAD Coulport (which is a storage and loading facility for nuclear warheads and located and protected behind miles of alarmed fence) is under extensive reconstruction and in part resembles a large building site. I was also reminded by a senior MDP officer the MDP should not be confused with any territorial police force who, unlike Coulport's MDP, do get involved in 'real police work.'

That senior officer mentioned a few derogatory names adopted by the MDP and often used by MOD staff 'and' the territorial police when referring to the

MDP. Names like 'glorified security guards,' 'armed gate keepers' and 'mod plod' being the most commonly used.

Those insulting tags are in reference to the hundreds of MDP officers who spend hours controlling entry/exit at many MOD establishments, where their main function is the security of the establishment and its personnel.

The words 'resembles a large building site' and 'glorified security guard' stayed with me for quite some time. I wasn't sure what to expect when I arrived at Coulport – surely I won't be working near the building site... police officers don't work on building sites, do they?

My introduction to the MDP started on a wet Monday, 2 April 1990, when I attended a one week (non-residential) induction course at RNAD Coulport. On my way to Coulport I drove past the psychedelic Faslane Peace Camp and Faslane Naval Base.

A permanent peace camp was established close to Faslane in the early 1980s, and still exists today. Campaign for Nuclear Disarmament (CND) protestors and other action groups regularly protest at and around both entrances to Faslane.

Driving less than one hundred yards further along the road from the peace camp, on the opposite side of the road is the start of Faslane's hideous and tall brown weld mesh, alarmed, security fence, topped with rolls of extremely sharp and dangerous razor wire. Razor wire also lies in wait, for any would-be intruders, at the bottom (inside) of the fence. Smaller chain link fences (also topped with razor wire) offer security at various points around the base. The base's security is strengthened by surveillance cameras which are mounted on tall criss-cross metal frames and can be seen at strategic points around the base. Clyde Marine Unit (CMU) patrols a protected channel in the waters off the west side of the base. RNAD Coulport is protected by a very similar security system.

From Faslane and driving approximately seven miles either west or north-west you'll find RNAD Coulport. Keeping to a more scenic route (west), following the

B833 takes you through some lovely villages and Loch Long is always visible on your left. I chose to take the north-west route that joins an unclassified road, which the MOD named the Northern Access Road. The high quality, relatively straight and level road was constructed to facilitate overland transport of nuclear weapons to the

Coulport roundabout

depot at Coulport. My final approach to Coulport's depot area was all downhill with a long, steep, sweeping right-hand bend before I reached the bottom and a roundabout with three exits. Turning left takes you along the B833 and the scenic route. Driving straight ahead takes you towards Coulport's first point of entry.

The B833

Many tourists have followed the B833 thinking they can turn left at the roundabout and continue to the North of Scotland. When they see the control barriers, gates and the armed police officers, heads get scratched and a new route is planned. The B833 stops for public access near those gates. The issue of where the public road ends has been a grey area for some time.

Sure enough when I approached the entrance gate (known as Kibble barrier) I was met by one, rather wet and hacked off looking PC whose function was indeed to control entry and exit. I rolled down my car window and handed him my introduction letter. A short conversation then ensued and I learned two PCs worked at that gate with one in position at the gate at all times. The other PC spent one hour inside a nearby portakabin (refreshment area) and rotated the duty with his colleague. Due to Coulport's constant inclement weather, many refreshment periods are spent drying yourself and your police uniform.

After being checked against a visitors' list I was permitted through the gates, which actually leads to the staff car park and another gate, the main gate. Coulport's main gate is around 200 yards from Kibble barrier and access was controlled by a number of armed and un-armed police officers who also looked a bit hacked off.

The area around RNAD Coulport was originally a village and had been best known as a summer holiday retreat for wealthy Glaswegians. *John Kibble* was one of several wealthy Glasgow merchants who had built large villas at Coulport in the nineteenth century either as permanent residences or summer retreats.

During the 1800s Kibble erected a glass palace at Coulport and in 1871 had it dismantled and moved by barge to the Botanic Gardens in Glasgow. Today the enlarged structure known as 'Kibble Palace' is one of the main features at the Botanic Gardens. However, when it was extended, no records were kept and it's not known how much of today's palace is part of John Kibble's originally creation.

Kibble Palace

It rained for most of the week during the induction course and most of my time was spent in an auditorium with sixteen other potential police recruits (most of whom are no longer with the force) along with a training sergeant, Ray Tidswell. With or without the rain, our movement inside Coulport was restricted as we had limited security clearance. Most of what I learned that week about the MDP and Coulport came from a very knowledgeable Ray Tidswell.

Construction of RNAD Coulport's Polaris nuclear programme started in 1963 on the east shore of Loch Long and was finished in 1968. The reconstruction and expansion work to support the new Trident missile programme started during the 1980s and was completed in 1995. Coulport, the village, with most of its houses and residents had all but gone. The last remaining building was demolished in 2005.

During a rain-hampered, escorted, windshield tour (in an MOD coach) of Coulport's depot area and new Trident site I counted around four internal gates where, between one and two very wet PCs controlled entry and exit. I also spotted several wet PCs walking in pairs around the depot and the ugly brown fence line. 'So,' I thought, 'is this what the MDP call "police work"?' Well, I was warned.

The driver of the MOD coach eventually arrived at and stopped in an area where construction was taking place on a new Trident jetty. He parked the coach just outside the entrance gates leading to a contractor's compound. During the reconstruction of Coulport a number of contractor companies were employed and accommodated in temporary contractor compounds. Those enclosed compounds were like mini villages (built within Coulport's big open-topped cage) where portakabins were erected and used by the contractors for refreshment breaks and, after work, to secure heavy machinery and other working tools.

Entry and exit to and from the temporary compounds was controlled by civilian security guards who were employed by a local (Strathclyde security) company. On occasions armed and unarmed MDP constables were also present at those gates. That whole new jetty area was extremely busy and extremely dirty. The falling rain and constant flow of site traffic (pedestrian and vehicular) in and out of those gates was making working conditions – especially under foot – extremely difficult for a Strathclyde security guard, who was controlling entry/exit at the gate where we stopped.

The security guards were employed to enforce Coulport's depot regulations and generally speaking were responsible for controlling entry and exit, checking I.D. badges, searching vehicles, personnel and baggage. When a guard wasn't present the MDP carried out those tasks. The security company's uniform was similar to a police uniform; however, the obvious giveaway was the flat cap's headband. It had Strathclyde Security embossed (in white stitching) along its front. That day the guard also wore a black waterproof jacket and a pair of muddy black boots.

Incidentally, one piece of uniform equipment that I received long after joining the MDP was handcuffs. It must have been around a year or so after my initial recruits' course before I was issued with the restraints. And in all my 22 years as an MDP police officer I never got the opportunity to try them out. I always wanted a signature expression like 'book em Danno' or 'you're nicked son'; however, it was not to be.

Heavy plant vehicles were trundling in and out of those compound gates and their wheels were throwing up loose chippings and dirty rain water which had settled in the deep, rutted, temporary road surface. The poor guard was very wet, very dirty and very dejected looking.

We were not allowed to get off the coach, in that area, due to health and safety regulations (hard hat area). This suited me fine; I didn't particularly want to take a soaking, plenty of time for that later on. Our escort on the coach was one of the early shift patrol sergeants and he was the only person who did get off; however, before doing so, he put on a heavy black rain jacket and an industrial hard hat. As he approached the compound gate I noticed one other person appear from a nearby portakabin (outside the gate). He was rather lively as he made his way in the supervisor's direction. That character wore a black oversized sou'wester hat and a long sou'wester coat and a pair of knee-high wellington boots.

Wellington-booted police

The three men now stood at the gate's entrance and the sergeant, who looked very irritated, was wagging a finger at the lookalike fisherman chappy. It was impossible to hear what was being said, the loud noise from construction vehicles

and heavy machinery was quite deafening. There was a lot of finger pointing and shouting and not only from the supervisor. Holding a rather large and heavy-looking, black oblong box in his left hand the irate fisherman wagged his right index finger just below the sergeant's bulbous nose. That black oblong box, about the size and shape of three stacked cigarette packets, was actually a cougar radio (*pictured left*) and was the radio system used by the MDP at that time; it was hideous.

After a couple of minutes the shouting match stopped and the fisherman handed the supervisor a small notebook. The sergeant wrote something in it before handing it back. The two, 'I assumed' security guards then disappeared into the portakabin and when they reappeared were both wearing white, industrial hard hats. The fisherman had changed out of his sou'wester dress and now wore a flimsy waterproof jacket and had replaced his wellingtons for a pair of black boots. Both 'guards' stood by the contractor gate as the supervisor boarded the coach and took his seat; he waited for a minute before turning to face his audience. 'The person who was off his "beat" and inappropriately dressed is a police constable,' he said. He also seemed quite happy to tell us, 'Coulport has many gates and you, if you last that long with the MDP, will get to know them all and Coulport's famous weather conditions.'

'So, standing at a gate is a beat,' I thought. I wondered how many more gates Coulport had to offer and if there were any decent 'beats'. I also thought back to Drumchapel and the cops who patrolled a proper beat.

On the way back to Coulport's Admin area I heard the sergeant calling up someone on his big, ugly, cougar radio and when he made contact with the call sign FUM8 all he said was 'Bravo Tango Kilo'. The answer he received was: 'will comply'. Just as the coach pulled into an admin parking bay the sergeant's crackling radio sprang into life and a voice came through with the message 'Kilo Bravo'. That was the first of many coded radio messages I learned whilst working at Coulport. If you haven't worked it out yet, Bravo Tango Kilo is boil the kettle and Kilo Bravo is kettle boiled.

Later that day and back at the auditorium there was no doubt in Ray Tidwell's mind about the name of the sou'wester-clad copper, Mike Harris, an old campaigner who'd been in the job twenty-five years, ten of them at Coulport. According to Ray, Mike treated Coulport with the contempt he said it deserved.

Mike often said, 'Like it or not, the MDP *are* just armed security guards and when it rains we should wear whatever waterproof clothing keeps our body warm and dry.' Ray told another amusing story about Mike, where he had a lucky escape from being disciplined.

During a morning shift at Coulport, Mike had to think fast on his feet when he was sitting (dozing) at a reception desk, eyes closed with his head resting on clasped hands (and elbows resting on the desk). Mike sensed someone standing by his side and keeping his eyes closed and arms still he lifted his head into an upright position and with a sigh and low murmur quietly uttered one word: 'Amen'. He then opened his eyes to see a confounded police inspector staring at him for a second before shaking his head, turning and walking back out the door he had just entered.

Towards the end of the induction week, during a lunch break in the depot canteen, I introduced myself to a few glum-looking PCs and mentioned the earlier antics involving Mike Harris.

Getting drenched from the rain was a regular occurrence at Coulport and if you didn't look after yourself, you usually ended up suffering in bed for a week. I learned Mike Harris had not long returned to duty after being struck down with a severe bout of flu. I also learned the waterproof sou'wester worn by Mike was, if they could get away with it, worn by most PCs during inclement weather.

One of the coppers said it was probably Mike's police pocketbook the sergeant was signing; either to note he'd visited that particular officer or to reprimand him for being dressed in the sou'wester get-up.

Those coppers had not long finished their two years' probationary period and agreed with Mike about being armed security guards. They were just biding their time at Coulport until something better within (or out with) the force came along.

Positions within the Clyde Marine Unit and the force Dog Section were often advertised. One of the cops was waiting on a potential dog handler's course at the Defence Animal Centre which is based in Melton Mowbray, east Leicestershire.

The last thing I was told by those coppers was, 'don't expect to come back to Coulport from your recruit's course and do *real* police work, it doesn't happen.'

'Real police work...', now where have I heard that before?

I still had sixteen weeks at the MOD Police Training Centre; plenty of time to get my head round the idea of spending my early career as an armed Ministry of Defence police constable guarding gates and patrolling a rain-sodden Ministry of Defence building site.

CHAPTER TWO
Police Academy

IT WAS MONDAY 9 April 1990 when I started week one of the initial (Scots Law) police (residential) recruits course at the Ministry of Defence Police Training School and Firearms Training Wing at Medmenhan, Buckinghamshire.

My particular course was the third course of 1990 (3/90) and was made up of four classes: two studied Scots law, the other two English law. The majority of recruits on the Scots law course were posted to Coulport and Faslane. The remainder were posted to other MOD establishments located in other Scottish regions.

As a mature thirty-one-year-old and one of the oldest MDP recruits on the course, I was immediately singled out by my course instructor, Sergeant Ray Peel, and elected class leader. My role as class leader wasn't difficult; I was basically the class spokesperson whose tasks included attempting to resolve any minor recruit concerns or bring the more serious of issues to the attention of the course instructor.

During that first settling-in week Ray Peel explained the course syllabus and mentioned possible expulsion from the course should anyone fail more than three weekly theory tests, fail to display a high level of competence during the three weeks of firearms training, which included a final qualification shoot, or fail to complete a physical test which included a mile and a half run in a specified time. My specified qualifying time was 11 minutes and 15 seconds. Before the end of the course I was timed at 10 minutes 44 seconds. The weekly theory tests, based on Scots law and the Ministry of Defence Police Act 1987, were carried out on a Friday morning with one final end of course exam.

For the first few weeks during training, all the instructors played at being the bad cop. They used any excuse to give recruits a good 'bollocking,' (telling off).Walking on grassed areas was not permitted and if anyone was spotted by a member of the training staff doing so, he was usually called upon to stop! And then balled out where he stood; even if he was one hundred yards from that trainer.

The training school practical scenarios were very realistic and very much what one may expect in a true life situation. Whatever the scenario, it would more often than not lead to an arrest followed by all the relevant paperwork. I was the arresting officer on a number of scenarios, breach of the peace, theft, assault, etc.

In between classroom work and the practical scenarios, drill practice took place. The drill instructor, Sergeant Andy Kirkwood is an ardent follower of Glasgow Celtic football club. One afternoon Andy had the 3/90 (Scots law) course congregate on the parade ground and had us line up forming four lines facing him (one behind the other). He then, starting from the first, walked along each line and asked each recruit one question, 'What football team do you support?'

The answers were a mixture of Scottish and English clubs until Andy stopped at an English recruit, Neville Horton. Neville, on hearing the question looked straight ahead and shouted 'Partizan Belgrade sergeant'.

I was one of the few who immediately understood the intentional ridicule of Neville's cheeky answer, which sent me into fits of laughter. Celtic had lost to Partizan Belgrade seven months earlier, in the European Cup Winner's Cup tournament. At first Andy was completely speechless, however, he then saw the funny side to the joke and laughed along with the rest of us.

Andy would ridicule the recruits during the practical exercises by dressing up as Rab C. Nesbitt; the alcoholic layabout from the BBC sitcom of the same name. When he was in character Andy annoyed and frustrated recruits by making their life difficult during arrest exercises. He would usually resist arrest and generally made life difficult for the frustrated recruits.

Although at times he was a pest, it is testament to Andy that during my recruit's course, Andy's recruit class (2/90) had t-shirts made and printed across the front were the words 'Kirkwood's Koppers'. Today, after twenty-four years, Andy (now retired) is still in touch with a few of the officers who were part of that recruit's course.

Less than three weeks into the course, when everything was going along fine, Ray Peel arrived late for the day's class. Normally he would walk in through the classroom door with a spring in his step. That morning, however, he looked visibly shaken and stood staring at the classroom's back wall for a few seconds before explaining his friend and colleague, Steve Gant, had been tragically killed (at work) by the accidental discharge of a pistol during an armed duty handover.

Up until that point in my training I'd never really thought about handling a potentially lethal weapon, 'maybe I am scared of guns after all,' I thought.

I started to get quite nervous about the firearms training. The thought of firing a gun, 'a real gun' with 'real bullets' started to play on my mind.

The Force policy regarding firearms changed after Steve Gant's tragic death and by the time my firearms course started a higher level of proficiency had been set. If any recruit failed in the safe handling of a firearm or the final qualification pistol shoot they would automatically fail the recruit course.

The first nervous week of firearms training was the introduction to a firearm (9mm Browning pistol), safe handling of a firearm and a weapons test at the end of that week. The weapons test included various exercises using practice bullets, more commonly known as *drill rounds*. A drill round is a round of ammunition that is inert, i.e., contains no propellant or explosive charge. It is used in training to check weapon function. Although a few people struggled with the weapons test, everyone did eventually pass. Fortunately the firearm instructors Steve Nicols and Bob Prescott were excellent. They were very patient and never hurried or pushed anyone to any extreme.

Live firing, for my class, was indoors at the training centre's (confined) twenty-five metre range. The other Scots law class were taken to a nearby outdoor range.

I was one of the first to be called up to the firing point. Standing to my right and just behind my right shoulder, stood Bob Prescott. He started shouting instructions about ear defenders, magazines and rounds and although I had been well briefed on the procedures, I was completely confused. Bob repeated his instructions and then told me to carry on in my own time.

Never before had I held a loaded gun. Now there I was, holding a 9mm Browning pistol loaded with ten real bullets. I stood trembling, just a little, ten metres away from a Figure 11 target. Looking straight ahead, with both arms outstretched and grasping the pistol with both hands, I took aim at the target.

For those of you who are thinking, 'why both hands; they do it with one hand in the movies?' Yes, maybe so, and for the doubters, try holding a bag of sugar in your (outstretched) hand. It won't take long for the arm to become heavy and begin to waver and droop. A bag of sugar weighs 2.2lbs; the Browning pistol without a fully loaded magazine (13 bullets) weighs the same. So, my two hands gripped the pistol. After taking a deep breath I gently squeezed the trigger with my right index finger. I saw the wood chippings fly up in the air before I heard the loud reverberating snap from the pistol; no coconut, for a dreadful miss.

Bob Prescott whispered in my right ear, 'low left into the sleeper, take your time and gently squeeze the trigger, all the way through.' I had anticipated the recoil of the gun and pulled my shot to the left blasting into a railway sleeper. As a safety measure, thick wooden railway sleepers were used to catch any bullets that went astray during live firing and prevented any ricochet.

I slowly fired off the next nine rounds, all into the centre mass of the target's body. My shooting and confidence kept improving and by the last week I was ready for the final test. On that final qualification shoot, held at the outdoor range, the entire course passed. We were now qualified to carry a 9mm Browning pistol.

With the pressure of the firearms training now behind me, I relaxed a bit more and enjoyed the rest of the course. Practical scenarios now took up a lot of the course work and one particular scenario starting from the initial crime was followed all the way through to a mock trial held in a room, which replicated a crown court.

I can't fault my police training at all; it was the bureaucracy at Coulport that for years stopped keen and enthusiastic PCs like me from putting our police skills into practise.

On the final week of the recruit's course the results of the final exam were announced; everyone was successful. Not everyone had passed all the weekly exams in the run-up to the final; I did and without any problem. I may not have used my police powers that much in the coming years but I studied whenever I could. Overall, the training I received at the police training school, both theoretical and the firearms, was excellent.

The night before the passing out parade the police social club was really busy. There were a number of PCs from Coulport who attended the training school for various courses. After getting involved in their company it became clear, like their Coulport colleagues whom I had met a few weeks earlier, they were also pretty dejected. None of them were really interested in attending training courses; they just wanted away from Coulport, and a jaunt to the police training school was one way of forgetting the Coulport regime.

The day of my passing out parade was a scorcher. I'd had a few beers the night before and was praying that I wouldn't wet myself or faint, luckily I avoided both.

After lots of marching, then long speeches and presentations from invited dignitaries, I heard those long awaited and welcome words, 'parade fall out.' I, along with the rest of the 3/90 recruit course respectfully complied before heading straight for the police social club bar.

After the excitement of the passing out parade subsided, I felt prepared, willing and able to give all my commitment to protecting Britain's nuclear deterrent and the defence community. I was also ready to put all my newfound police knowledge into practise according to Scots law and the Ministry of Defence Police Act 1987. It's just a pity I was being posted to an MOD establishment where much of my initial 'police work' would see me trudging round a building site.

Police recruits course 3/90

CHAPTER THREE
Behind the Wire

I FELT ELATION then triumph. Elated I had passed the final Scots law police exam and triumphant I had successfully completed the initial MDP police recruits course. Over the next five years or so that euphoria eventually disintegrated and gradually my joy turned to despair; I 'was' a glorified security guard after all.

I was a bit blind before I joined the MDP. I thought too much about becoming a police officer and didn't think enough about the police force I'd applied to join. And when I did initially join I never gave much thought to my posting or the type of 'police work' that was taking place inside that big open-topped cage surrounding RNAD Coulport. The warning signs were pretty obvious if I'd thought about them. I thought back to one of my interviews and being told Coulport was under extensive reconstruction and resembled a large building site; and I thought of the derogatory name calling, the coppers I met in the depot canteen and those at the police training school. Don't expect to come back to Coulport and do real police work, rung in my ears. Those coppers were all completely deflated. I saw their misery; it just didn't register with me at the time.

Recruits who were posted to Coulport were disappointed, although not all of them. Quite a few recruits came from jobs within the MOD and they knew the MDP salary was better than average; they knew and were pleased Coulport wasn't a busy place, not in the police sense of the word. They also knew Coulport was a nuclear 'guarding' station and not (really) a busy 'policing' station.

For a long time MOD contractors and civilian staff, and to a lesser extent the public and territorial police forces, 'have' looked on the MDP as, 'glorified security guards' and 'night watchmen'. I'm not sure where or when those derogatory terms originated except to say (in the 1990s) the MDP did spend many hours controlling entry/exit whilst operating manual and electronic gates. Walking around buildings checking the security of every external door and rattling padlocks on doors and gates was also part and parcel of life 'behind the wire' for the MDP.

Acquaintances, family and friends also ridiculed my new career and even though their comments were meant as light-hearted banter, it still struck a nerve. I'd meet people I hadn't spoken to in a while and when the conversation came round to 'Where you working these days?' I was actually embarrassed to tell them. If I said, 'I joined the police,' I got a few standoffish looks. Other people's immediate reaction was, 'Oh nice one, what station do you work at?' When I said I joined the 'Ministry of Defence' police, the reaction was usually the same, a wry smile and then, 'Oh them, security mob at the base.' Other people would say, 'Oh the mod plod, are they not just kid-on police?' This mockery did surprise me somewhat. The initial police recruit training, including the firearms was second to none. I think it was just the luck of the draw for me to be posted to a nuclear guarding station like Coulport and I knew I had to ignore people's ignorance of the force.

The temporary contractor gate, where I first saw *The* character Mike Harris, and the other contractor gates were the worst places to work. During inclement weather you could do nothing but stand, do your job, and take the pounding from the cruel elements. There was no leaving your 'beat' to take shelter and if you weren't as wise as Mike Harris, with his sou'wester get-up, you really did get a good soaking. Filthy rain water or, when it snowed, slush was churned up from the oversized wheels of the heavy plant vehicles making working conditions extremely muddy, slippy and extremely difficult underfoot.

During very dry and humid days and if it was at all windy, sand and gravel from temporary road surfaces swirled around you covering your uniform with a fine brown dust. Unlike the real cops on a *real* beat who, when the weather is bad, can skip into a local greasy spoon and take shelter whilst downing a warm mug of tea, there was just nowhere to escape Coulport's bleak and extreme weather conditions.

At Coulport you could not leave your beat until properly relieved; and that relief only appeared when the rain, hail or snow *disappeared.* Throughout static duty (on a morning or afternoon shift) at those contractor gates and during foot patrols I had to dodge various types of construction traffic, including hydraulic excavators, concrete mixers, road rollers and dump trucks as their heavy tyres splashed the dirty rainwater all around me. In the spring and summer one obstruction, and the smallest, impossible to dodge is the *Culicoides impunctatus* or to give it its more common title, the Highland (biting) midge. For those of you who don't know, the midge is a very small two-winged flying insect that usually attacks the ears and nose, or any exposed part of the body. Midges have been known to ruin people's holidays (in Scotland) with the amount of chaos they cause and it's usually only the females who bite!

After the contractors and civilian staff finished work for the day, the MDP carried out external and internal building security checks. During internal building checks, vacated offices were checked to ensure desks, unlocked drawers and unsecured cabinets did not contain important or restricted documents. If any windows were inadvertently left open, they were closed by the patrolling MDP. The internal checks were also a fire prevention exercise. All electrical appliances and outlets were checked to ensure no electrical plugs were left in sockets. Any fire hazards or building insecurities discovered were reported by way of a Building Insecurity Report.

Any breaches of building regulations were normally reported to a resident duty (civilian) officer followed by the submission of the Building Insecurity Report and a police occurrence report. Most of what happened afterwards was completely over the top. It didn't really make a lot of difference what the insecurity was, a 'police investigation' for a window being left open did take place and if the culprit was identified an interview with that individual usually took place. Another report followed the interview, and eventually a slap on the wrist was usually the recommendation for the offender. The amount of report writing required for an open window or a kettle plug being left in the socket was pretty ridiculous, although it did improve my police report writing and my interviewing technique.

Coulport's vast perimeter fence line meandering high behind the Trident jetty

During a nightshift, those internal building security patrols always took up at least half the shift. Many offices had big comfy chairs and after all checks were carried out, those comfy chairs were taken advantage of for an hour or three. Most nightshifts at Coulport were very quiet, with most coppers darting off to some dark corner in order to relax and keep out of the way of the more lively and alert patrol sergeant.

Foot patrols were carried out around Coulport's miles of road and its vast fenceline and on a night shift, if the weather was particularly bad, a warm vehicle or an insecure (unoccupied) building was an ideal way of escaping a good soaking or the regular high winds. Although most coppers working at Coulport did do a bit of ducking and diving during a nightshift, they would always respond quickly to urgent radio messages. Those Cougar radios may have been pretty ugly contraptions, but on full volume they certainly got your full attention when a call came in.

On occasions, and if I was lucky, I would avoid gate duty and long foot patrols by being part of the crew travelling with mobile patrol units. Occasionally I found myself being an observer with the internal and external mobile units, which, during the 1990s, included a Yellow Land Rover and a white Transit van. Both those vehicles came without official police markings or lights. The internal unit carried out mobile patrols, checked buildings and responded to any requests made by the control room staff. Most requests made were related to the checking of perimeter fence alarms (frequently false, caused by inclement weather) and the pickup and drop off of official paperwork; usually the daily shift rosters.

When police action and intervention is required at Coulport, it's more often than not due to some sort of disorder outside the entrance to Kibble barrier and usually caused by CND and those other action groups. The security of Coulport has also been breached with CND activists successfully cutting through the fence and gaining entry to the establishment. And I'm happy to add, on every occasion the intruders were apprehended and handed over to the local territorial police force. One thing I must say about my time working at Coulport; when any type of incident was reported which required immediate police action, the boys were up and at it without any hesitation or complaint. Depending on the type of incident they knew exactly what they should do and where they should be. All their training kicked in and during those incidents you never heard anyone complain about inclement weather, they just got on with the task in hand.

For years and before and during disturbances and demonstrations just outside Coulport's fences, Strathclyde police were usually in attendance and normally arrested, processed and charged any offenders. The MDP external patrol unit (the Transit) patrolled outside the wire on the Northern Access Road and the surrounding military lands; the unit included a sergeant and five constables. If a disturbance was reported at Kibble Barrier, the external patrol would attend and assist Strathclyde police when required. Which, to be honest, wasn't that often.

Although Strathclyde police dealt with most incidents requiring police attendance, the external unit, using its constabulary powers, was able to offer members of the public assistance until Strathclyde police arrived on the scene and took over. Again, through time, cooperation between Strathclyde police and the MDP did improve, so much so the external units were given authority to issue traffic tickets and deal with various offences without the need for a territorial police presence.

These days and with the local agreements between the MDP Chief Constable and other (territorial) Chief Constables, working relationships between the MDP and other police forces has improved significantly.

Getting back to my early days; quite a number of MDP officers became

The Northern Access Road

completely disillusioned working at Coulport with its filthy building site conditions, its busy gates, miles of fence line and doing next to no police work. The working conditions weren't made easier either by a minority of obnoxious supervisors. Several patrol supervisors insisted meal breaks were taken at specific times and would spend a lot of their time planning a meal break roster. If you weren't hungry at your nominated meal time, tough luck, you couldn't swap with a colleague who 'was' hungry; absolutely mental eh.

Disheartened and frustrated coppers resigned from the MDP to join territorial forces; others found new careers in police forces from other continents, a few even found jobs on building sites; no, they didn't, I jest. One cop, Mickey Michaels, from my initial recruit's course, lasted around six weeks before he gave up and went back to his former job working with an insurance company. Just about every shift Mickey worked was at a gate and more often than not the weather was horrendous. If I include every gate and exposed static post that was operated on a daily basis, I would say Coulport must have had around a dozen points where a copper could have taken a pounding from the inclement weather.

Me, I obviously stuck it out and I have to say, that fisherman's outfit and wearing wellingtons also helped me to overcome the frequent bad weather whenever I could get away with wearing them. Some supervisors sympathised with you and turned a blind eye, others were not so sympathetic. I didn't care; I wore my alternative police attire until I was ordered to take it off.

I can remember during a refreshment break (taken in a portakabin), sitting with a few of my former industrial colleagues (several welders) and just laughing at the ridiculous, yet similar, working conditions we escaped from. We left industry behind to get away from the difficult working conditions and avoid the constant noise from heavy industrial machinery. Now here we were; back in familiar surroundings with the muck and grime and, as some might say, masquerading as police officers.

Another point which probably helped us not to resign was, we were not young and immature boys when we started our MOD police career, several of us were married with young families and knew the conditions would improve.

The more downcast and dejected coppers took their frustrations out on their colleagues and during the designated refreshment breaks childish pranks were often played. Many a police cap was shrunk and ruined after being incinerated by a quick burst of a microwave oven's electromagnetic radiation.

Other bored and fed up coppers would spend their 45-minute meal break, drying their uniform, sleeping, eating and also planning the next prank or comedy caper. In the 1990s, Special Weapon Groups (SWGs) were formed at Coulport with six coppers making up one team. During an early shift when one team were together on a foot patrol in a rural area of Coulport, one copper, Frank Granger, who wanted to add a little humour to his day, dared one of the team, Allan (Barrsy) Barr (*left*), to do a pretty ridiculous and stupid stunt.

The area the team were patrolling has three miles of undulating concrete track which was constructed close to, and follows, Coulport's alarmed perimeter fence line. A large number of tall, criss-cross, metal-framed Pan Tilt and Zoom surveillance cameras were erected at intervals along the fence line and are activated by any disturbance to the sensitive fence.

When a fence zone is triggered a number of cameras will automatically swivel to the activated zone and scan the area. The cameras can also be manually operated by the MDP in the main police control room.

Now, at a flat section on that perimeter track two metal upright posts (around 10 feet high and 20 feet apart) were erected with an overhead cross beam; very similar in shape to a football goal frame. The thickness of the square posts was not very wide and a strong hand could easily manage a tight grip.

As the group strolled along the perimeter track and got close to that frame, Frank asked Barrsy if he could climb up a post and shimmy his way along the crossbeam then climb down the other side.

The wee man was on and scaling the first upright post in a flash. When he was half way along the crossbeam, arms swinging like a marionette, the others, now in fits of laughter, picked up some loose stones and pelted the sensitive fence. The alarm obviously activated which then saw a number of security cameras automatically swivel towards the activated zone. After checking the fence line, one camera, now being manually operated from the control room, panned towards the perimeter track in the general direction of Barrsy, who continued to shimmy along the frame. Now imitating a rabid chimpanzee Barrsy frantically continued his circus performance hoping to complete it before being spotted by the camera; he failed. The camera followed Barrsy until his safe touch down on terra firma.

Frank was the only one of the other four who could stop laughing long enough to transmit a radio message to the control room admitting to the alarm activation. Before being returned to its pre-set position the camera panned left and right a few times, like a disapproving mother shaking her head at her naughty child. Barrsy eventually transferred out of the Coulport mad house and, like Frank, a few years later volunteered for the UN mission in Kosovo. You'll meet Barrsy again later when he took on the more serious role as the Chief of Pristina Regional Support Unit.

Eventually, and to develop my so far boring career, I started applying for training courses at the MDP training school (now based at Wethersfield in Essex) and unlike my colleagues before me, I 'was' interested in the courses and the course curriculum. Three of those courses would later prove to be very beneficial during my overseas deployments when I was offered very rewarding positions.

Today the MDP's monotonous chores are shared or have been taken over by the Ministry of Defence Guard Service who take on guarding and security duties that do not require police powers or armed personnel.

CHAPTER FOUR
The Good Friday Agreement

OVER THE NEXT few years I tried to keep my nose in the Scots law book whenever I had the chance and on two occasions during the 1990s I was, unfortunately, unsuccessful at the constable to sergeant promotion (written) exam. I was also determined to make the most of what I had at the time and knew the MDP was, on the whole, making progress. Attending courses at Wethersfield helped me to forget the Coulport regime and made me see the bigger picture.

After ten years in the job and with many courses behind me I probably should have been more settled at Coulport. The reconstruction programme was complete and I was spending a lot of time, out of the rain, on mobile patrol duties. I was spending time as a tutor constable and was responsible for the progress of a number of probationers. I was also a First Aid trainer and qualified to teach five-day and one-day courses. However, during those years my police training and skills were rarely tested.

During a morning shift, sometime near the beginning of 2000, I was on duty at Kibble barrier and taking my break in the portakabin. I forgot to buy a newspaper that morning and after trawling through a couple of drawers looking for any reading material I found an old newspaper from December 1999. One of its headlines caught my attention: *Praise for RUC's Kosovo role*. Although the paper was more or less in bits, I could make out some of the report, it came from Northern Ireland security minister, Adam Ingram. 'Their work to build a sense of personal security among the people of Kosovo is essential to establishing a proper and decent quality of life,' he said. 'Wherever we went, people spoke highly of their work and professionalism,' he continued.

Like most of the world, I knew about the war in Kosovo and had followed most of the BBC's reports. After the war, I didn't know about the RUC's involvement. A short time after reading the newspaper article, I heard some confusing and conflicting whispers about MDP and a possible deployment to Kosovo.

The opportunity for the MDP to deploy its officers in Kosovo came about following a report which gave specific recommendations made by the Independent Commission on Policing for Northern Ireland (The Patten Commission) which was established in 1998 as part of the *Good Friday Agreement*. This agreement, after much discussion, was reached between Irish political leaders and the British government as a major step in the Northern Ireland peace process and combines two inter-related documents both signed in Belfast on Good Friday, 10 April 1998.

The Patten Commission, chaired by Conservative politician Chris Patten, recommended that the Royal Ulster Constabulary should be greatly reduced in number (over a period of time) from approximately 13,000 personnel to around 8,000. This report was published on 9 September 1999, two months before the RUC deployed sixty officers to the UN mission in Kosovo.

After the publication, Sir Ronnie Flannigan, Chief Constable of the RUC, strongly opposed the reduction plan commenting it could jeopardise future RUC deployments to Kosovo.

The UK government originally agreed to participate in the UN post-conflict reconstruction of Kosovo following the NATO intervention in 1999. And, as I've already mentioned, part of the UN Resolution 1244 was to provide an executive policing service for Kosovo whilst simultaneously creating a new and local police force. The original model for the Kosovo Police Service identified that there was a need for both the executive and new regional police services to be armed.

There was an agreement with the Association of Chief Police Officers (ACPO) that the Foreign and Commonwealth Office (FCO) would not poach home office Authorised Firearms Officers (AFOs) for the Kosovo mission as they were deemed to be in short supply. That did not include the RUC who, like the MDP, were 100 per cent armed, mainly for self-protection and not as AFOs.

The FCO then asked the MOD to provide a contingency should the RUC be withdrawn, the original plan being to use soldiers (the Royal Military Police). This was not acceptable to the UN as Resolution 1244 called for a move away from the military.

At that time the second Permanent Under-Secretary for Defence was the owner of the MDP, and he suggested the MDP as an alternative. The initial thought was that there would not be a need to send MDP officers and that the RUC would continue. However, the Policing Board of Northern Ireland instructed that the RUC be withdrawn.

MDP's Chief Constable, Walter Boreham, called a Senior Police Officers' conference at Wethersfield where the idea of sending officers to Kosovo, which had already been met with a lot of derision, was run down by the majority of those present.

Two superintendents who supported the Kosovo proposal were Tom Sloman and Geoff Heal. Tom became the first MDP overseas Contingent Commander (June 2000 to June 2001) followed by Geoff Heal who became my first Contingent Commander in June 2001.

Now that deployments to Kosovo seemed a reality for the MDP, it became quite a talking point. Who will be selected, what ranks, how many will go? And many more questions were asked.

A few of us agreed Coulport's PCs probably wouldn't be considered for such an important task; this was a job for at least a sergeant and other high ranking officers; not the inexperienced Coulport constable, we agreed. The MDP's Operational Support Units (OSU) is a rapid response unit tasked with operational support, public order and anti-terrorist search duties: 'They are much more qualified for this,' I thought. I'm glad to say, I was completely wrong, on most counts.

When the Kosovo announcement was made through an MDP Force Order, I had mixed feelings on the application criteria; there was no mention of which ranks could apply. 'Good,' I thought; however, I still didn't think I stood a chance of getting through the paper sieve. The first part of the criteria read:

> *The work is demanding and for this reason each individual person*
> *sent on a mission must meet the following criteria:*
> *Proven policing background, skills and experience (minimum of*
> *   eight years' service by date of deployment)*
> *Adaptability and resilience under pressure*
> *Team work skills*
> *Communication skills*
> *Genuine reason for applying*

Proven policing background skills and experience? Stop right there. After ten years in the job, the only crime-related entry in my police pocketbook was made after a practical exercise; on my recruit's course. And maybe the fear of being disappointed during the initial application process was one reason why many Coulport applicants never made themselves known; not, that is, until their name appeared on the official pre-deployment list. According to the MDP overseas deployment office many of those officers who did apply were, for various reasons, unsuccessful.

I also knew riot control was to be part of the pre-deployment training and the only experience I had with any type of public disorder was when I witnessed a chip shop proprietor batter six pieces of cod. However, just on the off chance I might be selected, I casually mentioned the opportunity at home only to get 'that look'. I declined from applying; on that first occasion.

When the list of names for the first pre-deployment training course was known, there were a few raised eyebrows. I was shocked as well as delighted. Most officers on the list were PCs and quite a few were from Coulport. I don't know how many officers applied or what ranks they were, I didn't care, I knew I had a chance when I did decide to apply.

I was reasonably happy to wait, and grind my wife down whilst the first contingent of Coulport guinea pigs headed east. Around late January 2001 the application and criteria for the second rotation was published. I'd had enough of arguing with my wife about can I can't I. I was applying and didn't care less who knew about it. I had spoken to my line manager and he helped me with the application. My role as a tutor constable also helped to tick some of the boxes. My evidence in support of the application was enhanced by my vivid imagination and my ability to talk for Scotland, as it were. Of the sixty or so police officers on my regular shift, I can only remember the name of one other PC, Gordon Campbell, who applied.

I forwarded the application and waited for a couple of weeks before I received a somewhat surprising reply:

> *Dear Colleague,*
> *You have been selected by the Foreign and Commonwealth Office for overseas deployment to Kosovo. Accordingly, on their behalf, I would like to invite you to a Pre-Deployment training course to be held at:*
>
> *The Ministry of Defence Police and Guarding Agency Headquarters Agency Training Centre, Wethersfield, Braintree, Essex CM7 4AZ*
>
> *The course is residential and will be held between Saturday 31 March and Friday 20 April 2001.*

That's just a small extract from a reply letter, confirming my successful application, and it also contained a list of names of those officers who'd also been selected for the next Kosovo deployment; Gordon Campbell was also included. I saw names I recognised from other MOD stations and some PCs I'd met during training courses.

When the contents of that letter sunk in I started to realise what I may be letting myself in for. I was going to be a real policeman, facing real and probably very dangerous situations. My life could be at risk. It was all a bit crazy, I was crazy; however, I wasn't backing out.

The next few weeks came and went; more gates and more rain. I spoke briefly to fellow PC Martin (Marty) Walsh who was also on the pre-deployment training list. Martin mentioned one Coulport PC from the first rotation, Tommy Coates; who was in a supervisory position and had applied to extend his mission. 'That's good news,' I thought. Conditions can't be that bad; if he's applied to extend he must be enjoying the experience. And he's a supervisor, how did that come about, he's only a PC?

CHAPTER FIVE
Pre-Deployment Training

WEEK ONE

It was 7.00 am, Sunday 1 April 2001, day one of the three weeks pre-deployment induction course.

There must have been around fifty anxious, Kosovo-bound, police officers gathered at the Police Training Centre for the pre-deployment training. That morning we ate breakfast in relative silence in the training centre canteen. My silence was caused more by fear than apprehension.

Those, like me, who flew down from Scotland the night before were knackered; our flight from Glasgow was delayed and we missed the MOD transport to PTC Wethersfield, which left Stansted airport 'promptly' at 10.30 pm. We waited over an hour before realising we weren't being picked up. I ordered the taxis, which made the forty-minute journey to Wethersfield.

After breakfast the pre-deployment 'hopefuls' were scheduled to attend the training centre's occupational health department where 'stringent medical tests' would be carried out throughout the duration of the day. I had the first appointment time, 8.10 am, which was a good time for me.

After the medical, the rest of the day was your own and I had agreed, on behalf of the alcohol-starved Scottish coppers, to pop down to the local licenced grocer and buy a few 'provisions'.

I sat nervously in the medical centre waiting room with a number of unfamiliar MDP officers. No one was in the mood for talking. Although we were from the same police force most of us were based at different defence locations spread across the UK. Formal introductions did come later.

During breakfast someone briefly mentioned a digital rectal examination and without probing him (pun intended) I thought, 'It's April Fool's Day, keep quiet'. After a long thirty-minute wait a young nurse appeared and, after looking at a clipboard, quietly said, 'Constable 4631 John Duncanson'.

'Here we go I thought.' For some reason I stood up and raised my right hand like the proverbial guilty school boy.

I was then introduced to the doctor who wore a pair of tight latex surgical gloves over his, huge, Lancashire sausage-looking fingers.

After a good going over and having blood samples taken the doctor then took off and discarded his gloves. He snapped on a fresh pair, which he then lubricated with a cold clear gel.

'I assume you know what's coming next,' he said. 'This ain't no April fool joke,' I thought.

As I lay on a bed, with my back to the doc, I heard, 'Bring both knees up to your chest and breathe in.' Huuuuuuuuuup!!

Although the violation of my chubby and clenched bottom lasted no more than a couple of seconds it was long enough to feel like a cold FAB ice-lolly had penetrated my insides, 'And breathe out.' Puuuuuuuuuuh.

The unintentional molestation and medical was complete and I left the medical centre with a definite squelching noise coming from behind me.

I waited half an hour after the medical before picking up those much needed provisions, which I stored in the communal fridge of our accommodation block. The one-storey accommodation blocks had around forty single bedrooms. Every block had four bathrooms and a communal TV room with a small kitchen.

Although females were housed in a separate block, it didn't stop the women from the Kosovo course dropping in for a cup of tea and the odd *cold* beverage.

I spent the remainder of that morning unpacking in the accommodation block, where gradually more people returned from Occupational Health.

A number of courses were taking place at the training school, including a Police Recruit Course. Happy memories. By late afternoon most of the medicals were complete and quite a few of my course gathered in the TV room, most preferring to stand, getting better acquainted.

During the evening, in the training centre bar of all places, the doctor privately announced individual results of the medicals. My results were pretty much perfect; including my blood pressure which the doctor explained measured 120/70. The doctor also mentioned a chest x-ray would be needed at some point during the course and also, if required, a number of inoculations. I received jabs for Hepatitis A and B, Typhoid, Polio, Diphtheria/Tetanus and Rabies.

Later that evening I heard two officers had actually failed their medical. I don't know why, but they had to return to their stations the following morning. Another was told to eat bananas as his potassium level was low. Apparently the average Chiquita banana contains about 422 mg of potassium (a little less than ½ a gram), making bananas a potassium super fruit; that's 13 per cent of the daily-recommended amount of potassium from only one banana, so there you are, interesting, eh.

The bar was packed with some thirsty coppers, especially those of us who followed the rules beforehand, as per the training school joining instructions for our particular course.

> *'You should abstain from drinking alcohol or taking part in strenuous physical exercise for at least five days prior to the induction training as either may produce an adverse influence on blood test results.'*

Quite a few of the Kosovo course remained in the bar until kicking out time and some of us were merrier than others. Questions were starting to be asked about Kosovo and it was those questions you think about but are afraid to ask. One particular question was 'Do you think they'll sell brown sauce'? At the time the company had a good laugh, however, I have never found a local shop in Kosovo that sells brown sauce.

One hilarious comment made by an inspector of all ranks was 'when I told my wife I was selected for Kosovo her face turned as white as a beetroot.'

That night we certainly got to know one another a little better and had a few more nights and laughs in the training centre bar.

LECTURES

Formal introductions took place in a classroom and for the duration of that pre-deployment course all officers were dressed in plain clothes. As it was a non-ranking mission, all officers were treated as equals and on first name terms. Most police ranks present were constables with a number of sergeants and inspectors. The highest ranking officer was a superintendent.

Along with everyone else I took the opportunity to explain where I was stationed, my rank, why I volunteered, and what expectations and concerns I had for the 'unknown journey' that lay ahead. Many of those coppers present had much more experience than the likes of me and had done quite a bit of police work. 'You're out your depth big man,' crossed my mind, after I listened to most of the others and their experiences.

A few of the England-based coppers had been involved in various crowd control incidents where many violent protestors and demonstrators were arrested. I can remember the Poll Tax riots (1990) where MDP officers were directly involved, with many receiving severe injuries. Protests and demonstrations were being held on a regular basis in Kosovo and I wasn't looking forward to either.

The rest of the first week was spent (with our two MDP course instructors) travelling between the classroom and a lecture theatre and the bar of course. Most of the lectures attended were boring and the PowerPoint presentations were tiresome.

The seats in the lecture theatre (a converted cinema) were a lot more comfortable than a rigid and upright classroom chair and it wasn't difficult to drift off to sleep, especially during those boring PowerPoints.

The curriculum for the week included:

- History and culture of Kosovo
- Control of UN property
- Map reading
- Media and radio
- Mine brief
- Monitoring introduction
- Monitoring report writing
- UN and KPS policy and procedure
- Officer survival
- Sexual harassment and HIV education
- Code of conduct
- Human rights
- Security briefing

Guest speakers from various departments within (and outside) the MOD were invited to present and discuss their specialised subject and during that week some really drove me to distraction with their monotonous voices and mind-numbing PowerPoint presentations.

One lecture, 'The History and Culture of Kosovo' was much less distracting and very informative. It was presented by a British UN official and two UN language assistants. Due to the multinational nature of peacekeeping operations, most peacekeepers will not be able to communicate with local people of the host country in their own language. The UN will typically employ local people as language assistants (LAs) to help peacekeepers with translation and interpretation. Although Turkish, Bosnian and Romany have official status in relevant municipalities, Kosovo's official languages are Albanian and Serbian.

The intent of the history and culture of the Kosovo lecture was to explain the historical origin and roots of the Albanians and the Serbians which went back to before the start of the Roman Empire. Both LAs, Valbona and Jelena spoke very passionately about their culture and beliefs and by the end of the lesson, and believe me it was a lesson, I learned Valbona was Albanian and Jelena was Serbian. Both LAs were born, and live, in Kosovo.

I also learned from both language assistants how completely different from one another the Albanian and Serbian languages are, when spoken and written. The Serbian language reminded me of Russian and as far as the Albanian language is concerned I couldn't really compare it with any other foreign language. Apparently it's comparable with Armenian and Modern Greek. The modern Albanian alphabet (36 letters) is a Latin alphabet. Serbians also use a Latin alphabet (30 letters) which differs from the Albanian alphabet; and they also use a Cyrillic alphabet (30) which does not have several letters used in other Slavic Cyrillic alphabets.

A number of our questions were answered at the end of the presentation and it was disconcerting to hear living conditions were not the greatest with the main electricity and water supplies being turned off and rationed on a daily basis. The question of job allocation was also raised and answered – vaguely – by the gentleman from the UN. We were told, 'Jobs are allocated after the successful completion of the UN induction phase which starts the day after arrival in the mission area.' That information as it turned out, was not entirely accurate. Week one of the course came to an end with Code of Conduct, Human Rights and a Security briefing.

After lunch each Friday the induction course broke up for the weekend and those flying back to Scotland caught an afternoon flight from Stansted airport.

On our return to the training centre, on the Sunday evening, we always headed

straight to the bar for last orders and a carry out. I tended to spend most of my time with those cops who I had more in common with and, apart from the obvious Scottish contingent, the football fanatics also stuck together; in the bar.

WEEK TWO

Week two was spent at the training centre's firearms training wing, where I was trained to safely handle, carry and fire a Sig Sauer P229 pistol, which was issued to me on arrival in the mission

Target used at a firing range

area and became my personal service weapon for

that first Kosovo deployment. In later deployments and after training, I was issued with a Glock 17, semi-automatic pistol.

During training, one day was set aside for attending the MDP stores department where officers were measured for a new (and modified) uniform, which included UN beret and UN and UK police (identification) badges. I was also given the opportunity to examine and check the contents of a personal issued (metal) travelling chest which was incredibly heavy and contained vital safety and personal equipment. Most of the equipment was supplied by the Metropolitan Police.

WEEK THREE

The training centre at Wethersfield covers a large area. A large grass area (including a football pitch and baseball diamond) separates the student accommodation from the main PTC and a small housing estate where MOD employees live with their families. It also has an area with empty houses and buildings which are used for training purposes. Three large runways are also used as training areas.

The RUC first deployed to Kosovo in November 1999 and the MDP Head

Typical electric arc welder

of Firearms Training, Andy Kirkwood (the former training school drill sergeant and now a chief inspector) was sent to Belfast to share and compare notes with RUC trainers.

Through the RUC's knowledge and experience of the Kosovo mission, Andy put together a training programme for all Kosovo candidates. Four RUC instructors were then invited to assist with the first MDP contingents' training.

The training involved high level firearms tactics in built up and urban scenarios. Improvised Explosive Device (IED) search training, mine awareness and hostile environment inputs came from the British military.

A fairly basic level of Public Order training was also carried out and took place at the Operational Support Unit. The borrowed police protective equipment was excellent and included limb protectors, polycarbonate transparent shields and rigid batons. Personal issued ballistic helmets and tactical (stab proof) vests were also worn; both of which travelled to and were issued in, Kosovo. Although it was entitled basic training, I still found the public order training extremely strenuous and also very compact. Tactical applications were taught in crowd control during non-violent and violent protests and demonstrations.

Practical scenarios were based on real life occurrences in Kosovo and included situations where the police (local and international) were involved in building entry, corridor and room search, disarming suspects and vehicle searches. Normally those exercises involved small groups of the pre-deployment officers and role actors. A number of scenarios took place indoors using a Fire Arms Training Simulator (F.A.T.S). The F.A.T.S system is entirely interactive and uses a computer programme, a large screen and very realistic firearms that are loaded with computer chips instead of ammunition. In fact it looks like a big video game.

After each strenuous and exhausting day it was back to the block for a few cans of Heineken, a warm bath, an early dinner and then across to the bar for a few more beers.

Near the end of the last week of the practical scenarios, one final exercise was organised involving the entire pre-deployment course. The course was examined in several areas, again using role actors who delivered a variety of compliant and non-compliant scenarios. By the end of that day, we were exhausted, however, we were also very well trained for the potential dangers ahead of us.

On the second to last day of training the course gathered in the classroom where the course instructors introduced an unexpected guest.

Jed Hunter, a PC just back from Kosovo, on home leave, had volunteered to pay the training school a visit and, on behalf of the current Contingent Commander, tried to answer some of our original questions.

Jed was nearing the end of the MDP's first, one year, Kosovo deployment, before he was due to return to duty in the UK. However, an extension request had been granted and Jed would complete a further six months. In future Kosovo deployments many MDP officers would complete a two-year secondment.

At first I couldn't take Jed seriously; he stood addressing my course in his full UN peacekeeping attire. He wore the Blue UN Beret with a gleaming enamel UN badge; a short sleeved, sky blue shirt with an embroidered canvas (rectangular) patch displaying the word 'police' above the left breast pocket.

On the right arm of his shirt was a circular embroidered patch also bearing the UN insignia and on the left arm another circular embroidered patch bearing the Union flag and United Kingdom Police. He also wore dark blue trousers and a pair of immaculately (bull) polished black Pro-boots.

Jed worked in Pristina, as did hundreds of other internationals (not only police) and according to Jed you could do a lot worse than be deployed to Pristina. 'Try and stay away from the Mitrovica region,' we were warned. Apparently Mitrovica was one region to be avoided at all times. 'Mitrovica is a hot spot where trouble can kick off in a matter of seconds,' Jed continued. Jed also answered most of our questions and his knowledge of the UN system seemed to be quite good.

Jed made attempts to answer a few main questions by telling us what happened during his one week UN induction course held at the UN Police Training Centre (PTC) in Pristina.

On arrival in the mission area, hotel accommodation was provided, however, it wasn't free of charge. The local UN hotel where Jed stayed was 95 German Deutschmarks per night. In January 2002 Kosovo replaced the Deutschmark with the Euro. The exchange rate was roughly 1 Euro = 1.92 Deutschmarks. Apart from the burea de change offices, 'money men' loiter on Kosovo's city street corners and will exchange most currencies for Euros and the Serbian dinar.

Jed explained the initial week at the UN Police Training School was taken up with mission checks which involved a pile of paperwork and the issue of UN equipment, including a UNMIK POLICE ID card (like a police warrant card). More lectures and PowerPoint presentations were held and also an English language test, a 4x4 driving assessment and finally the safe handling of a firearm and a shooting proficiency test, which was carried out with your personal issued weapon. The induction week was also an opportunity for new arrivals to secure a job. The previous comment by the UN representative regarding job allocation was quickly dispelled by Jed.

During breaks from the lectures CIVPOL Heads of (various) Departments and unit team leaders would be milling around the training centre. Those selective supervisors waited for an opportunity to speak with new mission arrivals with a view to recruiting those officers who they considered to be suitably qualified. Those supervisors were usually from specialised units that sought a particular brand of police officer.

Officially the UN representative, I mentioned earlier, was following the rules when he explained the job allocation, however, poaching CIVPOL during the induction week was an acceptable wrong. When Jed's induction training was complete the Contingent Commander produced a list containing the names of all UK contingent members, what region they were being deployed to and a contact number of that region's personnel department. Re-deployment papers were also produced for the attention of the region's Chief of Admin Services.

As far as living accommodation was concerned, you basically found your own. Local UN language assistants and small estate agents were the main source of information. There were plenty of local householders only too willing to take your money. Most owned empty furnished accommodation, whilst others offered accommodation in their home which was usually below or above their own occupied family home.

After coming to an agreement with the householder regarding rent and utilities the lease agreement was signed by the UN staff member and his new landlord before being forwarded to the regional personnel department.

I found Jed's talk very informative and I think my upbringing on the Glasgow Clydeside helped toughen me up for the whole process of working and living in Kosovo; which was now just six weeks away.

PTC staff

Winter whiteout in Kosovo

PART TWO

KOSOVO

JUNE 2001 to DECEMBER 2002

WITH THE TEMPORARY transformation from MDP police constable to that of a UNMIK civilian police officer just about to take place, it's important to mention the following details and explain a little more about working in Kosovo and the territory itself.

UNMIK received its initial operational idea based on a report from the then Secretary General, Kofi Anan, on 12 June 1999, and announced its authority by its first regulation. The procedures of the international communities were included and a chain of command was set up. Under UNMIK four pillars were formed whose administration and lead responsibility was allocated to different international agencies:

- Pillar one, Humanitarian Affairs, was entrusted to the UNHCR.
- Pillar two, Interim Civil Administration, was given to the UN.
- Pillar three, Institution Building under the control of the OSCE.
- Pillar four, Economic Reconstruction – the task and responsibility of the EU.

On 22 May 2001, Pillar one was changed and renamed '*Police and Justice*'. Although my main focus of attention will obviously be centred on Police and Justice, in order to provide an overview of the challenges faced by international agencies, I have mentioned a little of Kosovo's political and humanitarian situations.

In 1999 the security problem in Kosovo was largely a result of the absence of law and order institutions and agencies. While KFOR was initially responsible for maintaining public safety and civil law and order, its ability was limited due to the fact that it was still in the process of building its own forces. The absence of a legitimate police force was deeply felt.

Three main targets of the UN's effort in Kosovo were:

- Deploy an international civilian police force with executive authority.
- Create and train a new local (armed) Kosovo police service before handing over authority.
- As soon as the new Kosovo Police Service are entirely functional, UNMIK will transfer more and more responsibility for law and order and will revert to training, advisory and monitoring functions.

UNMIK Police consist of International Civilian Police (CIVPOL), Special Police Units (SPU) and the Border and Boundary Police (BBP).

This was the first executive police mission in the history of the United Nations.

Executive authority: UNMIK police will retain the power of arrest and seizure. They will have the power to intercede into the operational duties of the Kosovo Police Service to cease any violation of policy or an abuse of authority.

Deployment of CIVPOL was very slow. Rosters of police officers who would be ready and able for quick deployment, from their home force, to overseas assignments were not compiled as the UN first thought. In the case of Kosovo, the CIVPOL unit working in New York started to panic and with less emphasis on quality, attempted to find police officers who could head off to the Balkan peninsular at very short notice.

UN Selection Assistance Teams (SAT) were deployed (for pre-deployment screening) in over forty countries with the aim of assisting the police contributing countries in their selection process of their national police personnel. The selection process produced the standard UN test, English language test, 4x4 driving assessment and the shooting proficiency test. Those who passed were approved to travel; those who failed remained in their country. That process helped to improve the quality of officer selection. Nevertheless, several officers whose oral English was well below the standards set did manage to slip through the net.

I personally met many CIVPOL whose command of the English language was less than satisfactory. I can remember working with one Turkish CIVPOL officer whose ridiculously poor understanding of all aspects of English caused him to seek out and have other Turkish CIVPOL act as his language assistant and translator.

I also met a CIVPOL officer from Bangladesh with no formal police qualifications or experience whatsoever; he was actually an architect. The reason for his UN secondment to UNMIK, where he would no doubt have earned a small fortune, was to reward him for designing a Bangladeshi police station.

And incredibly several CIVPOL officers from the USA, who normally drove automatic vehicles in their home country, could barely drive a manual transmission vehicle. One officer, who knew I was a former driving instructor, actually asked me for driving lessons.

Many CIVPOL complained about their colleagues stating they would much rather have a smaller unit of good quality CIVPOL than the same number of quality officers dispersed in a larger, less capable unit. They were also of the opinion that supervising and correcting the mistakes of the less able draws off energy and morale; and the less qualified officers gave CIVPOL a bad image.

During late 1999 and early 2000 the image of UNMIK police was also being tarnished by patrolling CIVPOL officers who preferred to frequent and remain (for long periods) in the relative safety of the local café bars, mainly in Pristina, to the potentially dangerous streets of Kosovo's cities. Local citizens began to believe some CIVPOL were in Kosovo JUST to make money and have a good time. Some CIVPOL were even reluctant to leave police stations or their police vehicles if faced with the smallest of incidents.

CIVPOL management was made aware of the lack of officer motivation and participation and promoted and demanded a more assertive approach. Higher profile and aggressive policing and an increase in contact with local and minority communities came into force. The RUC with their deep experience of policing Northern Ireland was particularly effective in Kosovo. RUC officers frequently carried out joint patrols with KFOR and conducted many searches of vehicles, people, buildings *and* cafés, looking for illegal weapons. They also formed firm community contacts by being proactive in various non-police-related deeds, including building playgrounds and collecting toys for local children. This show of charitable goodwill was also adopted by members of the MDP, including me who, with a few MDP colleagues raised thousands of Euros through the simple task of organising a weekly pub quiz.

By mid-2002, there were around 5,000 Kosovo police officers (and growing), including mid-level and higher level managers as well as specialised personnel in criminal investigation and training. Sixteen per cent of KPS were ethnic minorities who police in their local communities, and seventeen per cent were women.

The total number of UNMIK police was around the 4,000 mark and included over 3,000 CIVPOL and around 1,000 BBP and SPUs.

According to Kosovo's demographic profile its population since 2000 has been between approximately 1.8 million and 2 million. Of this figure, 92 per cent are Albanian with 8 per cent consisting of non-Albanians; the majority of that 8 per cent are Serbians. Other ethnicities include Bosniak, Gorani, Roma, Turk, Ashkali and Egyptian.

The main religions followed are Islam and Catholicism (Albania), and Serbian Orthodox. The main languages spoken are Albanian and Serbian, with others being Bosnian, Turkish and Romany.

To Pristina (capital in the south), Northern Kosovo (predominately Serbian communities), marks a land which is left alone to function autonomously; to Belgrade (capital of Serbia), the entire region remains subject to the terms of the Kumanovo Treaty.

The Kumanovo Treaty is a Military Technical Agreement between the International Security Force (KFOR) and the Governments of the Federal Republic of Yugoslavia and the Republic of Serbia.

Although not an official Eurozone member, the Euro is the official currency of Kosovo. Kosovo adopted the German Mark in 1999 to replace the Serbian Dinar and later in 2002 replaced it with the Euro, although the Serbian Dinar is still used in some Serb-majority areas (mostly in the north).

CHAPTER SIX
Journey to the Unknown

06 JUNE 2001

The six weeks after the pre-deployment training came and went, not surprisingly, nothing of any significance occurred at Coulport. Oh, except Gordon Campbell broke his leg and never made it to Kosovo, which turned out to be a blessing in disguise for Gordon. After recovering from his injury Gordon was offered a deployment to the Pitcairn Islands as an alternative to Kosovo. Whilst travelling to Pitcairn via New Zealand Gordon applied to join the Auckland police. His application was successful and he is now settled in Auckland.

One check-in desk at London Stansted airport had been opened specifically for the Kosovo-bound officers and a sign above the check-in desk, along with two armed Essex police officers, turned a few heads. The sign read, 'Ministry of Defence police Kosovo deployment'. I had a good look at the sign before handing over my passport to one of the two very sombre-looking ground staff who were checking us in. After checking in my five pieces of luggage I was told to have a nice trip. I pondered the words 'nice trip'.

Those being deployed were escorted through the airport, by the two armed Essex cops, to a VIP lounge where we were met by the MDP Chief Constable Lloyd Clark. I didn't need to be asked twice by the boss to help myself to a drink. I had a large vodka and diet coke followed by another large vodka and diet coke.

After a short stay in the VIP lounge and a good luck speech from Lloyd Clark we were escorted through the departure lounge to an awaiting coach that transported us to the waiting plane.

Two hours after check-in and I was sitting alone (three seats from the back) on an aisle seat of a Boeing 737 aeroplane bound for Kosovo and Pristina International Airport. Along with the rest of the UK2 contingent (and a few others from the international policing office), this was it, there was no turning back. There were plenty of empty seats on the plane and, like me, quite a few of my colleagues preferred to sit alone and ponder their thoughts.

My stomach was churning and my palms were sweating, normally that is pretty much par for the course when I fly, however, that morning a combination of other concerns was adding to my nervous. As soon as the seatbelt sign was switched off I headed straight for the toilet. I felt sick, I was anxious, I was sweating, I was a wreck. I sat in the toilet's small compartment and tried to compose myself. A few minutes later I heard the unmistakable deep tone of Ross Gaines coming from outside the toilet, 'John, flying is not dangerous; *crashing* is dangerous.' I just about managed a half-hearted smile. 'Maybe if the plane did crash my chances of survival would be higher than surviving a year working in Kosovo,' I thought. I did feel a little easier when I got back to my seat. Ross and Pat Kearney (both constables), who were sitting across from me, were having a little chuckle at my expense.

Pat actually became my housemate for the entire eighteen months during our

Pat Kearney

first mission. Pat was kind enough to share a little of his own mission experiences and will be mentioned again in later chapters.

During the flight I moved about the plane speaking with a number of colleagues, including PCs Martin Walsh, Harvey Denton and one PC, Matthew Chinnery, who worked at one of the small English MOD stations. Matthew, or Matt, was friendly with and had kept in touch with a number of coppers already in mission and seemed to be pretty well versed with current events in Kosovo.

Over the last three months tension had increased in a number of towns and cities, most of whose names I recognised through attending the pre-deployment training. Continuing ethnically, politically motivated violence and organised crime were the main causes of concern.

Matt mentioned a number of incidents and I was so engrossed in what he was saying, I was completely oblivious to the turbulent weather conditions which the plane was now bumping its way through. I could've been listening to a film critic analysing the latest *Hollywood war blockbuster* for all I knew. Now I was getting worried again. This wasn't a movie, it was real life and I was about to take on a supporting role.

A recent bomb explosion in Pristina city centre killed one person and injured four others. In Kamenice/Kamenica a region of Gjilan/Gnjilane a Russian KFOR soldier was shot and killed. I started to think and ask myself questions, 'The Kosovo War ended in 1999, what is going on over there?' I really wasn't expecting to hear of bomb explosions two years later; I was more used to seeing exploding police hats in microwave ovens.

One other recent incident which occurred in North Mitrovica really brought home to me the civil disobedience and complete disregard of police authority. Not long after the arrest of three Serbians in North Mitrovica, an angry crowd, also Serbians, showed up at the UNMIK police station holding the detainees and demanded their release. When that didn't happen the crowd turned on CIVPOL which resulted in the injury of twenty-one officers. Later, several vehicles and rented CIVPOL accommodation were damaged. As a consequence of that incident UNMIK temporarily suspended CIVPOL patrols in the north part of Mitrovica, which lasted several weeks. When the patrols resumed, joint patrols were carried out with CIVPOL and KFOR.

I just couldn't have imaged such disorder and violence; was I being naive? Yes, very. In a future mission myself and two other MDP PCs would become part of a nightmare when a violent incident, also in North Mitrovica, saw hundreds of Serbians, armed with guns, hand grenades and Molotov cocktails, turn on UNMIK police and KFOR.

From the beginning of 2001 and up to our arrival on that day in June, over 120 alleged murders and attempted murders (Kosovo-wide) had been reported. One other frightening statistic covering the same period of time was the number of burglaries – over 2,300. The international community had also become a very big target for organised gangs of burglars.

The last thirty minutes of the flight was similar to the Mad Mouse (roller-coaster) at Blackpool's Pleasure Beach; too much bumping and jolting for my liking. The plane's descent started with a bank to the left and a long spiral downward path towards Pristina airport. I was now sitting at a window seat looking out the window, rubbing my sweaty palms, my forehead and my thighs. I was panicking and I didn't know if it was because of the turbulence or the sight of Kosovo below.

I could see mountains and to my left I could see a massive steam of sinister looking yellow smoke bellowing from what looked like a concrete chimney. I later learned the chimney is 70 metres high and is sited at one of two coal-fired power stations belonging to the Kosovo Energy Corporation, KEK. The power stations are a short drive from the centre of Pristina and very close to the small town of Obiliq/Obilic. For at least eighteen days a year, the city of Pristina suffers from dust clouds and smoke brought over by wind from the power plants.

Just as the plane landed to my right I could see a number of small buildings and the airport terminal. To the right of the terminal I saw a number of green vehicles with flashing blue and red lights. They appeared to be moving fast and pursuing our plane, which had now come to a halt at the far end of the runway.

It didn't take long before all the passengers were allowed off the plane and told by Contingent Commander Geoff Heal to gather and wait on the tarmac until given further instructions. Just before I took my last step off the plane and onto Kosovo soil, so to speak, I just thought of Coulport and its fences and gates. Coulport suddenly didn't seem that bad after all! This 'glorified security guard' had better get a grip of himself,' I thought.

When those pursuing green vehicles arrived I could see they were occupied by Russian KFOR, which was our welcoming party. As far as I can remember, those Russian troops were acting as border control and custom officers. Although we were now surrounded by a bunch of rather tall and stern-faced Russian soldiers carrying AK-47 assault rifles and submachine guns, they never really did much; they just looked on as we unloaded the plane.

A UN bus was parked (on the runway) a short distance from the plane and on board were those MDP from the first Kosovo rotation who were returning to the UK. The UN bus would transport the incoming rotation to Pristina; that was after they emptied the plane's hold of its contents, including all of the contingent's metal travelling chests. That back-breaking task was made ten times worse by the searing heat which felt like a furnace inside the plane's hold. Just before she boarded the plane, I spoke very briefly to one of my returning MDP colleagues, Bernice Woodall. I only had time to ask if she enjoyed the experience and her reply was, 'Find an office job and stay away from Mitrovica.' After hearing about the recent incident in North Mitrovica, I fully intended to stay well clear of that unpredictable city.

CHAPTER SEVEN
Pristina

THE CITY OF Prishtina/Pristina has a majority Albanian population along with other smaller communities including Bosniaks, Romani and Serbian. In February 2000 an estimated census had the population at around half a million. It is the administrative, educational and cultural centre of Kosovo. The city is home to the University of Pristina and is served by Pristina International Airport.

PRISTINA 2001

The journey from the airport to Pristina city centre took around ninety minutes and was a real eye opener of what to expect whilst travelling (on the right hand side of the road), on the pothole ravaged and largely unpaved roads. Heavy traffic was moving slowly in both directions in long queues but this didn't prevent several crazed motorists from attempting, and just about managing to complete, ridiculously dangerous overtaking manoeuvres, which included passing vehicles on both sides and over grass verges and makeshift pavements. The driving was unbelievably atrocious.

One strange looking vehicle that caught my eye was a modified tractor. The front axle of the tractor (with two small wheels) was separated from the rear axle (with two large wheels) with a longer than usual drive shaft. Basically the tractor was cut in two to make it longer. A large seat, where the driver sat, was attached in the middle above the drive shaft and the tractor was controlled by an extended pair of handle bars. That vehicle and others modified to similar and personal specifications is known as *The Kosovo Harley.* The Kosovo Harley is used to transport all kinds of everything; from a 3lb bag of potatoes to a 500lb Busha cow.

Head-on collisions are a regular statistic on road traffic accident reports. On two occasions that first day, on a main highway I saw two red and white UN Toyota 4Runner police vehicles being driven erratically and at high speeds with a total disregard for other road users. Both passed the UN bus and appeared to be racing each other. Neither was displaying the flashing blue light on the vehicle's roof.

The Kosovo Harley

I saw a number of minor road traffic accidents between two vehicles which seemed to be caused by the following vehicle being driven too close to the vehicle in front, causing a minor shunt. I lost count of the rotting carcasses of dead dogs lying on roads and by the roadside; obviously victims of other road traffic accidents.

Occasionally the UN bus driver of the vehicle I was travelling in swerved frantically to avoid potholes, animals and pedestrians. During the journey I saw a small kid walking along the road keeping well to the right. He was clinging to a long rope and at the end of the tied rope was a very large cow. The practice of walking cows on a highway seems to be the norm. The cows are usually guided from one field to another for grazing purposes.

Today I drive on the same roads and the only conditions that have improved are the road surfaces. Major road construction has been on-going for years, with a motorway being built that will eventually lead to Albania.

Our first port of call, before Pristina, was the UN compound where mission check-in took place and the issuing of UNMIK photographic I.D. cards. Numerous amounts of paperwork were also completed; so far so good.

As the UN bus arrived on the outskirts of Pristina, the traffic grew as did the traffic jams. Vehicles were parked along the streets, with most being parked at right angles to the pavements. Many vehicles were parked on the pavements, forcing pedestrians to walk on the road. The unfamiliar and peculiar parking positions seemed to be acceptable to most road users, including the local police.

Examples of random car parking

The bus eventually turned into Police Avenue, a road where UNMIK MHQ was located along with other International and KPS buildings and institutions. The road was one way and parked bumper to bumper on both sides was a long line of red and white UN police vehicles, which incidentally are nicknamed Coca Colas, the inference being to the red and white colours of Coca Cola cans.

UNMIK MHQ in winter

Our final destination was the UN hotel, my temporary accommodation for one week, and located just off Police Avenue. After spending two hours of unloading the bus and a truck which had transported the metal chests to the hotel, I was free until 7 am the following morning.

Before heading to the nearest pub, a few of us new arrivals decided to go for a short walk and have a look at where we may be spending the next year or so.

The main language spoken in Pristina is Albanian although many young local people do speak some level of English. The city centre was smaller than I first thought, it's around two and a half square miles, however that small area is packed with shops, cafés and lots of small stalls which sold fast food and very salty popcorn.

Navigating around the city (on foot) was quite easy, however, I was very aware of those crazy motorists. Crossing the road on Ramiz Sadiku Street was a nightmare. Most roads are heavily congested and drivers have no respect for pedestrians, road signs or markings. Zebra crossings meant nothing to the average local driver. I literally had to run across the road in front of oncoming cars and buses.

The city centre also has a football stadium, home of Pristina Football Club, and has a capacity of around 16,000. During our walk we strolled down to have a look at the stadium and couldn't really get near it because of the hundreds of market stalls close to and all around it. Markets in Kosovo are very popular and

89

you'll find them in most areas that are flat and have spacious open ground. Like the smaller street stalls, the markets sell everything.

The shops and street stalls sold everything from A to Z

I also noticed more dead dogs and several strays, that I was later told, ran in packs and were extremely dangerous.

Most of Kosovo's towns were overrun by stray dogs that had basically been abandoned (during the war) and thereafter became savage scavengers. At times they became so hungry they would turn on and kill the weaker pack members. I don't think I need to explain what happened next. Men, women and children were also attacked by these strays and also one big ugly Scottish guy. Yes, the first time I had to draw my service pistol it was to scare off a pack of ravenous dogs. Luckily I didn't have to open fire. The situation with strays became so severe, dog culls were introduced and organised by local municipal hunters. Those culls took place every few months and locals with domestic pets were always advised weeks in advance.

On the way back to the hotel along Police Avenue, one side of the road was lined with café bars. Just about all those cafés, inside and out, were full of UNMIK police and KPS. That probably explained why so many Coca Colas were parked along that street.

CHAPTER EIGHT
Settling In

BACK AT THE hotel I met big Jim Holme and Martin Walsh and we headed off to a local bar which we'd heard about from other colleagues. The weather was still very hot when we took the short walk from the UN hotel to the *Kukri bar*; a British themed pub which opened in June 1999 and was owned and run by John Foreman MBE, a guy from Sunderland, England. The bar staff were a mixture of ethnic Albanian and other ethnicities including Serbian, which was very unusual under the current circumstances. Many Serbians who fled Pristina during and after the war were scared to return to the city. Those who did stay or returned were accommodated and normally remained in areas protected by KFOR. Although the Serbians who worked in the Kukri bar knew their life was more at risk outside the protected areas, they took their chances all the same.

A busy Kukri bar

The Kukri bar was the main social attraction for all working and visiting internationals and that first day it was particularly busy, both inside and out (in the small beer garden), with MDP, after members of the first rotation (who had extended their mission) congregated to meet and greet the second rotation.

A quiet Kukri bar

Several MDPs were holding court, offering advice *and* jobs to those who were prepared to listen. And it was obvious a few of my contingent had already secured jobs. They were being introduced to their *new* team leader and being told when they would officially start the job. I was told later that was the reason why so many MDP kept very quiet about their initial mission application and never spoke about it. Their colleagues in mission had a job for them, however, they (the applicants) were told, 'But don't speak about it or tell anyone, just in case.' Whatever!

At that point I was just glad to be sitting in a pub beer garden surrounded by friends and colleagues, sipping a beer and biding my time, no rush. That beer garden overlooked a pedestrian walkway and that day was the first of many (during the first mission) where I'd sit and watch some of the most beautiful women in the world go by. I also noticed the number of CIVPOL toddling around; just about every third person was an international police officer wearing a different uniform, but with very familiar headdress. In a mission area, UN police can be easily recognised by the official UN light blue beret (or cap) donning that enamel UN badge. Other than the UN beret (or cap) and UN badges, uniform worn by UN police officers is usually of the officer's home country of police authority.

Many of the international staff based in Pristina were regular visitors to the Kukri which hosted many regular social events. That first day ended late into the night after the Kukri bar became packed with many assorted internationals, some of which rarely ventured out at night. On that occasion, however, the soccer World Cup qualifiers had coaxed them out. The only home country who didn't play that night was Scotland and I was left to watch as England beat Greece two nil.

After a good night, a few beers and a good laugh, I fell into a very small and smelly UN hotel single bed. The poor conditions made no difference, I was out like a light and the next six nights were exactly the same. At 7.30 am on that first morning the new rotation gathered, in full UN attire, outside the UN hotel before walking the half a mile or so to the UN Police Training Centre. We walked along Police Avenue and although it was early morning, the cafés were starting to get busy with CIVPOL and KPS.

The week's UN induction course was nothing special and fairly straight-forward. The material presented was basically the same as that of Wethersfield. The UNMIK instructors were from various countries of the world and all with different levels of oral English. Ironically, one instructor from Turkey who presented radio communication, was particularly poor. One other lecture which I thought important to mention now was policy and procedure. The UN and KPS policy and procedure lecture was repeated during the UN induction week and I think it is important to include a little of what was explained.

Both the UN's and KPS' policy and procedure manual (PPM) is a set of rules and regulations designed to provide significant officer guidance on how they should perform their duties and how to provide professional democratic policing.

The UN's source of authority comes from the following authorities and is applicable to all UNMIK police officers whilst performing their duties:

- The UN Security Council Resolution 144 (1999), dated 10 June 1999
- UNMIK Regulations of the Special Representative of the Secretary General
- The UN Civilian Police Handbook, dated October 1995

UNMIK Police is headed by the Police Commissioner and consists of Civilian Police, (CIVPOL) Special Police Units (SPU) and the Border and Boundary Police (BBP).

The Police Commissioner's responsibilities of UNMIK are comprised of a Main Headquarters (MHQ) with support staff to facilitate UNMIK field operations.

UNMIK regions are supervised by a CIVPOL Regional Commander with support staff. UNMIK Police Stations (also occupied with KPS officers) are supervised by a CIVPOL Station Commander with support staff.

Executive police authority was retained by UNMIK who could overrule an act of duty by a KPS officer in order to stop a violation of human rights, stop a serious breach of authority or violation of rules and regulations, and to protect human life.

UNMIK police officers deployed within the mission and in cooperation with the Organisation for Security Cooperation in Europe (OSCE) were responsible for training and organising the KPS (who are also armed), including the BBP.

It was the job of the UNMIK police to ensure the actions taken by the KPS were consistent with the principles of policing in a democratic state and rule of law. The applicable laws throughout Kosovo in 2001 were the Criminal Code and the Criminal Procedure of the Socialist Federal Republic of Yugoslavia, however, nearly all UNMIK police followed the rule of law bound by their own country.

During the week, and as Jed Hunter had previously mentioned, CIVPOL supervisory staff from various UNMIK police stations, units and departments attended PTC. By the middle of the week the majority of the contingent, including those who had secured jobs prior to coming into the mission, knew which region they were being deployed in and which unit they were being deployed to. I heard a few names mentioned, neighbourhood unit, RPU, border police, station operation, PFTO, communications officer, regional crime and station patrol officer. Most of them didn't mean anything to me.

Two days before the induction course ended Tommy Coates met with several (new) contingent members and offered a vacant position, to no one in particular. Tommy was the Chief of Communications in Pristina's main control room and the position of radio control room operator was available. I was the only person who was interested and with a couple of thoughts in mind – 'Office job and not in Mitrovica' – yes please. Tommy sorted out all the paperwork and all I had to do was make sure I passed the shooting proficiency test, which I duly did; from a target that was placed at a distance of seven then ten metres.

The final day of the induction course saw most of the contingent going their separate ways and to various regions. During the eighteen-month mission, those officers who were deployed outside the Pristina region only occasionally paid the city a visit and that was usually once a month when picking up their UN salary (around £2,800) which, until January 2002 when the Euro was introduced, was paid in German Deutsche Marks and withdrawn from a local bank in Pristina. When the entire contingent was required to meet, it was for a contingent meeting, a shooting day or the UK medal (presentation) parade. Qualifying time of service for the reception of a UNMIK medal is six months.

The UNMIK medal was established in Sept-ember 1999. The ribbon has two outer bands of light UN blue, symbolising the presence of the United Nations. The inner band in dark blue symbolises the International Security presence and the cooperation and support received from it. The two bands in white symbolise the overall objective to promote peace for all the people in Kosovo.

Pat Kearney and I agreed to share a house and found accommodation together in a hilly area on the outskirts of Pristina town centre. The area, known as Dragodan, was the most popular location for international staff working in Pristina to reside and was also the location of various embassies, including the British. It was also a target area for gangs of burglars. Pat and I were lucky to escape being burgled, however, many internationals' accommodation was broken into and at times car keys were stolen along with private and police vehicles.

We had rented a two bedroom house (350 Euros per month each) with a very small sitting room, kitchen and bathroom. It also had a small balcony which was on the wrong side of the house to catch much of that first summer's glorious sunshine. In anticipation of the power cuts, the landlord supplied a very small and inadequate generator which lasted for about fifteen minutes before it required more fuel. Owing to ageing equipment and the lack of investment, serious difficulties with the supply of electricity in Kosovo was a major cause of concern and meant it had to be rationed. Power was cut every day with a rotation of two hours on then two hours off. At times it was four off, two on. At other times it was a hit and a miss affair whether it was due off or on. With support from the European Agency for Reconstruction, efforts were made to solve the problem by training staff, restructuring the management of Kosovo Electric and carrying out a comprehensive overhaul of the power generating units. Problems with the energy supply in Kosovo are deep rooted and complex, that's probably why the problem has never really been resolved. Water supplies were also rationed and switched off on a daily basis.

I had no objection to Pat having the more spacious of the house's two bedrooms. To be honest, I never knew Pat very well then, and didn't want to create any immediate animosity in a home that we'd be sharing, bar any unforeseen circumstances, for at least one year. My bedroom was very small and cluttered with a bundle of architectural equipment (belonging to the landlord's daughter) and the narrow, wooden, pine bed was six inches smaller than my five foot eleven inches body. One consolation though, I did have the balcony.

Pat was far more domesticated than me and thought more about what was needed for daily household chores. The main item required though, according to Pat, was an ironing board, good call; let's head to the nearest haberdashers. In a local market, Pat found a small store that supplied most of the items we wanted, however, he couldn't see an ironing board. He was struggling to communicate and demonstrate 'ironing actions' to the Albanian proprietor when he, the proprietor, suddenly disappeared into the back of the shop. A little boy, maybe aged eight, appeared and asked Pat in the strongest Glasgow accent, 'Can I help you mister?' Pat laughed and explained what he wanted and the young lad quipped up, 'youfaeGlesga?' Pat laughed and said, 'Aye and you sound like you've been there at some point in your young life.' The wee lad explained he was evacuated to Glasgow during the Kosovo war and was now back home in Pristina. Pat got the ironing board.

The first night in that home was completely different to the UN hotel, where, for that first week, I'd return from the Kukri, merry and tired, and immediately fall into bed and fast asleep.

First thing I needed to do was empty that metal travelling chest which contained numerous items of uniform clothing and a bundle of expensive survival and safety equipment. By the time all the bits and bobs were removed, I had enough kit to carry out an intravenous infusion in the dark whilst keeping my patient warm. If necessary, I had the means to administer mouth to mouth resuscitation, and if all else failed, I could dig a big grave. Seriously though, I had all sorts of gear. The intravenous drip came with various syringes. I had two first aid kits, one Maglite, a sleeping bag, a Laerdal pocket mask and a British Army double folding spade.

When I'd emptied the chest, I had to fill it up again. I discovered there was no space in the room's wardrobes to store a pair of socks, let alone my equipment and uniforms; the two wardrobes were packed full with female clothing.

On that first night I went to bed late and noticed a key in the lock of the bedroom door, which I made use of. The bedroom windows had wooden (exterior) shutters, also utilised during the night. Close to my bed was a small three-legged stool where I placed my loaded service pistol.

I lay in bed and could hear all sorts of noises, near and far, coming from outside. Dogs barked constantly and by their gnarling sound I assumed they were fighting one another; maybe even attacking people. I also heard gun shots, which became a regular occurrence and which I later learned could have been 'happy fire'. Special occasions are sometimes announced and celebrated by a quick burst of automatic gunfire, usually from AK47 assault rifles, especially births and weddings.

During the coming weeks in Kosovo I lay in that small uncomfortable and inadequate bed at night, and in between listening to all the familiar and unidentifiable scary distractions I couldn't help but feel very scared, vulnerable and at times sorry for myself. When I was very young, during the night, I would get so scared that I'd wake my brother and ask him if I could get into his bed. Can you image Pat Kearney's face if I did the same? 'Pat I'm scared can I sleep with you tonight?' What would the poor guy have thought of me?

It took me quite a few months to get used to that house with all its creepy night time shadows and all the unnerving noises wailing from outside. It also took me a while before I could sleep without keeping my pistol on that stool or under my pillow.

The following morning I woke early and had a long, nervous stretch before I got myself prepared for my first day as a CIVPOL radio operator in Pristina's main control room. After showering in relative darkness (due to the power being off) I joined Pat in the sitting room.

With the power being off the sitting room was dark, even with the curtains open the sunlight didn't illuminate the room. The eerie darkness just added to the nervous and peculiar situation I found myself in. It wasn't just the fact I was starting a new job. The whole experience was obviously new; Kosovo, its unfamiliar and unpredictable citizens, the UN system and of course my new living arrangements. I looked over at Pat who was studying me; we both laughed at the same time.

Pat was one of the many (newly deployed) CIVPOL who started their mission life in UNMIK police stations. He would become a patrol officer in one of four police stations situated in various districts of Pristina.

On that first morning I felt very strange walking Pristina's streets with a holster and gun strapped to my right leg; and it was very uncomfortable. The loose pistol holster was tapping my right leg every time I took a step forward. The tapping sound also reminded me, if I ever found myself in a life threatening situation, help wasn't far away.

CHAPTER NINE
Pristina Control

JUNE 2001 to DECEMBER 2001

My first day of work as an UNMIK CIVPOL officer started at 3 pm on 13 June 2001. Tommy Coates introduced me to that afternoon's staff which included two CIVPOL from the first UK rotation, Chrissy Gibson, Pristina control Deputy Chief, and Mick Slater, Duty Officer. Later Mick escorted me to the logistics department where I was issued with my first items of UN equipment, a Motorola hand-held radio, battery and charger.

Mick also helped me prepare an evacuation plan which included all my personal details and a map and grid reference to my accommodation. The evacuation plan was necessary in the event of being evacuated from the mission area. Whenever the safety and security of international staff is threatened and depending on the circumstances, a number of security phases are put into force. The last phase to be considered is evacuation from a mission area; a scary thought, but a potential reality when working in Kosovo. I was also added to a Warden's Chart which is also part of the evacuation process. Wardens are appointed to ensure proper implementation of a Security Plan in a predetermined zone of a large city.

Excluding supervisory staff, around twenty CIVPOL worked a three eight-hour shift system; morning, afternoon and night shift were worked by five radio operators. The KPS shared the control room with CIVPOL and worked similar hours but on a separate radio system and frequency. I mainly worked the afternoon 3 pm to 11 pm shift.

Twelve local staff (LAs) were also employed in the control room and between four and five worked per shift and also followed the eight-hour system. Of those twelve LAs, eleven were Albanian and one was a minority Serbian. The Serbian LA (Aleksandra), who was originally from Pristina, lived just outside the city in the small Serbian enclave town of Gracanica. During the war Aleksandra's family, like many Kosovo citizens who fled their homes, were forced to relocate to other towns and villages.

When Aleksandra was on shift, she was always picked up from her home and always escorted home after every shift. During the shift she rarely ventured from the confines of the control room. I picked her up and dropped her off on several occasions. Gracanica was one of many towns and villages within Kosovo where KFOR checkpoints and patrols ensured a safe and secure environment for all Kosovo minority citizens.

Other families fled from Kosovo and took refuge in other parts of the world, including the UK, Germany and Switzerland, before those countries forced them to return to Kosovo. The UNHCR and the International Organisation for Migration (IOM) were the chief humanitarian agencies to assist hundreds of thousands of forced and voluntary returnees. Temporary accommodation was provided by the UNHCR whilst the returnees reconstructed their homes. Many of those families who were internally displaced and through fear of reprisal have never returned home.

Aleksandra was a very pretty lady and eventually one of the American CIVPOL, from Pristina control, asked her out. Today they are married with a young family. I know of six MDPs who met and married partners whilst working in Kosovo; all of them, at one time or another, worked at Coulport. I also know several other cops from other MDP stations who met and married partners also as a consequence of working in Kosovo.

It was the language assistants who introduced me to some of the local fast food shops and stalls. Most mornings or afternoons I would have Burek, which is a baked filled pastry, made of a thin flaky dough known as phyllo (or yufka). It's usually filled with cheese, spinach or my favourite, mincemeat. It reminds me of a sausage roll, however, unlike the sausage roll, it contains very little meat. Another local favourite is Cufte (pronounced Choofty) which are little circular pieces of fried pork or beef mince, stuffed into a half slice of thick pita bread; I'm not a big fan.

Burek before being cut   *A cut Burek containing meat*

Cevapis with pitta bread and rice, another local fast food dish

Pristina control room was extremely busy and of the five rotating CIVPOL radio operators on duty, two shared the responsibility of operating the much busier secondary radio system whilst one operated the less busy primary system. The two remaining operators were the relieving officers. The operators usually rotated every hour or so.

When messages were received on the secondary system, mainly from the downtown cycle (police) patrol units, one officer was responsible for all radio transmissions, whilst the other was responsible for maintaining the radio log and making phone calls to tow truck companies. The cycle units patrolled Pristina's hectic city centre streets and issued traffic tickets to illegally parked vehicles. Other vehicles that were blocking entrances or found to be parked in a dangerous position were towed away by local contractors. The request for a tow truck was constant; every five or ten minutes and that is no exaggeration.

The tow trucks literally followed the police around. However, when a tow truck was required, the bike unit had to follow the procedure of contacting Pristina control, who in turn kept a record of which tow company was next in line to be contacted. That way most companies were given a fare allocation of the work and usually, although not always, that practice prevented tow drivers from being arrested for fighting one another over who was next in line.

For my first week I sat and watched my colleagues, who were from all corners of the world, including, India, Pakistan, Bangladesh, USA, Fiji and the Philippines and quite a few of them struggled to cope with the volume of radio traffic. And bearing in mind that it was an English-speaking mission, and taking into account some very broad accents, radio transmissions with other nationalities (including native English speakers) soon developed into long drawn out and epic dialogues.

The longer it took the operator to understand and comply with the radio message, the more frustrated the transmitting unit became. On several occasions Chrissy or Mick stepped in and took over the transmission.

I watched several operators and at times I didn't know if they were unsure about radio procedures or just plain lazy. Every UN computer is linked up to the internet and in between radio transmissions those characters would be distracted as they played on-line games or trawled the internet. At times transmissions were missed and on many occasions I heard Mick answering (and dealing with calls) over his personal hand-held radio. Other times the operator would answer a call from a unit and after maybe four or five minutes communicating with one another, the radio log would remain blank. The issue of not completing the radio log caused important information to be lost and police reports to be inaccurate and incomplete. Quite often, and after an incident, police units would rely on the dialogue from the radio log in order to complete the police report. When the responsible operator was asked why he didn't complete the radio log at the time of the transmission, there would be a blank look and no real explanation. At times the excuse would be, 'The unit was talking too fast' or 'I can't write very fast'.

On other occasions stations would phone Pristina control and ask, 'Is anyone working today?' One American officer who had reported a missing four-year-old child had been waiting for over forty minutes after asking for police assistance in searching for the child. The receiving operator was so caught up on the internet, he had either ignored or forgotten to contact a unit to assist the American officer. Such was the American officer's frustrated wait for assistance, he came back over the radio to announce, 'Pristina control, can you note, the child we are searching for is now five years old!' It was then that I first realised many CIVPOL seemed to show little interest in their job; all they wanted to do was play games or trawl Japanese websites looking for cheap cars or at estate agents to price houses. Others were logged into Yahoo chat where they would spend most of their shift chatting to complete strangers. I had no intention of letting my police force or myself down.

Before getting behind a radio set I felt it was very important to thoroughly know my new role and get to know the region I was deployed in, and so over a number of weeks I studied the control room's Standing Orders (SOs) and other important procedures. It didn't take me long to get the hang of operating procedures and by studying maps I was able to build up a picture of the Pristina region and its municipalities.

After a short time, and before reporting for my afternoon shift, I'd visit Pat Kearney at Station Four and travel as an observer with Pat during his city and surrounding area mobile patrols. I was also given permission to travel with a regional CIVPOL traffic unit, which allowed me to see more of Pristina and of Kosovo. Those familiarisation tours gave me more knowledge and understanding of the areas around the city and made my job so much easier when dispatching units to an incident.

I was able to assist units with shortcuts and guide them away from the heavily populated traffic areas. I applied for access to the Kosovo Police Information System (KPIS) which is similar to the UK Police National Computer. I soon learned how to search for and enter wanted persons and vehicles and how to navigate mapping systems. I memorised important phone numbers and kept a list of important contacts by my side. My self-appointed 'on the job' training was later recognised and became compulsory for all new CIVPOL on being deployed to Pristina control.

In the control room the KPS and CIVPOL were separated by a thin partition and communication and cooperation between both was generally good.

At the beginning of August 2001, the KPS was just two years old and had no rank structure; however, team leadership courses to build middle management were held later in the month. By October 2001, around 265 KPS were trained in supervision and management. Several of those supervisors were deployed to the control room.

The turnover of CIVPOL in the control room was quite high with most officers redeploying after two or three months. Like me, several were deployed to the control room directly from PTC. However, as soon as they possibly could, they were on the lookout for a less busy position that offered personal comforts, like their own office, a computer and an assigned vehicle.

Not that long after I started work in the control room, Tommy Coates redeployed to the Weapon Authorisation Card unit and Chrissy took over as Chief. At that point I was happy to continue learning about the mission area and assist my CIVPOL colleagues who still struggled to cope with, and understand, the English language and accents over the radio. One Indian officer in particular was finding it difficult to understand a few native English speakers and their local dialects.

I can remember one occasion when Gordon Peters, another of the UK contingent, transmitted a message requesting one unit to attend a minor road traffic accident close to Station Three, a perfect landmark. Most radio transmissions were used by giving a map grid reference, or a landmark, close to the reported incident or event.

Gordon, who was himself responding to a more serious incident, also gave a precise grid reference (using a GPS tracking device) before informing my Indian colleague he was heading away from the accident en route to Podujevo. The reply he got back was, 'Do you want to report a fire in Podujevo?' After Gordon repeated his message word for word, he was asked for a precise location. He then said, 'I have already given you the location twice and a grid reference to within one metre of the incident.' I had already contacted Station Three and told my now agitated Indian colleague to relax; a station three unit was on its way. One week later that colleague was redeployed to a very cushy office job where he was responsible for authorising and approving Compensatory Time Off (CTO) and annual leave requests, submitted by CIVPOL.

On one other occasion a CIVPOL officer came over the radio and was received by another operator from India. The CIVPOL officer immediately responded by saying, 'I want to communicate with the British guy.' I was working on that day and after apologising to my college, I took over the call. It was quite an embarrassing moment.

During every shift 'flash reports' were faxed to Pristina control. Those police reports contained initial and basic information (before the full report) of major incidents which could attract public and media attention.

Kosovo-wide situation reports were also collated by the control room and I could read at a glance what was going on mission wide. Those daily reports covered a twenty-four hour period and contained information regarding the general situation in a region. Almost everyday reports of ethnically motivated violence against Kosovo minority communities continued to occur in all regions and included – intimidation, harassment, assault, arson and murder. Political violence was also a major issue.

The situation reports also brought home to me how dangerous a territory Kosovo continued to be, even after being flooded with thousands of UNMIK police and KFOR. UNMIK and KFOR had been very busy carrying out joint operations to seize weapons and seek out those believed to be members of armed groups. KFOR reported from May to September (2001) that 1,000 suspects had been detained and 1,000 rifles and pistols seized. Other assorted weaponry was also seized, including hand grenades and anti-tank weapons.

I kept mental notes of where the hot spots were and what type of criminal acts were taking place. Mitrovica was the biggest hot spot, just about every night disturbances of various types were reported from there and most times the incident involved big crowds and firearms. Hand grenades, used in Mitrovica, were also a favourite weapon used against UNMIK and KFOR.

The number of reported murders in my first few months was twenty-five and fifteen of those were reported during my first month. The number of burglaries was just under 1,000 and thefts were just under 2,000. Many thefts against UNMIK occurred in public car parks when unattended police vehicles were broken into and personal belongings stolen by organised gangs. Several gang members prowled around car parks waiting for UNMIK police who were careless enough to leave valuables on display in the vehicle.

Having access to those daily crime reports and statistics was certainly a good way of keeping track of all the trouble and situation mission wide; and I was thankful I had an office position which kept me in a safe environment and that was a big factor in me seeing out my eighteen months contract. Several MDP decided six months in mission was more than enough time away from home and headed back to the UK. I know one officer who lasted just three days before going back home.

I suppose I was extremely lucky not to be in the firing line (so to speak) during my time in the Pristina control room. I was literally on the edge of my seat when I was the radio operator during many serious incidents. And I could only listen (and comply) as many of my CIVPOL colleagues radioed, and sometimes screamed, for back-up during violent demonstrations. On numerous occasions I received messages from my MDP colleagues as they faced dangerous and life-threatening situations unfamiliar to most MDP officers. The majority of those officers declined my request to share their mission experiences and I respect their decision.

I received reports of intimidation, harassment, assault, arson, ethnic murders, hand grenade attacks and other crimes characteristic of a post-conflict territory.

I was also on duty when the first KPS officer was killed in the line of duty. Death threats and assaults or other forms of violence are not unusual fears for KPS officers to face on a regular basis, or UNMIK police. Minor offences from the issue of a traffic ticket to a vehicle being towed often produced obscenities and threats, and in some cases, physical assaults took place.

One incident which I found extremely disturbing was when I received a flash report regarding the brutal murders of four persons from the same family. Only the youngest daughter (age seven) survived the machine-gun attack on the family's vehicle which took place on a dark, rural road.

The day after the attack the vehicle was brought to Station One as a murder inquiry began. I saw the car (a small Yugo) which was completely riddled with bullet holes, caused by, according to the police report, one or maybe more AK47s. Empty bullet casings from an AK47 were found around the crime scene. I looked inside the car and on the back seat I saw one very small blood-covered training shoe. On the dashboard I could see a piece of skull with blooded, long, dark hair. I gazed into that vehicle for a quite some time before the horrible stench of the thick, matted blood-stained seats got the better of me. I was faced with a similar situation during a future mission; however, on that occasion I was staring at a very different and much more horrific scene.

I read the police report of that family's brutal murder. The father and mother were found shot dead in the Yugo's front seats. Their son (age nine) and daughter (age twelve) were found shot dead on the back seats. The daughter who survived with no physical injuries was found under her brother. No suspects were immediately identified and I never found out if any arrests were ever made.

The reports received when working in Coulport's control room were rather different to Pristina control. Most of the routine messages received were: 'commencing foot patrol of the admin area', 'west perimeter fence checked correct or commencing mobile patrol of the explosive area'. Quite often the external mobile patrol officers would ask the question, 'Can you inform the farmer that six of his goats have wandered onto the Northern Access Road?' On a Saturday evening, the external mobile patrol officers did get busy, when picking up orders from the local Chinese takeaway restaurant.

Okay, I'm having a dig at the MDP, however, I've already mentioned my excellent police training and if it wasn't for that training and all the career development courses I attended, I would never have been offered a secondment to Kosovo in the first place.

During November, when the weather was turning very cold, and to reinforce the UNMIK police presence, I, along with other UNMIK office staff, was detailed to monitor crowd control and deal with any civil disorder at a polling station in Pristina. That day, during the 17 November elections, was my first real test of policing and controlling large crowds and I, along with one American CIVPOL and several KPS officers, controlled the lively, but reasonably well behaved, voters as they pushed and jostled one another whilst waiting in line before entering the polling station.

If I said I wasn't nervous on that day I'd be lying. From what I'd heard about Kosovo and how peaceful situations can quickly escalate I prayed that I'd get through the day unscathed. Luckily the day passed with no real incidents to talk of.

One thing that did happen that day which surprised me was when a young Albanian kid, no more than eight years old, walked slowly through the gates leading to the polling station as he carefully carried a metal tray containing two glasses of black tea, and a packet of lemon puff biscuits. He offered me and my American colleague the tea and biscuits and told us, in English, the gesture was from his grandfather who had been watching us (from his home) all day and thought we must be very cold and possibly hungry. He wanted to offer us tea to warm ourselves. I've never been so grateful for a 'glass' of tea. The biscuits also went down a treat.

The November 2001 elections, which led to the transfer of authority by UNMIK, were parliamentary elections to the Assembly of Kosovo. The Assembly was an institution within the Provisional Institution of Self-Government (PISG) established by UNMIK to provide provisional, democratic self-government in advance of a decision on the final status of Kosovo. Unlike 2000 when Serbians didn't vote in municipal elections, the parliamentary elections proved different and many Serbians did vote. The establishment of new self-government institutions represented a significant landmark in the post-conflict development of the province. The powers of new institutions were limited and despite the devolution of responsibility for the day to day running of affairs in many areas of government, the ultimate powers of the SRSG were undiminished. Kosovo's new President was Ibrahim Rugova and the new Prime Minister, Bajram Rexhepi.

Towards the end of the year I toyed with the opportunity of becoming Deputy Chief of Communications; no interview or test was necessary. Chrissy and Mick were preparing to end their mission in December 2001 and if I wanted the position, it was mine. That offer didn't go down too well with a few of my control room colleagues.

CHAPTER TEN
Moving On Up

THE DEPARTURE OF Mick and Chrissy, along with a few other CIVPOL, caused a minor reshuffle of control room staff. A new duty officer was appointed, I took over as deputy chief and an American officer, Mary Beth Lovett, took over from Chrissy and became the new Chief of Communications.

After a staff meeting with Beth and the duty officer, Beth agreed with my recommendations to enforce operating procedures regarding the radio log. She also agreed with me to restrict internet usage to quiet periods during a shift. Night shift officers were permitted full internet access but to use their discretion during busy periods.

Those changes didn't go down well with most operators, especially as I was now paying closer attention to those officers I knew abused the system. I made sure the radio log was completed during transmissions and Beth usually checked the log after each shift.

One operator who was a habitual visitor to the Yahoo chat rooms got the fright of his life when he spoke with a person who went by the name Lushlips 69. The clown was very open about his chats and I knew his user name was Papa Lazarou. On this particular occasion I registered with Yahoo chat and when the lechers on-line saw that provocative user name I was bombarded with private messages, including of course, Papa Lazaru. He asked me where I was from and I told him Australia, however, I worked overseas. When he asked whereabouts overseas, I said 'not far from you'. The look on his face was a picture as he started to look around the control room. Appearing to shrug that comment off he then asked me how I knew where he was and I shouted across the control room 'because I'm behind you'. He was mortified when he realised what had happened. After my little bit of fun, using Yahoo chat whilst on control room duty was temporarily banned.

I knew that practically all CIVPOL, bar maybe one or two working in the control room, were of a higher rank than me, with several being two or three ranks above my UK rank. They knew about the MDP and the role it plays in the UK, especially at Coulport where Tommy Coates works. Being a PC, Tommy

Coates found it amusing to be supervising much higher ranks and wound a few of them up. One Senior Inspector of police from Pakistan complained constantly about being told what to do by UK 'underlings'.

Several high ranking officers, from different countries, seemed to think they should have been selected (irrespective of mission experience) for a supervisory role on their arrival in mission, and when they were not they took exception to a lower ranking officer being their supervisor. UNMIK's non-ranking (mission) policy was something many CIVPOL did not agree with as it allowed *all* CIVPOL officers (regardless of rank in their home police force) to apply for most (advertised) supervisory positions and many MDP constables filled many supervisory posts.

If I'm to be completely honest, during the early period of the Kosovo mission, there was a lot of job fixing and plenty of positions, like mine, were filled without interviews. Apparently recommendations from other CIVPOL were good enough. It was Mick Slater who recommended me to the Pristina Chief of Operations and he was delighted to appoint another British police officer into a supervisory position.

Of those who challenged my rank, experience and especially my new position, I challenged them to answer questions on station operation and mission emergency procedures. They didn't have a clue what I was on about. I met CIVPOL who had no idea what was contained in the UN policy and procedure manuals and my daily UN-based quizzes often baffled them.

And to use a phrase straight from the MDP book of competencies, I showed resilience, even in difficult circumstances. I was prepared to make decisions and had the confidence to see them through. That positive MDP attitude helped me achieve other supervisory positions in later missions.

My duty hours were usually from 8.30 am to 5 pm, which saw me have more of a social life. Now that I was working normal hours I got out more. And if I got back to the digs and the power was off, I had a quick change of clothes and headed down to the Kukri Bar. On one of those rare nights when I did decide to 'stay in' I managed to catch up with Pat who I didn't really know that well prior to meeting him again at the Kosovo pre-deployment course.

I first met Pat at Coulport after he transferred in from The Royal School of Artillery, Larkhill. RSA Larkhill is the principal training establishment for artillery warfare in the British Army.

Pat's experience with the MDP is wide and varied and, unlike me, he had been involved in quite a bit of real police work. He was involved in large scale public order demonstrations such as the summer solstice which takes place every year on Salisbury Plain. His role with the MDP prior to Kosovo was with the Clyde Marine Unit where he was responsible for providing water-borne security to HMNB Clyde.

He was revelling in his job at Pristina Police Station Four. He was in the thick of things straight from his first night shift and told me an amusing story about an old lady and several pairs of sturdy boots.

Pat's first few days on shift at Station Four were uneventful as he accompanied his shift team leader on a familiarisation tour of the patrol area around *Dardania*; a neighbourhood in downtown Pristina.

Being a patrol officer Pat worked mainly with other CIVPOL. Most KPS working from UNMIK police stations were still under training and carried out their duties accompanied by an UNMIK Primary Field Training Officer (PFTO), who was responsible for training, advising and evaluating the KPS station patrol units. On completion of their initial twenty weeks' police recruits course the KPS received a further fifteen weeks' training, at their station, with a PFTO.

After three days working at Station Four, Pat carried out his first joint house search with Station Four CIVPOL and KFOR. Pat was told by his new team leader, CIVPOL officer Rod Wagner, to attend as an observer and he could see how the search was carried out.

Pat teamed up with two Fijians, one Bangladeshi and one Indian CIVPOL along with three KPS and one LA. From information received the house was identified as a possible location for supplying drugs and concealing weapons.

All CIVPOL officers met KFOR troops close to the house and Pat immediately noticed the troops were British. Similarly two KFOR soldiers noticed Pat's insignia and focused their attention on him.

Pat's first thought was to say, 'Sorry guys I'm the newbie, speak to the others,' but he saw the expression on his colleagues' faces and knew they were happy for him to take the lead. Pat's brief was straightforward: gain entry and provide scene security. KFOR do the actual systematic search.

With his heart pounding Pat knocked on the door with all sorts of thoughts passing through his mind, especially the thought of armed bad guys on the other side. An Albanian female's voice shouted something from inside and the LA quickly translated to Pat, 'What do you want?' Now speaking through the LA Pat shouted, 'UN police open the door.' In Pat's own words, 'This wee wifey, who reminded me of my granny, opens the door about four inches. I repeat, "UN Police" and she tries to shut the door but I managed to wedge my foot in and I pushed the door open and this wee granny starts going nuts. Standing behind her is a young girl around fifteen years old who turned out to be the granddaughter. As I tried to step over the threshold this wee granny grabs both sides of the doorway to block my entrance while still going berserk. The LA tells me the problem is our boots.' The woman didn't want anyone in her home with outdoor foot wear; removing outdoor shoes is customary in Kosovo and many householders take serious offence if you don't.

It was explained to the woman the purpose of the visit, however, Pat's CIVPOL colleagues were already untying their boot laces. Pat shouted at the other CIVPOL to keep their boots on and by now he was quite nervous and worried. The woman was told the boots weren't coming off and that the quicker she cooperated the quicker the search would be over.

Pat said, 'The wee granny stood firm with a vice-like grip on either side of the door frame. I tried to gently push past her but no chance, when I say *vice-like*, John, I mean clamped. Now I'm thinking this wee granny is gonna make me look a right idiot. "Hi lads how did the search go? Eh sorry, couldn't gain access because of a seventy-year-old granny, I would never hear the end of that." I reached around her waist, clasped my hands together lifted her off the floor and pushed as hard as I could to break her grip; I kid you not mate it took all my strength to do it, she was as strong as an ox. After breaking her grip she started scratching and punching me around the head. I carried her into the living room and quickly, but gently I should add, deposited her on the sofa, but she continued to struggle to get up still trying to stop the rest from getting in. At one point I thought I was gonna have to sit on her to keep her down; thankfully it didn't quite come to that. I remember thinking at the time, there must be some stash in here with the way she is kicking off. The LA was great at calming the wee granny down and between both of us we managed to calm and console her, although she just cried her eyes out, poor soul. I asked KFOR if they could be as quick as possible while still being thorough. They said they would do their best. As me and the LA continued to talk with the old lady I learned that she lived there alone with the granddaughter. Now I'm starting to think something is fishy here, something's not quite right. Then I learned for the first time that the old lady's apartment block was situated close to a block of flats occupied by Serbians.'

Under the protection of KFOR, Serbian families lived in a cluster of drab concrete apartment buildings, financed by the government (and known as the YU project) in Belgrade.

Pat continued, 'It turned out there had been an argument a few days earlier between the granddaughter and one of the Serbian families, and as you will recall, John, this was one way that both sides could mess each other around by calling KFOR and making accusations about weapons and drugs etc knowing that KFOR will come round and rip the house apart. I spoke with the KFOR lads and they said that they felt it was a tit for tat argument. They both agreed with me, to go through the motions as quickly as possible and get out as soon as. I remember leaving there heading back to the station thinking, "I didn't come here to tackle grannies." Thankfully, although I was involved in many more house searches; I never had to bear hug or wrestle any more old ladies.'

One night Pat arrived from work with a rather large white board. He'd been in town and bought several bits and bobs he thought would 'ease Station Four's budgetary constraints'. Pat's in the habit of getting the job done quicker and on that occasion, as a teamleader, putting his hand in his own pocket and spending over one hundred Euros, temporarily solved a KPS logistical issue.

On the white board Pat created a colourful bar chart where the monthly crime figures were entered and readily available for all Station Four's CIVPOL and KPS officers to view. With all its fancy colours, and by checking the chart, every officer could see, at a glance, what was going on in their area of responsibility.

Pat is definitely a creative character; he would also spend hours drawing up exercises, both written and practical, for Station Four's newly recruited KPS and those officers who, although considered to be more experienced, were not all together conversant with Kosovo law and procedure.

As a team leader Pat also spent money on arranging social nights out for his KPS officers. At the end of the evening he never gave a second thought to paying the food and drinks bill for the entire company.

I also knew by reputation how well Pat was doing at Station Four. His name frequently cropped up in conversations during drinks in the Kukri. Station Four was in an area where serious criminal and ethnically motivated incidents were regularly reported. Pat had investigated everything from car theft to murder and even football violence.

Just like Pristina control room, Station Four had a few CIVPOL who were lazy and uninterested. Pat said of the stations operations officer, 'To say he was good at the role would be a gross over statement.'

During a morning shift team brief Pat read out an operation order which required a police presence at a local football match. The order simply stated the time of the match and that a police presence was to be maintained until the completion of the match and the dispersal of the match crowd.

Although that type of operation was new and unfamiliar to Pat, he was surprised at the lack of operational information. There was no mention of actual numbers of police resources to be deployed and no background history regarding both football teams and any crowd disorder during any previous meetings. There was nothing in the operational order to suggest any type of trouble.

With KPS resources already stretched to the limit and assuming no crowd trouble was anticipated Pat detailed two KPS units (six officers) to attend the football stadium thirty minutes prior to kick-off. When the match kicked off the police presence would be reduced to one KPS unit; that single KPS brief was to observe and report any early signs of crowd disorder. If trouble did occur more units would be deployed. All going well, the second KPS unit was instructed to return, along with Pat's CIVPOL deputy team leader, to the stadium fifteen minutes before the end and make sure, on completion of the match, both sets of supporters dispersed in an orderly manner.

What Pat didn't know was the match was between two teams whose supporters are fierce rivals and fighting between them was a common occurrence. That was a significant and important point which was not written into the operational order.

Later in the day Pat was returning to Station Four from a bogus road traffic accident when he noticed the time was getting close to the end of the football match. He radioed his deputy team leader and asked for an update on the situation at the ground. The deputy had left five minutes before the final whistle and reported all was well. Pat was livid, his instructions to his deputy were clear and to make matters worse he was still unaware of the rivalry between the both sets of supporters.

Pat, along with his LA, attended the stadium just as the match finished and as both sets of supporters flooded out the stadium together (no segregation) all hell was let loose. Pat told me, 'Bottles were flying through the air along with sticks and stones. A large crowd of visiting supporters from Gnjilane clashed with a group of Pristina supporters, with fights breaking out all around us. I and the KPS tried to break up the fighting and shepherd the Gnjilane supporters towards their coaches in order to get them boarded and out of Pristina.'

Things were really getting out of hand and at one point Pat and his LA were surrounded by home supporters. Pat radioed for back-up and in the meantime had a savage crowd to contend with. 'I genuinely thought we were both going to be torn apart, however, I pulled a big container of CS spray off my utility belt and pointed it towards the angry faces staring back at me. I was surprised when they seemed to think twice about what they were intending to do and the closed circle of people broke up, allowing me and my LA a way out.'

'I think two CIVPOL units arrived from Station Two with two American CIVPOL and eight KPS officers. They deployed in full protective riot gear and with riot shields and batons. As they attempted to control the situation I was deafened by the crack of two gun shots. I remember looking at the CS spray in my hand thinking I had made the wrong choice. I couldn't see my LA and within a couple of seconds the CS spray was on the ground and I had my service pistol drawn. I spun around and there was Fitim, my LA still standing (thank God). And beside him was a little Indian CIVPOL from Station Four (Sindhu Kumar). Sindhu had just arrived, drew his service revolver and fired two warning shots into the air. John, I wanted to have his babies, such was my relief, and thankfully that feeling only lasted a split second… ha ha.'

'The unannounced warning shots caused so much confusion and immediately on hearing the shots, both American CIVPOL also drew their pistols; they were now pointing their weapons towards an angry but scared crowd.'

Pat continued, 'I thought, this is gonna turn into a bloodbath, I was screaming at Mick Slater (in Pristina control) via the radio to broadcast that the shots fired were warning shots by a CIVPOL and that all officers were to holster weapons. I had to de-escalate this as quickly as possible. Although I knew Mick was Duty Officer and not normally heard on the radio, I was glad he had the sense to man the radio and he did a sterling job in conveying my message. Eventually, and without any further incident, we managed to disperse the home supporters and get the visiting supporters onto their coaches and escort them out of Pristina. Incidentally, little Sindhu Kumar later went on to become my deputy when I took over as Chief of Operations. What a character he turned out to be. I've never seen so many scars on one guy in my life; turned out he earned most of them fighting the Taliban in his home country. I never ever thought of having his babies again though.'

If I were to compare myself with Pat, one aspect of my character which differed to his would be when returning after work during a late night power cut to our darkened accommodation, I really was a big fearty. And Pat, well Pat could sit contently in total darkness and wait patiently for the power to click back on.

One night after a back shift I was walking back to the house when the power went off. I got out my Maglite and followed the beam up the dark Dragodan hill.

When I was inside the house's hallway it was in complete darkness. There was no sign of any life or any flickering candlelight coming from the sitting room.

Just as I put my Maglite down so I could unlace my boots, I heard a creaking door open and a deep voice coming from inside the bathroom, which was immediately to my right.

'Heeeeeeeeeeelllllllllllllllllllloooooooooooo,' said a chuckling Pat Kearney. For a split second I was rooted to the spot and then the inevitable shiver ran up my spine at the same time my body hair came to attention.

Pat was actually having a bath during that power cut and as he held open the bathroom door looking out at me the chuckle had developed into full blown laughter. I managed to get both my boots off and stagger into the sitting room where I sat shaking for about ten minutes. I obviously did see the funny side to that scary prank but, my God, what a fright Pat gave me.

I remember visiting Station Four one afternoon, just to say hello to Pat and have a coffee. Pat, as the recently appointed Station Commander, was too busy inspecting the Station's KPS officers who were lined up in three ranks in the courtyard of the station. A local television company was also visiting and filming that day on Pat's invitation.

The inspection of officers was immediately prior to a presentation, organised that day by Pat, where one officer was identified as 'officer of the month'. The award was part of a new and clever scheme, created by Pat, which encouraged all KPS officers to realise the importance of their role and encourage them to carry out their routine duties in a professional and ethical manner.

Pat ended his mission as Station Four Commander. Quite a commendable achievement when you consider he started as a patrol officer just eighteen months earlier. As far as other MDP constables were concerned, reaching the position of Station Commander was not unusual.

CHAPTER ELEVEN
The Newbies

DECEMBER 2001 to MAY 2002

On 6 December 2001 the new Kosovo rotation arrived in Pristina and I gave myself an unofficial day off to greet a good friend from Coulport, Reyburn Logie, and a few other friends and colleagues. They were spending the first week in a city centre hotel rather than the UN hotel.

Rey, and the others, had already arrived when I reached the hotel; he was puffing and panting as he shunted his heavy treasure chest up a flight of stairs towards the hotel reception, along with the rest of the tired looking contingent. There was no hug or any other usual form of informal greeting from Rey; just his usual greeting of 'awright mucker.'

I recognised several of the new faces including, David Rodden, who I had worked with at Coulport, and Christian Linetty, who left Coulport in 1994 for (London) Whitehall Area Policing Team. However, I never spoke with them at that point, they seemed a bit caught up in the moment; a wee bit overawed. It wasn't the right time to start rambling on about the city, the trouble or anything else for that matter.

After he checked in and dumped the chest, Rey knocked on the door across from his room; a voice within shouted 'five minutes'. Rey gave me the thumbs up and whispered, 'John Pearson, good guy'. John Pearson (*left*) was a constable from Faslane who Rey had got to know during the pre-deployment course. We stood outside the hotel having a cigarette as we waited for John; I had arranged to take Rey and introduce him and a few others to the Kukri bar.

When John appeared and after Rey introduced me we headed off to the Kukri. Within ten minutes of being in the bar John Pearson must have asked me more questions than Bamber Gascoigne ever asked in his twenty-five years as University Challenge quiz master. The wee man was quite nervous to say the least. I told John to chill out and any needs or concerns he had could be addressed during his induction week. Davy Rodden and Christian Linetty joined us later and we spent a couple of hours catching up and basically just 'chewin' the fat.'

After their UN induction week, Rey started working with me in the control room. John (now looking a bit more relaxed) and Christian were deployed to the Regional Protection Unit and Davy Rodden started working with the Border and Boundary police at Pristina airport.

Less than a month after the new contingent arrived attacks against KFOR and UNMIK increased. One of the worst incidents came following the arrest of three former Albanian members of the KLA on charges of war crimes 'against' fellow Albanians during 1998 and 1999. Angry protests in Pristina finished with serious injury to several UNMIK police and KPS and many police vehicles were damaged.

Like many CIVPOL before him Rey Logie didn't last long as a control room operator and after a few months redeployed to the Pristina Regional Support Unit. John Pearson wasn't cut out for Regional Protection and shortly after joining the unit he redeployed to Station Four and became a patrol officer. Pat Kearney was still working at Station Four and was now a patrol teamleader. Davy Rodden was happy working in airport security at Pristina airport and Christian Linetty, was settled with the RPU.

I was also content working in the control room, however, around April 2002, during a conversation with a CIVPOL (and MDP) colleague and good friend, Alasdair (AJ) Stewart, AJ asked me if I'd ever thought about a change of scenery. Although he had no formal training or experience, AJ was a driving instructor at the KPS police training school and was about to redeploy to the Police Air Support Unit as a police observer, where he would be hanging out the door of big UN helicopters high up in the sky; not my ideal job.

As a vacancy would be coming up, and as AJ knew I was a former qualified driving instructor, he asked me if I'd be interested in replacing him. I asked about qualifications and found out all potential trainers must successfully complete an OSCE International Instructors Development Course, which did appeal to me. The OSCE course lasted two weeks and two certificates were awarded which I thought would enhance my CV. I was relatively happy working in the control room, however, as a former driving instructor, a qualified first aid trainer and police response driver I reckoned I had something more to offer the KPS. One other good side to joining the driver training unit was the current chief was just about to end his mission and a UK CIVPOL officer was taking over. I had around one month to think things over, but in the meantime I was happy working in the Pristina control room.

Although I was the Deputy Chief of Communications, it didn't keep me away from the control room radios, especially when I had to step in and assist a few of my colleagues. One UK CIVPOL (station investigator) from Newcastle (North East England) was a rascal when he came over the radio and used his broadest Geordie accent and dialect at every opportunity. And at the end of his transmission instead of using proper radio procedure like 'copied your last message', he would always say, 'ye knaa what ah mean leik', meaning, 'do you know what I mean, like'. The baffled operators rarely did.

One early evening when I was standing in for a colleague, who had taken a break, I acknowledged a call from the unmistakable and dulcet tones of Christian Linetty. Along with five other RPU colleagues Christian, who was RPU team leader, was on his way to Mitrovica and was informing Pristina control he was leaving Pristina region and switching radio channels from two (Pristina region) to four (Mitrovica region).

When any UNMIK police unit travelled from one region to another, it was normal practice to switch radio channels. In Christian's case, all further radio communication was through Bravo control, the Mitrovica main control room call sign. What happened that evening to Christian and his team certainly brought home to me how a quiet situation can suddenly explode into extreme violence. I really was glad my job kept me safe and indoors.

Christian's detail of six CIVPOL, Personal Protection Officers (PPO), three occupying a soft-skinned Toyota 4Runner and three occupying an armoured Scout RG32, were on their way to a French KFOR camp in North Mitrovica where they were instructed to seek a French Colonel and transport him, under their protection, to Pristina; a common and routine task for the RPU.

I'd first met Christian in 1994 when he transferred from Greenham Common to Coulport. The big Welshman suffered Coulport for eighteen months before escaping to the bright lights of London with a transfer to The Duke of York's Headquarters, Chelsea. Three years later he was on the move again and transferred to the busy Whitehall Area Policing team.

On first meeting: 'Linetty, Christian Linetty,' you'd immediately think, 'sounds like James Bond.' A James Bond sound-alike maybe, although he certainly doesn't have the characteristics that Bond writer Ian Fleming gave the M16 agent – extremely dull, an uninteresting man and a blunt instrument. Christian has the qualities of that other fictional (occasional police agent) character, Simon Templar, boyish humour, cool and debonair.

Christian's a very proud police officer and is always immaculately dressed, both on and off duty. He's also the type of individual who, when other police would be wearing black combat trousers, Christian would be wearing black surplus Raw Vintage Airborne Combat Pants. Sorry Christian, just my little joke.

It took Christian just two months to become the RPU team leader and he became responsible for the supervision and welfare of thirteen bodyguards from a variety of nations including, Russia, Italy, Canada, USA, France, Germany and Jordan.

The RPU detail used the Mitrovica by-pass road that would see the unit turn back on itself and arrive in North Mitrovica via the small town of Zvecan, which is around two miles from the KFOR camp. That night Zvecan was deserted with not a single CIVPOL unit on patrol. Then, the KPS had still not deployed in North Mitrovica. Christian had asked Bravo control for a situation report and was informed the Mitrovica area was calm and quiet.

When both vehicles arrived at the camp gates the French soldiers were shocked to see the RPU officers who refused to allow them entry. A quick exchange of words took place with some confusion before Christian got the message; he was not getting through those gates.

What Christian didn't know was, days earlier, serious rioting had taken place following the arrest of a Serbian who was also one of the North Mitrovica *Bridge Watchers*. The Bridge Watchers basically act as an early warning system and keep a lookout near Mitrovica's main bridge, which separates north and south Mitrovica. Any irregular activity on or near the bridge is monitored and 'investigated' by Bridge Watchers, who are held by some members of the Serbian community in high esteem.

After the arrest of the bridge watcher, around 300 Serbian protesters armed with stones and hand grenades confronted CIVPOL and a Polish SPU unit. Twenty-two officers were injured and one seriously wounded Polish officer required surgery. Four other Serbians were detained and a restriction of movement implemented in North Mitrovica. Basically what that meant was North Mitrovica was a no-go area for all international police and Christian, for whatever reason, was not aware of that.

A small crowd had gathered around 100 yards from the RPU vehicles with some people darting off behind buildings and cars. Others arrived and a few were using mobile phones. Christian knew he had to get his team out of Mitrovica and the only way to do it was through a gauntlet of angry Serbians, who were now armed with bricks and iron bars. Not knowing Mitrovica at all, Christian could only depart the way he came in from Zvecan and that direction was going to take him straight towards his adversaries.

In Christian's own words: 'They had welcome parties waiting for us all the way out through the North route as they had used their mobiles to communicate. We faced rocks, iron bars, cars trying to run us off the road. I was driving on the pavements at one point and on the wrong side of the road most of the way out. My 4Runner's windows were all completely smashed and the vehicle had several deep dents, caused by boulders being dropped from high rise buildings.

Two of my officers held their Beretta pistols and Heckler and Koch G36 rifles out of the windows and considered opening fire on several occasions. Those rifles carry sixty rounds and if used would probably have caused fatal injuries.

Fortunately I kept the vehicle upright when mounting pavements at speed and a blowout would have gotten us killed without doubt, but we managed to get out of Mitrovica and assess the vehicle damage and injuries. The two vehicles were written off and our injuries included cuts and grazes from shattered glass and rocks as they penetrated the windscreen and side windows.' Christian and his officers were very lucky indeed.

The shock and reality of the incident didn't deter Christian and he continued to work with the RPU, who later became known as the Close Protection Unit (CPU). It did, however, make me even more determined to stay clear of Mitrovica.

One month or so after that incident involving Christian in Mitrovica, I was again asked about the position at the KPS training school. Although I was enjoying my supervisory role I also wanted to experience new opportunities and being a KPS trainer did appeal to me. I could have remained in the comfort and safety of the control room, however, the role became very repetitive and I was getting lazy stuck behind a desk. Not long before I made a decision on whether to join the driver training unit or stay put, I was asked by the Pristina Chief of Operation (American CIVPOL) Dave Paton if I would take over the Chief's responsibilities. This unusual request was made after complaints were received by Dave against Beth Lovett regarding her tact and diplomacy when dealing with her staff. I do actually remember one incident where Beth entered into a short argument when she complained (in full view of other staff members) to a radio operator about his scribbled handwriting. The radio operator, who just happened to be the Filipino Contingent Commander, was not a happy man. Other members of the Filipino contingent worked in the control room and I think the Contingent Commander was completely mortified to be chastised in public. That incident may have led to a complaint by the Filipino officer, however, I don't know if it was ever reported.

I agreed to Dave's request and, although Beth retained the title of Chief of Communications, her power had all but gone as I had now taken over her responsibilities. CIVPOL visitors to the control room looking for the Chief were directed to Beth who in turn informed them to 'Talk to John, he's the Chief.' It became a very confusing and awkward situation for both the radio operators and of course me. There was really only one way for me to resolve that embarrassing situation; redeployment to the KPS training school.

In May I was deployed to the KPS training school and within a few weeks I was causing havoc.

Written off UNMIK police vehicles

CHAPTER TWELVE
Wacky Races

MAY 2002 TO DECEMBER 2002

Working in the Pristina control room certainly helped me to get to grips with and get used to reports about the continuing violence in Kosovo; I now took the frequent murders and grenade attacks and protests in my stride. The flash reports and daily sit-reps were my daily newspapers and I knew the areas to avoid and those areas where I had to be extra vigilant. However, the opportunity to qualify and train as an international police instructor at the KPS training school in the town of Vushtrri/Vucitrn (which is around six miles from Mitrovica) was too good to turn down. And it released me from that difficult situation I found myself in with Beth Lovett.

Part of my role with the MDP as a police response driver allowed me to drive at speed (with safety in mind) with the blue lights revolving and the siren wailing. I found the three-week response driving course incredibly intense and difficult as I tried to concentrate on my driving technique while at the same time giving a full running commentary on my drive. Commentaries were given by MDP students during normal and high speed driving conditions to describe the road and weather conditions, point out driving hazards and generally speaking just to make sure the student was completely aware of what was going on around him.

As well as theoretical presentations and tests, a student spent around two to three hours behind the wheel every day, and for continuity, was always accompanied by the same instructor. Those students who failed to reach the required standard failed the course and expulsion could occur during any section of the three weeks. I was lucky enough to pass all weekly driving assessments and one final end of course written and practical test. The practical test was conducted by a sergeant from a territorial police traffic unit.

During the three week response course my instructor, Graham Scott, was excellent. What I was taught gave me a completely different outlook on driving in general and definitely made me a much safer driver. Being aware of and quickly spotting potential hazards was one important aspect of safe driving. On one occasion when I was driving, Graham pointed out a long hedgerow separating

Me with PTC staff members – David Keefe, head of PTC, Joe Robson,
head of driver training, and Dave Pape, PTC instructor

two fields. Graham then said, 'That hedgerow is probably running alongside a concealed road or dirt track, which probably leads from this main road to that farmhouse up on that hill. Make sure you spot these potential hazards early enough to consider your options should you spot a moving vehicle over the top of the hedgerow.' Sure enough as I got closer to the hedgerow I could just about see the top of a tractor and its exhaust pipe. It was travelling away from the main road towards the farmhouse, so no danger at that particular time.

At the start of the week my commentary was quite poor, however, on that course and travelling in the same vehicle as me was MDP colleague (Constable) Ritchie Henderson who was (maybe still is) a member of the Institute for Advance Motorists (IAM). Ritchie's commentary was fantastic; he didn't miss a trick and spotted every possible hazard. When Ritchie was at the wheel I certainly learned how to improve my observations and commentary. Near the start of the first week when Ritchie was driving I remember him saying, 'Ahead I can see several wheelie bins on both sides of the main road, this tells me it must be collection day, so I must look out for bin lorries and be aware of any refuse collectors who may step onto the road.' Before that course I never gave such potential hazards a second thought. Not surprisingly, Ritchie eventually became the MDP Force Driving Instructor.

KPS DRIVER TRAINING

The chief of KPS Driver Training was now that UK CIVPOL officer, Joe Robson, a retired police officer, formerly of Northumbria Police. A small group of retired territorial police were also seconded by the UN and became part of the UK contingent.

Joe was a complete character and didn't have a care in the world. He wasn't very interested in how the driver training department functioned and was really in Kosovo to increase his bank balance. I have to say he was also one of my drinking buddies in the Kukri bar; he wasn't a bad guy, just a wee bit uninterested and greedy for money.

Before I could officially join the driver training unit I was required to take a written and practical test. The written test was very straightforward. In fact I couldn't possibly have failed; I was handed the answers to all ten questions. My driving test was conducted by a CIVPOL driving instructor who obviously had a good memory. He didn't take any notes during my twenty minute drive around the centre of Pristina; he did, however, complete a driving assessment form back at PTC after my test was completed. I passed.

My first trip from Pristina to the KPS training school, which takes around forty minutes, was on a Monday morning and, like just about every Monday afterwards, I was stopping drivers of private and KPS vehicles for speeding, inconsiderate and dangerous driving. Most vehicles I stopped were driven by KPS officers travelling to the training school for 'a driving course.' I didn't have a ticket book, I just gave the offender a telling off and if it was a KPS officer on his way for a driving course, I often singled him out and he became my new student. Monday seemed to be the one day when most people travelling to the training school drove much faster than the 80km (around 50mph) speed limit. Apparently they didn't want to be late for the first day of their course.

When I arrived at the training school I was met by Joe Robson and introduced to eight CIVPOL instructors, five LAs and maybe around half a dozen local driving instructors. The CIVPOL instructors were from countries far and wide and all had different views on driving techniques. Incidentally, if my memory serves me correctly none of the CIVPOL driving instructors had any formal training as a driving instructor. I met colleagues from Nigeria, Russia, Turkey, Germany, USA, Ukraine, Italy and one officer, Asad Shaikh from Pakistan. I already knew Asad from Pristina control where I had been his supervisor. That was the crazy thing about that Kosovo mission, you could be nobody one day and a big boss the next and vice versa. And, as you will find out, during my future Kosovo missions, one MDP constable rose from patrol officer to Regional Commander, back to patrol officer then back again to Regional Commander.

Meanwhile back at the ranch. During the day I learned a few of the LAs were also driving instructors after they too completed the OSCE instructor's development course. After taking a tour of the training school I returned to the instructor's office and had a look at that week's course curriculum.

When I studied the course curriculum I became a bit anxious. At that particular time there was only one type of KPS driving course available: 'Emergency Response Mode' (ERM), which was similar in content to the three weeks MDP response driving course. When I say similar in content, I'm specifically referring to high speed driving and not a lot more. The ERM course lasted just 'five days' (Monday to Friday) with fifty per cent theoretical training and fifty per cent practical training. Being a former driving instructor and knowing how much training and driving is involved in a police response course, gave me every reason to be concerned. A guide to the week's curriculum is laid out below, however, I'll explain later how the week actually panned out.

Monday
Course introduction by Course Commander and introduction to instructors followed by theoretical and practical exercises.

Tuesday
Driving assessments carried out all day. One instructor accompanied by two KPS students and if required one LA.

Wednesday
KPS are in the classroom all day with selected instructors. The remainder of the instructors were free for the day.

Thursday
Emergency Response Mode (training and assessments) carried out all day. Again one instructor accompanied by two KPS students with an LA if required.

Friday
Theoretical followed by practical tests.

In fairness to Joe Robson, he only took over as the driver training supervisor days before I was redeployed to the unit. So I suppose I can only blame his predecessor for the way business was conducted in the unit.

Okay, so here's what really happened during my first few weeks at the KPS training school.

Mondays

A maximum of twenty KPS students attended one classroom within the KPS training school. After being introduced to the Course Commander (American civilian Sam Brown) and the training staff driving licences (the paper type) were then collected and examined for validity and forgery. Just like forged education and degree certificates, several KPS officers also possessed forged driving licences. The KPS officers were naive enough to think the Course Commander would turn a blind eye to any forged licences. Sam Brown examined the driving licences using basic methods to detect any forgeries. If he became suspicious the suspect's licence was immediately sent off to forensics (for further checks) at a nearby UNMIK police station. All KPS officers found to be in possession of a forged licence were excluded from the course and ultimately dismissed from the KPS.

The course started when one instructor presented the first of numerous theoretical lessons, including pre-driving vehicle checks, poor weather conditions, safe speed and so on. After each class presentation the student was given a handout on that lesson. The handouts were basically homework for the student to study in preparation for the theory test. If an instructor was not required for a class, he was free until after lunch.

After lunch, the instructors and KPS students gathered in a large car park where various traffic cones were set up and used for a variety of training exercises and manoeuvres, for example 'parallel parking' and 'three point turns'. Every day, and before every practise, all vehicles (Skoda Felicia) were checked for roadworthiness. The instructors then (from a safe distance) observed the students as they followed a set (timed) course and carried out the driving manoeuvres.

Tuesdays

A Tuesday was the day when basic driving skills should have been examined with any minor and major faults identified, explained and corrected during the course of the day. It should have been that simple. Driving assessment forms were supplied and as a guideline for the instructors contained headings such as use of controls, speed and positioning while driving. The idea was for the instructor to mark the driving fault as it was made and correct it when possible. Several instructors chose not to use the forms until that day's driving was complete.

I usually made sure any vehicle I was travelling in was fitted with dual controls and eventually I refused to travel or instruct without them. For the first few courses, and until I passed my OSCE instructor's course, I travelled with instructors 'mainly' as an observer just to get used to the driving routes and to see how the instructors used their driver training skills.

What actually happened just about every Tuesday was, all vehicles with a KPS student behind the wheel departed the training school at five to ten minute intervals and slowly headed for the main highway. Following the same route, and after many crunchy gear changes, dodgy overtakes, and rivers of nonstop distracting and irritating chattering, they eventually arrived at the scenic Batlava Lake. After one, sometimes two, cups of coffee the KPS students swapped over the driving and slowly headed back to the training school for a long lunch. In the afternoon another leisurely drive took place with lots of nattering between the LA and the KPS students; they were usually complaining about the vehicle windows being open and how cold they were. That was during a very hot summer when temperatures reached 90°F. With those windows rolled up the smell in some of those vehicles reminded me of boiled cauliflower.

It didn't take me long to realise quite a few KPS students lacked basic driving skills and good road sense; in fact quite a few had no road sense at all and their awareness of other road users was, let's just say, not good. Even though most students may have received some sort of prior basic driver training, there was no way that after only one day's assessment they were ready to be trained in ERM.

Generally speaking most KPS students displayed classic 'experienced driver faults,' improper gear selection, changing direction, misuse of the handbrake, steering, misuse of mirrors and other minor faults. The drive to and from Batlava Lake was very straightforward and not many KPS students committed any major faults. Those who did were spoken to at the time and usually agreed where and why they went wrong. Dangerous overtakes were the most common fault. The day ended with assessment forms being completed and signed off by the instructors and any driving faults committed and noted at the time were discussed.

Wednesdays

The students spent all day in the classroom where the remainder of the course material was explained by PowerPoint presentations. One instructor (with one LA) normally presented one lesson before handing over to a colleague for the next lesson and so on. Instructors who were not required for the classroom work usually headed back to Pristina and PTC where they could complete any course paperwork or carry out any other relevant tasks.

Thursdays

On a Thursday morning after a CIVPOL team briefing, all instructors and students assembled in the school car park. Following on from the previous Tuesday's 'driving assessment' and now assuming that all remaining KPS students were deemed competent and safe drivers, the target for that 'one' day's driving was to further train the students until they reached the standard required to drive (safely) at high speeds whilst responding to an incident or when pursuing a suspect vehicle.

After my first Tuesday and the leisurely jaunt in the countryside with a CIVPOL instructor I decided to team up with one of the LA instructors whose name is Alban. Alban explained to me the students don't necessarily travel with the same instructor as they had on a Tuesday, and that particular Thursday was no exception. My immediate remarks to Alban were, 'That is ridiculous, where's the continuity?' And 'How does the instructor know how good or bad these students are?' Well, the assessment forms were the answer. If, on a Tuesday, the assessment forms had ticks in the right boxes, everything was good to go on a Thursday.

I decided to say nothing more and, after making sure the vehicle was clean, fit to be driven and fitted with dual controls, I told Alban I would sit in the back seat, take some notes and keep quiet. Alban explained a few minor details to me and after ten minutes we set off with one KPS student driving while the other sat in the back with me. After an uneventful fifteen minutes travelling on the Mitrovica to Pristina highway Alban told the KPS student to pull into a fuel station. A short conversation in Albanian then ensued before Alban turned to me and said, 'Have you ever been to the Marble Cave in Gadime?'

Completely confused I said, 'No, why?' Alban then explained to me what was going to happen next. 'In a moment we will be leaving the gas station with head-lights, blue lights and siren on, heading for the village of Gadime and the Marble Cave,' which is around 25 miles from that gas station. Alban further explained it was part of the training exercise. He had just explained to the KPS student, 'For training purposes you are required to drive to Gadime where a serious incident has been reported. You must drive in Emergency Response Mode until I tell you to relax. The only other question I asked was, 'Will we be travelling at high speed all the way?' I didn't like Alban's answer. Thank God for rear seatbelts.

As soon as those blue lights and siren were activated all hell broke loose. It was as if the KPS student under 'instruction' thought he was invincible and expected everyone and everything else using the road to see those flashing blue lights and hear that annoying siren and immediately move out of the way. He was travelling around 85mph and never put a lot of thought into what he was doing or what was happening around him. There was not a lot of slowing down when approaching crossroads or traffic lights, a quick look left and right seemed to satisfy him before he put the boot back down. Slowing down for corners, blind corners and blind summits were just not part of his course of action. During one misjudged overtaking manoeuvre, and with oncoming traffic fast approaching, he was forced to swerve sharply to his right causing other vehicles to brake sharply as he forced his way back into the flow of traffic. All the while Alban hardly uttered a word.

That was it for me. After around twenty minutes or so, I told Alban to stop the exercise and find somewhere safe to park, and as a joke I said, 'Preferably near a toilet!' I had only managed to write two words on my note pad, *Wacky Races*. Unfortunately, neither Alban nor the two KPS students had ever heard of Dick Dastardly and Muttley. During our unexpected pit stop, I couldn't really get my point over on how dangerous the student's driving was. And Alban really did think I needed to use the toilet.

After at least half an hour explaining different aspects of safer driving, anticipating other road users and everything else I could think of to delay this crazy guy from continuing his drive, he (the student) asked if I could give a demonstration. With pleasure my friend; I drove at intervals in ERM all the way to the Marble Cave and commentated on my driving techniques. I also spoke about those hedgerows and other potential hazards. Alban and the two students were very impressed.

Alban's original plan was to travel to the cave, take the guided tour and afterwards have lunch. After lunch, we would swap students and travel back to the training school. He told me sightseeing trips and other excursions were not unusual on a Thursday. I must admit I thought the whole set up was hilarious. Where on earth did driver training come into this scenario?

We did have time to take a quick tour of the cave and I must admit it was fantastic. The cave was found by a villager in 1966 and is made from karst limestone. Much of it is still unexplored. I also spent half a Thursday visiting a Kosovo winery.

Before we left for the training school I took over the training from Alban. Each student drove, within the speed limits, and rotated the driving every twenty minutes and I corrected their driving faults at the time they were made. I did this

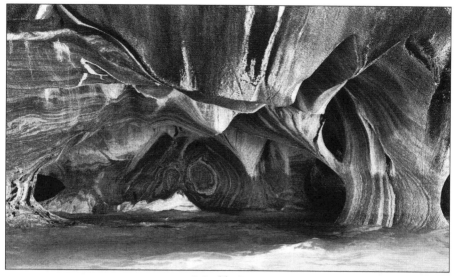

Marble Cave

all the way back to Vushtrri/Vucitrn. With two hours remaining in the day, and a little more informed, I allowed both KPS students, under instruction, to drive in ERM. Luckily they were quick learners and safe drivers. I was confident both students would pass the ERM test. The following day all students passed the test, very rarely did any fail. Several instructors were far too lenient and very reluctant to fail students, even if they were poor or dangerous drivers.

Fridays

Friday mornings were spent in the classroom where a theory test was conducted. After lunch those students who successfully passed the written test (60 per cent pass mark) were then examined (within the school car park) whilst being timed on the various driving and parking manoeuvres; one three point turn was also part of the test. If the student completed the course within the stated time they were presented with a police response or pursuit scenario which required them to drive, under test conditions, at high speeds (ERM) on an urban highway. Incredibly, the ERM test lasted on average, around six minutes. There was no set rule on who tested who. KPS students preferred some instructors over others and no one objected to the student selecting which trainer he wanted for his test.

On the few occasions that I conducted a Friday test my right foot was never far from the dual brake. As soon as I noticed the KPS student getting over excited and preparing himself for a crazy or dangerous manoeuvre the game was up.

Before he had the opportunity to make me and the rest of the vehicle's occupants a road traffic statistic, my foot was on that brake and my left hand had a firm grip on the bottom of the steering wheel. On those occasions all students knew exactly what was happening. Before setting off on the test I gave all students a safety brief and explained what action I'd take if I felt they were about to put any lives in danger. At that point the test was terminated and the failed student was asked to pull over at a safe location. I then drove back to the training school and completed my report. I have no idea what happened before or after I arrived at the training school, but a few of my colleagues seemed a little surprised that I was actually failing students. They were even more surprised when I failed several students during the Tuesday assessment.

YOU AINT SEEN THE BEST OF ME YET

During an afternoon break at the training school I mentioned to a senior OSCE instructor (Mike Cole) who was on a secondment from his home police force (PSNI), the current driver training programme was in need of a severe overhaul. I explained to Mike the poor standard of training, KPS driving and my near misses and feared someone would be seriously injured before too long. Mike told me if I could devise a programme that would improve the programme and the driving skills of the KPS students, he would make sure of its approval.

After several weeks of planning and using my prior knowledge and experience, I devised a more formal driver training programme which helped the instructor to follow a more structured training plan and it really took the student driver back to driving basics. Joe Robson gave me his full backing and after several meetings with Joe and Mike Cole, often in the Kukri, the Course Commander approved my changes.

On a Tuesday all students were now briefed before each drive and told they would be under assessment any time they drove. Idle chit chat was to stop and students should concentrate on their driving and follow all instructions given by the trainer. It made no difference what route the instructor followed or when and where breaks were taken, the important point was to play the game when you're driving the vehicle and listen to your instructor.

I produced new assessment forms which were more detailed and covered more driving competencies. The last section on the assessment form was used to comment on the overall assessment and development needs.

On a Thursday morning the student continued to be assessed and developed, however, more emphasis was put on his development. If the student appeared to be competent, ERM was taught on that Thursday afternoon after demonstrations from the instructor. Long drives under ERM conditions were stopped with much shorter journeys being introduced.

Basic Driver Training courses were eventually introduced and became a stepping stone to the ERM course. KPS non driving licence holders who had completed thirty hours with a local (civilian) driving school were also invited onto those courses and after one week of intense training at the school, and if they reached the required standard, the students were examined by an approved driving examiner. Those examiners were authorised to issue pass (or fail) certificates which in turn could be exchanged for a full (and valid) driving licence.

I'm sure my improvements to the structure of the driver training programme helped the CIVPOL officers to be more respected, as instructors, by the KPS officers and the local instructors. In my opinion too many CIVPOL instructors were far too relaxed and used driver training as a way of getting free sightseeing excursions around Kosovo. Other instructors thanked me and were very happy that I had made those much needed improvements. A few told me they were long overdue and that they would have made changes themselves, but just didn't know how to do it.

Now that I had completed my new driver training programme I started to get out and about more with the KPS students and on several occasion I ventured as far as South Mitrovica. I was very curious to see what all the fuss was about and why Mitrovica should be avoided. The city wasn't any different to any other in Kosovo and the local citizens went about their day to day business like any other city I've visited. When I visited Mitrovica I always stayed on the south side of the city, however, I didn't expect the north to be that much different.

Out with driver training and during my relatively short term at the training school no major incidents were reported in Kosovo, although in August a number of protests took place in Peja/Pec and Pristina after the arrests of several former KLA members. A total of twenty-two protesters were arrested and twenty-three UNMIK police were injured.

I plodded on at the training school and as I neared the end of my mission, one American and one Danish CIVPOL instructor followed my example of improving the driver training programme and the KPS driving skills. They introduced motorcycle and PSV training which became very successful. An indicator of the general progress being made at that time by the KPS was the fact that one class of new recruits graduated and several of their course classes were conducted solely by local police instructors and not UNMIK.

CHAPTER THIRTEEN
The Kukri Bar

MY FIRST DAY in mission really started in the Kukri bar and my last day in mission ended in that same bar. In between times, I spent many occasions meeting new and current friends and colleagues and I'll never forget the great times and some very special moments we shared in that place.

The Kukri bar which was without doubt not always the safest place to be, but absolutely the friendliest and liveliest place to be.

Although driver training was a bit of a nightmare, the job did have its advantages; unofficial weekends off. The KPS training school worked Monday to Friday with weekends off and as far as UNMIK was concerned, Saturday and

This is where the Kukri was situated

Sunday were administration days. What that meant was CIVPOL trainers used the weekend to prepare all lesson plans for the coming week. I spent my weekend in the Kukri, although I seldom ventured out until the Saturday (and Sunday), Scottish Premier League and English Premiership football matches were due to start (4 pm local time). Well, if a game started early, I was out early; usually before 1 pm. The Kukri showed Sky Sports on three or four TVs, which obviously came in handy during the football season.

My Contingent Commander who was now Andy Kirkwood would often visit the Kukri with CIVPOL colleagues for lunch. If I did appear early on a Saturday out of uniform and Andy was in the Kukri, he would always acknowledge me with a nod but with a seemingly disapproving look on his face. I did explain my fortunate position and the admin days, however, I don't think Andy was impressed by my early drinking sessions. I'll give Andy his due; he rarely questioned my social habits, although, one day he did jokingly and sarcastically ask me, 'John, what is it that you do in Kosovo?'

With many of the MDP courses I volunteered for taking place at the MDP training centres, I would more often than not meet Andy, especially during firearms courses. It was during some of those courses and other social occasions that I got to know him reasonably well. He was a great instructor, very firm but very fair and when and where appropriate, he always included lighthearted moments, like his Rab C Nesbitt character, in his course material.

Andy is also a very forgiving individual as I found out during a one-to-one meeting which took place in an office in Pristina when he was the UK2 Contingent Commander.

During a UK medal parade and after an alcohol fuelled afternoon, I had a go at Andy and blamed him for refusing an earlier (pre-deployment) request I had made, asking to be deployed to Prizren region rather than Mitrovica. Rey Logie was on his second mission and working in Prizren and had set me up with a position in the Prizren main control room; however, it was not to be.

I gave it to Andy with both barrels and as I was verbally abusing him in full view of the UK contingent, my MDP colleague and fellow CIVPOL, Alun Ferguson, intervened and led me away.

No more was said that day and no action was taken. On my return to work two days later later I received an e-mail. It was addressed to Constable Duncanson and sent by Superintendent A. Kirkwood. I knew I was in big trouble. I was to attend a meeting in Pristina with Andy and in attendance would also be Inspector Paul Jordan.

I asked Alun Ferguson to travel to Pristina with me as my MDP federation representative, that's how bad I thought the situation was. I was sure I'd be sent home and I needed Alun to fight my corner. At that particular point in time my personal life was just beginning to crumble and Alun, who knew about my situation, wanted to use this as a defence for my erratic and unruly behaviour.

Once in Andy's office Alun asked to speak with Andy alone, he agreed. I waited outside and prayed the big man would convince Andy not to take any disciplinary action against me.

After ten minutes Alun came out and told me to go in. Paul Jordan hadn't arrived yet and it was just me and Andy. I couldn't believe Andy's first words. He apologised to me for *his* inappropriate behaviour and said he was out of order. I couldn't remember Andy saying anything. I thought it was only me who was dishing out the abuse.

After about five minutes apologising to one another Paul Jordan burst in the door and what a look he gave me. Andy told him he had everything in hand and that Paul wasn't needed. Paul simply glared at me and left.

Although Andy had apologised he still laid it on thick about my over indulgence with alcohol and the fact I could have been sent home for my misbehaviour. Andy wasn't the only senior rank present that day and any of the others could quite easily have spotted me before big Alun stepped in.

The incident was discussed and forgotten about in Andy's office; I was forgiven. It could have been so very different and if I had been sent home early I've really no idea how my life would have panned out. I owe Andy big time for his, let's call it *understanding*, and will be eternally grateful to him.

Socialising in the Kukri bar was always a great way to end a busy, quiet or dangerous 'day at the office'. You could have a good blow out, make a clown of yourself and no one was bothered. It was also a great place for getting to know those fellow internationals from around the world and educating one another on each other's home country and favourite football (soccer) team. From Glasgow and Ghana; from Finland and Fiji, from Pakistan and Poland, I met and drank (not always alcohol) with them all.

Christian Linetty (*right*) wasn't a regular to the Kukri but he did pop in now and again and actually suggested starting a quiz night to break up the week. Christian, me and fellow MDP PC Ian Barwick, who compiled the quiz questions, spoke about a quiz night

John Foreman and Allan Barr

for some time and eventually owner John Foreman, who received an MBE for his charitable work in Bosnia, agreed.

The Wednesday night quizzes became very successful and raised thousands of Euros for various charities (mainly Serbian and Albanian) and also offered several donated prizes for quiz winners. I remember Austrian Airlines offering two flight tickets from Pristina to New York, if it could advertise the airline during one quiz night. The winner of that prize was able to change the original departing airport and left from his home town of Liverpool (UK) to JFK, New York.

Rey Logie and I eventually took over the organising and running of the quiz, and John Foreman took over from Christian Linetty as quiz master. After a busy quiz night, Rey and I would catch up on the few beers we'd missed out on and eventually the bar security guard would demand that we leave the 'empty bar'. John Foreman had security cameras installed inside the bar and would phone the security guard if he saw Rey and I overstaying our welcome. On a few occasions the sun was rising by the time we left. Eventually Allan Barr, who joined the mission in 2003, took over as quiz organiser. Like those before him Allan raised thousands of Euros for charity.

In an ideal world the Kukri bar was possibly everything Kosovo would want to be, free from ethnic hatred. The Kukri's walls and ceilings were covered with a mass of flags and football team pendants and scarves. It sold draught beers, including Guinness and Kilkenny; however, my particular favourite was Amstel.

Mounting anger over the Kukri's existence had seen locals throwing eggs at customers and dropping rotting rubbish from the balconies above the pub, setting off tear gas canisters on the premises and issuing death threats to its staff. Most nights John Foreman had to escort his Serbian bar staff home for fear of them being attacked. John was frequently told all the problems would disappear if he was to 'get rid' of his Serbian staff. John who speaks fluent Serb-Croat was even accused of being a spy, involved in war crimes and a Serb masquerading as an Englishman.

Local gangsters loathed John Foreman and his employment policy and had already made one attempt on his life, after his refusal to pay them protection money. John, who regularly carried an authorised firearm for personal protection, was a big guy and said he would never give in to the local mafia.

The UN issued a public notice putting the bar under the protection of security forces. The notice was stuck to the bar's main entrance and John would read it aloud when troublemakers came in. At the time several UN officials admitted life in Kosovo would be a lot easier if the bar ceased to be in existence.

Near the end of my mission I was in the Kukri with Rey Logie and a number of other MDP constables who worked in the Pristina region. Due to work commitments and different shift patterns, I hadn't seen much of them in mission. John Pearson was there, Pat Kearney, Davy Rodden, Christian Linetty and a few others.

That evening we were all crammed in a corner and most of the conversation was about how we and others enjoyed and coped with the mission and how we managed to achieve the senior positions that all of us had or still occupied. Regional Commander, Deputy Chief of Communication, Station Commander, Chief of Traffic, Chief of Operations, team leaders and more.

Copper John Kane had been the first MDP officer to achieve a region's highest position, Regional Commander, in Gjilan/Gnjilane.

I've got to hold my hands up; I spent just about every night of my last six months in mission enjoying the atmosphere in the Kukri and sampling many more Amstel beers. I was also very fortunate to have attained two positions with UNMIK police, which kept me well apart and away from the mayhem and violence.

I was really on the wind down during my last few weeks at driver training. The courses were now being operated in a more professional manner and there was a much better looking structure to the weekly course curriculum. I was happy with my input, the OSCE were happy, and so too were the KPS who were now completing courses, feeling good, looking better and turning out safer drivers.

During those last few weeks and after Monday morning briefings, Joe Robson always had a 'special task' for me, which kept me away from most of that week's driving course. Joe and I would leave the training school after a morning coffee and head down to Pristina. The Kukri bar was always our first port of call where we would tuck into a full English breakfast (with brown sauce) and during the occasional Monday afternoon I'd return to the Kukri for a few special teas. 'Special tea' was always ordered by a CIVPOL officer in uniform and was always served in a ceramic mug. The Kukri bar staff were familiar with the term and knew my special tea was a vodka and coke light.

The Kukri bar was the obvious choice for the UK contingent's end of mission knees up and I can tell you there were a lot of emotional people that night.

My three-day UN check-out took all of five minutes. The only piece of UN property I had to return was that Motorola radio, battery and charger.

On the morning of my departure I wasn't ready to return home and back to the MDP and Coulport regime; I was also quite upset. In fact, the airport transport left without me and John Pearson had to drive me to the airport. I left the Kukri without saying goodbye, I knew I'd be back. As soon as we boarded that plane the UN berets were well and truly off and most of the MDP supervisors were once again addressed according to their rank.

John Pearson finished his one and only UN mission in June 2003 as Station One Commander. Pat Kearney ended his first of three UN missions in December 2002, as Station Four Commander. Davy Rodden was another mission junkie and in December 2003, he finished his first of three UN missions as Pristina Airport Deputy Station Commander. Before Christian Linetty completed his first of two UN missions, he was still RPU team leader.

Incidentally, John Foreman sold the Kukri in 2004 and moved to Cyprus with his Serbian wife Suzie where they opened a bar and named it, *The Kukri Bar*. The venture never really worked out and John and Suzie returned to Kosovo. The new owners of the original Kukri Bar closed it and after refurbishment it was reopened and renamed *The Phoenix Bar*.

On landing at Stansted airport the contingent was picked up by MDP transport and driven back to PTC Wethersfield. We spent one week at the MDP training school being reintegrated back into the old routine. The reintegration course included re-qualification in personal safety and firearms. During the week all post-deployment officers were treated to a slap-up dinner at a local golf course and afterwards a certificate of recognition (for outstanding police work in the service of the UN Police in Kosovo) was presented to each officer by a senior MDP officer.

Although I felt fit and healthy with no obvious post-mission ill effects, I thought a routine medical followed by a 'wee talk' with a post-mission counsellor may have been on the week's agenda, however, they were not. I'm sure there must have been a few coppers who would have experienced unfamiliar and maybe very disturbing events that could cause some sort of stress or anxiety disorder. And coppers like Christian Linetty (who was still in Kosovo) and who experienced pretty terrifying encounters must surely have been affected in some way or other. Personally speaking the only post-mission problem I suffered was sadness. I was saddened by the fact I'd be returning to the Coulport regime.

CHAPTER FOURTEEN
From Kosovo to Kibble

ON MY RETURN to Coulport very few coppers were curious to know about my jaunt abroad. Some even thought I'd been on long-term sick leave. My first duty on my return to work was Kibble barrier and during a visit by the patrol team sergeant, Les McQueen, the first thing he said to me was, 'You haven't submitted any 260s for a few months.' A 260 is a self-maintained log of an MDP police officer's daily or monthly duty times, including overtime which is submitted to the station's admin department.

I looked at him for a moment, waiting for the laugh, which never came. 'I've spent the last eighteen months in Kosovo, how was I expected to submit a 260?' I asked.

'It's your responsibility to submit your 260 on time,' he said before driving off.

That brief conversation summed up Coulport in sixty seconds. Some of the old school supervisors were still more interested in harassing you than asking about your welfare and wellbeing.

I stood at Kibble barrier in the driving rain and at one point the rain hammered down on my flat police cap so hard it felt like a rapid paradiddle from a crazed and demented rock drummer. I was soaked all the way through to my thermal underwear which clung to my body and by the end of my shift had me walking around like Herman Munster. There was no question in my mind after that first shift back at Coulport, when the right opportunity arrives, I'm off, back to Kosovo.

During my time back home I had to work hard to convince my wife going back to Kosovo would be good for my future career and I'd have a better chance of gaining promotion with the MDP during the mission. Truth was, I just missed working in Kosovo and wanted another taste of mission life.

Davy Rodden meeting US president Bill Clinton and Angelina Jolie

PART THREE

MITROVICA

DECEMBER 2004 TO
DECEMBER 2006

AS FAR AS returning to Kosovo was concerned, the UK policy was, no applications would be considered for a further secondment until one year had lapsed. Although I could have gone back at the first opportunity, I decided to wait a little longer. I returned to Kosovo on 6 December 2004 and already knew where I'd be deployed to; the dreaded and troubled city of Mitrovica. During the MDP pre-deployment training for that particular mission I, along with my participating colleagues, was told which region I'd be deployed to. I was terrified and the thought of pulling out of the deployment did cross my mind. I was thinking of an easier life somewhere else. It was actually during that pre-deployment course when I made the request to be deployed in Prizren, where a job in the main control room was waiting for me. My deployment request was refused.

My two years deployment was a big test of my character and resilience. After just a few weeks in the mission I found myself up against groups of idle CIVPOL officers who seemed to forget why they volunteered for the UN mission in Kosovo. My working practices didn't seem to go down too well with certain CIVPOL officers and I eventually found myself battling to save my reputation.

As the KPS became more effective and self-sufficient the crime rate began to decrease; however, attacks on minority areas including murder continued to take place. Tragically during my two years back at home six KPS officers had been killed in the line of duty bringing the total to seven. To date eleven KPS have lost their lives in the line of duty.

After my arrival in Kosovo on 6 December 2004 the UN's key targets continued to be met. The transfer of authority from UNMIK to the KPS was well under way with most RHQs and police stations now being managed by KPS supervisors, under the watchful eye of their CIVPOL (monitor) counterpart.

At transitioned RHQs the CIVPOL Regional and Deputy Regional Commander Monitors continued to co-locate with their KPS counterpart and would later become known as Regional Commander Liaison Officer (RCLO) and Regional Operations Liaison Officer (ROLO).

At transitioned police stations the UNMIK Station Commander and Deputy Station Commander Monitors would also continue to co-locate with their KPS counterpart; their titles would become KPS Station Commander Liaison Officer (SCLO) and KPS Operations Liaison Officer (OLO). Both those positions would be the only two CIVPOL positions assigned to a KPS police station.

During the transition period of the UNMIK police stations (to KPS authority), CIVPOL patrol officers, PFTOs and all other CIVPOL would be redeployed elsewhere.

Most UNMIK police were no longer directly involved in the daily workings of the KPS, however, they did retain police powers to act to preserve life or property, or to prevent the commission of a crime. Several UNMIK police stations had been handed over to the KPS and 85 per cent of KPS training at the KPS training school was managed and delivered by KPS officers and other staff from Kosovo.

The UN induction course had introduced new lectures and PowerPoint presentations relating to the monitoring programme, including an introduction to monitoring the Kosovo Monitoring Information System (KMIS) and monitoring report writing. An operational bulletin was published and updated on several occasions, however, the general purpose and policy of the bulletin virtually remained the same:

GENERAL PURPOSE
The purpose of the bulletin is to put forth the rules and requirements that the UNMIK Police will follow to serve as Monitors/Mentors/KPS Station Commander/Operations Liaison Officers for the Kosovo Police Service (KPS). International officers will not be directly involved in the daily workings of the Service, but will retain police powers to act to preserve life or property, or to prevent the commission of a crime.

POLICY
This will establish the procedures in which the UNMIK police will adhere, in order to perform as Monitors/Mentors/KPS Station Commander/Operations Liaison Officers for the KPS after direct control of operations and patrol is transitioned to the Kosovo Police Service.

UNMIK had not yet started the KPS handover in the Mitrovica region where the command staff continued to be a CIVPOL Regional Commander, Deputy Regional Commander and the Chief of Operations. Regional Crime, Regional Traffic and all seven police stations also continued to be under CIVPOL command.

The number of UNMIK police in mission was around 3,600 and KPS numbered around 6,280. The composition of the KPS was 84.5 Albanians, 9.4 Serbians and 6.0 were of other ethnicities. The number of police officers from the UK was somewhere in the region of 100.

Other significant points to note:
On 25 November 2003, UNMIK established its administration in North Mitrovica which meant its authority had now extended throughout all of Kosovo. That was after an agreement of the authorities of the Federal Republic of Yugoslavia to discontinue the financing of parallel structures, including parallel security structures. This included the support of UNMIK in assuming control of the

administrative functions and developing the KPS in North Mitrovica. Several institutions did continue to receive financing from Belgrade, especially in the health department.

UNMIK started to implement certain provisions in North Mitrovica, which included static and joint KFOR patrols on the main bridge. The KPS (non-Albanian) were deployed in the north and started to carry out regular patrolling.

On 15 March 2004, a young Serbian was killed in a drive-by shooting. On 16 March, four Albanian children were reportedly chased into a river by a group of Serbians as an act of revenge for the young Serbian's death. Three of the Albanian children drowned with one surviving.

The surviving Albanian child's version of events differed from that of two other Albanian children who had also been in the river. A UN spokesperson said there were very significant inconsistencies in the accounts given by the child during two separate interviews, and a lack of corroboration of his story. The spokesperson said, 'In fact, it is logically at odds in several respects with other evidence.'

Demonstrations and protests took place which led to violent unrest and on 17 March tens of thousands of Albanians took part in widescale attacks on the Serbian people.

In Mitrovica Albanians and Serbians clashed on Mitrovica's main bridge which led to the injury and death of a number of people, including Albanians, Serbians and UN peacekeepers. It was the largest violent incident in the province since the Kosovo war.

During the violence many Serbian houses, Serbian public facilities and a number of Serbian Orthodox church buildings were desecrated, damaged or destroyed.

Approximately 100 KPS were identified as the subject of allegations of misconduct during the March violence. It was reported some KPS may have taken no action to prevent violence or, worse still, may have participated in it. However, the overall professional conduct of the KPS during the violence was a significant indicator of the professional growth of the service.

Following the violence, UNMIK police shifted resources in order to establish the full facts of what occurred during the violence. A Task-Force and incident room was set up at UNMIK police headquarters supported by task forces in all other regions.

CHAPTER FIFTEEN
North Mitrovica

MITROVICA

Mitrovica is a city and municipality in northern Kosovo. It's the administrative centre of the District of Mitrovica. The city is multi-ethnic although Albanians, mainly living in South Mitrovica and form the absolute majority. With no accurate statistics for the present time, approximately 70 per cent of the inhabitants are ethnic Albanians, with Serbians being the second largest group. Other ethnicities include, Roma, Ashkali, Bosniak and Turk.

The Serbian community is heavily concentrated in the north of the city across the River Ibar, in an area known to some as North Kosovska Mitrovica and to most as Mitrovica. The population of Mitrovica is around 71,000.

MITROVICA 2004

On the last day of my induction course I knew I was being deployed to North Station in North Mitrovica and later that night in Pristina I was picked up by the North Station, Station Commander, CIVPOL Roger Phillips, a retired territorial Police officer and CIVPOL Alan Phillips (MDP constable from Coulport), the Mitrovica Chief of Operations. After having a coffee in a small café bar we headed up to Mitrovica.

On the way up to Mitrovica through light snow, Roger spoke about the March riots and although the violent clashes were six months old, the situation in Kosovo remained tense and further clashes were possible. In view of this, KFOR *had* reinforced its presence by deploying approximately 2,000 additional troops on a limited engagement. Both KFOR and UNMIK were maintaining a high level of visibility and presence, particularly in minority areas. Roger also mentioned, after the March violence, the minority Serbians living in North Mitrovica were now a bit more tolerable of the UNMIK presence and many now felt more protected.

Another reason for tolerating UNMIK and other international staff was obviously financial. Serbian families, like any other in Kosovo, relied on UN staff to rent their properties and like my first mission, rent was usually negotiable and the cost depended on the number of potential occupants. I must say, after a few months living in Pristina I would say Pat Kearney and I were ripped off. Paying 350 Euros each for that house in Dragodan was way too much. First mission naivety I suppose.

Three internationals sharing one house could make one family around 600 Euros (around 500 pounds) per month. Local café bars made a good profit, especially at weekends, and especially in the small town of Zvecan, where I rented a small flat.

Roger spoke about one pub in particular, a local pub in Zvecan, *Xponto*, and said it was packed at the weekends with both locals and internationals, which was a bit different to the Kukri, where it was mainly frequented by internationals.

The journey to Mitrovica, in pitch darkness, took forty-five minutes along the main Pristina Mitrovica highway (which had very limited street lighting). I was quite nervous when Roger took the turn off for South Mitrovica; nevertheless, I was also quite excited at the thought of passing over the Main Bridge into North Mitrovica which I'd obviously heard a lot about.

It wasn't that late, maybe around seven o'clock, however the dark winter night and evening power cut made sure all of Mitrovica was shrouded in complete darkness.

Roger soon arrived at Mitrovica Bridge, or the main bridge, where French KFOR and CIVPOL were present at either end. Roger, who was driving a white UN Toyota 4Runner, was motioned to slow down by the torch light of one CIVPOL. As soon as he saw Roger, he waved him on. The CIVPOL on the North side seemed to recognise Roger immediately and also waved him on.

After crossing the 100 metres or so steel truss bridge, we were in North Mitrovica, where the power cut continued to prevail. From the main bridge, it was a short drive, around two miles, to the centre of Zvecan. Just before Zvecan and near the local railway station is the lead and zinc smelting factory Trepca. It has a large smokestack which is just over 1,000 feet tall and the tallest structure in Kosovo. Unfortunately, due to the serious environmental pollution from the factory, the UN and KFOR shut it down. The only ongoing operation is alloy production for batteries and battery recycling. At one point the workforce was around 4,000 and today in the municipality only around 500 people are employed.

Roger drove slowly through Zvecan and I could see candlelight through the window of one small café bar that had a few people inside. That cafe was called *The House of Art* and it was mainly students who gathered there. On one side of the road there were a few small prefabricated metal cabooses with only room inside for the proprietor. All customers were greeted through a small front window. Those small cabooses were erected in every town of Kosovo, most without any type of licence to trade. Eventually the municipalities had most of them dismantled and destroyed. Roger pointed out a few buildings and shops that I might want to visit – post office, barber and other types of amenities.

Trepca smokestack

The municipality of Zvecan covers forty square miles and has thirty-five villages, three of which are Albanian. The population is around 17,000 with 95 per cent being Serbian, and 5 per cent of non-Serbian.

Martin Walsh, who I barely saw during my first mission, was now back and working in Mitrovica as a traffic patrol officer with the Mitrovica Regional Traffic Unit. Marty and Alun Ferguson, who worked with Regional Crime (Trafficking and Prostitution Investigation Unit), shared accommodation in Zvecan and had already arranged for me to look at a small ground floor flat. I would have preferred to move in with them, however, they had no room, so I had to go it alone. On my first night in Zvecan, I moved in to the flat which was directly opposite my new CIVPOL colleagues and Scottish compatriots. I had no hang ups about living alone and although I knew all about Mitrovica and its violence, I did settle very quickly. I think the fact Marty and Alun were literally across the street and I spent most of my spare time with them, was a big contributor.

I met Roger Phillips the following day and was assigned to work in the North Station duty office, which was a radio control room. I must admit, I was quite happy to once again be working indoors and in a control room. I was responsible for transmitting and receiving messages to and from all North Station CIVPOL. Any major incidents were reported to and dealt with by Bravo control.

I worked with two LAs but no other CIVPOL. The LAs were a great help and it was mainly through them that I was introduced me to the station's policies and procedures. The station was due to transition in mid-2005; however, in the meantime three CIVPOL teams working three eight-hour shifts (three nights, three afternoons and three mornings) patrolled the north alongside the KPS. The other CIVPOL working in the Mitrovica region also worked alongside the KPS in the other six UNMIK police stations.

CIVPOL officers working in two UNMIK stations in the north, Zvecan and Leposavic, were preparing for the stations to transition and had started to monitor the KPS patrol officers and forward *daily activity monitoring reports* to Mitrovica RHQ. During late December the UNMIK Transition Unit Monitoring Team had become extremely busy with updating the entire monitoring programme and the daily activity monitoring reports would be replaced by a new computer database system, the Kosovo Monitoring Information System (KMIS)

The monitors worked according to the policy set in *Operational Bulletin 0.66* and the purpose of the bulletin was to put forth the rules and requirements that the UNMIK Police would follow to serve as monitors, mentors and executive advisors to the KPS.

The latest version of Bulletin 0.66, 5.3, was basically the monitor's bible and it was important to keep right up to date with its contents. Although at that point I was not a monitor, I wasn't going to sit back and ignore the bulletin. I knew that sometime soon North Station would transition and I would be looking for another job which would either be as a monitor or possibly with community policing. Being a tutor constable at home and being used to monitoring and evaluating probationary constables, monitoring appealed to me more.

It didn't take me long to settle back into mission life and working in the North Station duty office helped with that. It also didn't take long before my nose was stuck back in the KPS and UNMIK PPM just to refresh my inquisitive memory.

As far as the criminal codes were concerned the KPS were no longer working according to the Criminal Code and Criminal Procedure Code of the Socialist Federal Republic of Yugoslavia. From April 2004, the new law was in accordance with the Criminal Code and Criminal Procedure Code of Kosovo. I battered into that as well. I even had a look at the Kosovo Traffic Law articles. It wasn't all work though.

I was working early shift on Christmas Day, a Saturday, and later that evening Marty and Alun took me, for the first time, to Xponto to sample the local night life and of course the local beer, *Jelen* (deer) and *Lav* (lion) being the most popular. We couldn't get through the bar's only door. The place was absolutely heaving with people, crammed into a very small, loud and lively bar. Eventually Big Alun, and he is a big lad, managed to excuse himself all the way to the bar whilst Marty and I followed close behind. We didn't speak to each other, we screamed to be heard and what I was screaming was 'Let's get out of here.' Alun just laughed and shouted, 'Welcome to Mitrovica.'

Throughout the evening the (rock) music didn't get that much quieter, however it did become more recognisable and the loud noise became more tolerable. Most of the bar's tables and chairs had been deposited outside the bar to make more space for the continuous flow of people who were determined to get through that door. We put up with the music and constant jostling for an hour then headed back to Marty and Alun's accommodation for a few Heineken and some peace and quiet. The fact it was Christmas had nothing to do with Xponto being so busy; as Roger Phillips had told me it was always busy during the weekend.

On New Year's Day I was working night shift and missed out on a few parties, however, I did celebrate another Christmas and New Year's Day in January 2005. Being Orthodox Christians, Serbians follow the Julian calendar and celebrate Christmas day on 7 January and New Year's Day one week later.

Both Marty and Alun had been in mission since June 2004 and straight after PTC were deployed to Mitrovica. They had the same fears as me but both agreed they would never redeploy to any other region. They got on really well with the other CIVPOL, LAs and KPS. To top that off, the local Serbians seemed to like Scottish people much more than other nationals from the UK.

The next time the three of us got together was during a 'curry night' in Marty and Alun's house. Curry nights were a regular feature with the guys and they always invited a number of other CIVPOL as well as LAs from their respective units. Marty usually brought back curry powder or curry paste when he'd been on CTO. Both he and Alun were also keen visitors to the British PX (Post Exchange) in Pristina where they could buy various British goods, groceries and beers. During my first mission I rarely visited the PX, mainly due to a lack of transport.

Marty and Alun worked on morning shift whilst I worked the three shift system, so initially we never really saw a lot of each other; not until I received a phone call from Alan Phillips who asked me if I was interested in becoming the Mitrovica Transition Monitor Liaison Officer (TMLO). Before I had a chance to quiz Alan about the position he told me he had no idea what the job description was, except it was a day job and the Deputy Regional Commander (American CIVPOL) Alice Holmes (whom I had yet to meet), was the person I should speak to. This I did on the phone but she was just as clueless as Alan. However, a meeting was set up and in early January I met with Alice.

Alice's office was located on the top floor of Mitrovica RHQ, South Mitrovica, which is less than a ten-minute drive from North Station. Since arriving in Mitrovica region I'd never been into North Mitrovica town centre or travelled over to the South side.

My job kept me behind a desk in the North Station duty office and all my free time was spent in Zvecan, either in Marty and Alun's house or one of the bars, usually Xponto.

Another first was driving a Coca Cola. Believe it or not, I'd never driven an UNMIK police vehicle either. Pristina Control had access to a small Sherpa van and KPS Driver Training normally used the Skoda Felicia.

Turning left out of North Station gates took me onto the relatively wide King Peter Street (turning right takes you to Zvecan) and down into the mayhem of Mitrovica town centre. Cars parked, nose first, on the pavement forced pedestrians to walk on the road. Shops, café bars, small market stalls and cabooses were erected below many of the high rise flats, all the way down either side of a partly tree-lined stretch of road covering just over quarter of a mile. At the bottom of the road was a T-Junction and the Main Bridge straight ahead. Turning left at the junction takes you to Little Bosnia, a multi-ethnic area; turning right takes you to the Three Towers and Suvi-Do, another multi-ethnic area. Also at the bottom of the road on the right side of the T-Junction, and diagonally opposite the main bridge, is café bar *Dolce Vita*, a bar which was usually frequented by UNMIK police.

When I arrived promptly at the arranged time, on the top floor of RHQ I headed towards Alice Holmes' office. Standing in the office doorway with arms slightly raised, body slightly bowed turning right then left was the rather small Alice Holmes. Her first words to me were, 'I forget what I was about to do, you must be John?' That semi-gyrating motion became typical of Alice; she was always busy dealing with numerous tasks at the same time.

We spoke in Alice's office in between several interruptions whilst she answered both her mobile phone and the landline. Alice explained the region required a transition liaison officer to the MHQ transition unit, and the primary task was to convey all information regarding the monitoring programme between RHQ and MHQ.

Alice also assured me the Mitrovica TMLO would be responsible for organising other important tasks; tasks with responsibilities that she and the Regional Commander, Joachim (Joe) Schaeck could not commit to. Mitrovica region was very busy with various sensitive operations and as far as both Alice and Joe were concerned the new TMLO position would take the pressure off them.

The TMLO's position or job description did not feature in Bulletin 0.66, 5.3 nor did it feature in any of the regional chain of command charts. It later became apparent the title of TMLO was just a way of describing a go-between who (whilst having a full-time position) kept a regional RHQ up to date with transition and monitoring issues. However, in Mitrovica this position included 'other important tasks'.

I was given a number of memos by Alice and she asked me to read through them before giving her my final answer on the position that was on offer. The more I read the more excited I became. The job was a real challenge and I couldn't turn it down. Later that day I contacted Alice and agreed to become the Mitrovica TMLO.

The transition from the Mitrovica UNMIK police stations to KPS authority was drawing close and, in preparation for that event, two Regional Monitor Base Stations (RMBS) had to be established by the TMLO, in the region – one in North Mitrovica and one in South Mitrovica.

Each RMBS would then be occupied with an as yet unspecified number of qualified CIVPOL monitors made up of one supervisor, three team leaders and three teams.

When my task was complete, Joe Schaeck and Alice Holmes agreed I would be appointed as the overall supervisor to both RMBS, however, I obviously knew the TMLO was not an official position never mind a command position.

When I questioned Joe about my concern, he said words to the effect of: 'I am not involved in the monitoring programme. I am not the Mitrovica Regional Commander Liaison Officer; I am the Mitrovica Regional Commander and I have delegated you to act on my behalf. You are only answerable to me and have my authority to supervise both Mitrovica RMBS and make any decisions you deem necessary for the good of both base stations and the Mitrovica monitoring programme in general.' Was I being a little naive – probably?

CHAPTER SIXTEEN
The Monitoring Programme

I SENT E-MAILS to all of the Mitrovica (UNMIK) Station Commanders introducing myself as the new Mitrovica TMLO and supplied them with information regarding my position, my task, my authority and the imminent redeployment of the station's CIVPOL officers. Redeployments would take place immediately before the station was handed over to KPS authority.

During the transition period, and when the handover from UNMIK to KPS was complete, only two CIVPOL officers were appointed as monitors to KPS stations. The monitor titles were KPS Station Commander Liaison Officer (SCLO) and KPS Operations Officer (OLO). Both the SCLO and OLO worked on day shift, normally 8:30am to 5:00pm. Here are the job descriptions of both those CIVPOL monitors.

KPS STATION COMMANDER LIAISON OFFICER (SCLO)

Once operational command of a station has been transitioned to the KPS, the senior UNMIK police officer assigned to that station would hold the title of KPS Station Commander Liaison Officer.

The KPS Station Commander Liaison Officer will advise, mentor, monitor and work alongside his KPS counterpart (Lieutenant or Captain depending on class of station). The KPS SCLO will be responsible for coordinating with the Regional Monitor Base Station (RMBS) supervisor and team leader ensuring the adequate monitoring of all KPS activities, carried out within his area of responsibility, on a twenty-four hour basis.

The KPS SCLO will ensure that the UNMIK police KPS Operations Liaison Officer (OLO), under his supervision will advise, monitor, evaluate and report on every aspect of KPS performance.

The KPS SCLO retains both the administrative and operational responsibility for the KPS OLO and himself while assigned to the station.

The KPS SCLO will review all monitor reports and Non-Compliance reports regarding the KPS officers assigned to his station and will ensure each report is accurate.

The KPS SCLO is responsible for formulating and submitting a weekly report of KPS performance to his UNMIK Police Regional Commander through the Kosovo Monitor Information System (KMIS).

KPS OPERATION LIAISON OFFICER (OLO), advisor to the KPS Operations Officer.

This officer will assist the KPS SCLO in his daily duties. This officer will also deputise for the KPS SCLO during periods of absence. This officer will also be responsible for advising, mentoring the KPS officer in charge of station operations (sergeant or lieutenant depending on class of station). This will be the only other UNMIK police officer working out of a transitioned KPS police station.

One point I mentioned in the e-mail was 'my authority' and it didn't go down well with one or two station commanders. Phone calls were made to the Regional Commander to clarify my and their position after a UNMIK station was transitioned. An agreement was made whereby I and the Mitrovica SCLOs, post-transition, would be equal to one another; CIVPOL monitors would be answerable to the TMLO and a SCLO as well as RMBS supervisors and team leaders.

Most CIVPOL officers were redeployed to a Regional Monitor Base Station (RMBS), a Regional Community Base Station (RCBS) or to another region. A few CIVPOL secured alternative positions due to the end of a mission of other CIVPOL. Here is an overview of a RMBS and its staff members.

REGIONAL MONITOR BASE STATION (RMBS)

Through the use of UNMIK police officers as monitors and mentors the programme, which will also offer advice and oversight to all KPS officers, from patrol officers to the patrol supervisory staff, will include station investigations. Each region within Kosovo will have Regional Monitor Base Stations that will be staffed by a supervisor, three team leaders for each shift and the patrol monitors.

RMBS Supervisor

The RMBS supervisor is the senior UNMIK police officer assigned to a RMBS. This officer is responsible for the operation and administration duties of the UNMIK police assigned to the station.

The RMBS supervisor is directly responsible for all administrative tasks of the base station, assignment of monitor team patrol locations (within the area of responsibility) and the coordination with each station SCLO and OLO of any operational plans, KPS patrol assignments and special details.

The RMBS supervisor will have access into the KMIS and review the monitor reports, generated from the RMBS, for accuracy and completeness. Additionally, the supervisor will ensure that the RMBS team leaders, under his supervision, are active in the management of the UNMIK patrol monitors assigned to their respective shifts and that pro-active monitoring is enforced by the team leaders.

Obviously the Mitrovica RMBS supervisors, according to the Mitrovica Regional Commander were answerable to me.

RMBS Team Leader

The RMBS team leader is an UNMIK monitor, designated by the Regional Commander and under the direction of the RMBS supervisor, who will supervise the UNMIK police monitors assigned to a particular shift. The team leader will ensure the accuracy and submission of all relevant reports generated by monitors on his shift. The team leader will ensure the pro-active patrol of the monitors assigned to his team.

RMBS Monitor

All UNMIK CIVPOL officers assigned as KPS monitors will actively engage in the monitoring of activities, actions and behaviour of the KPS and its officers throughout Kosovo at all police levels and to include all ranks with the KPS organisation.

The CIVPOL monitors will ensure that the process and procedures used by the KPS are consistent with democratic policing principles and the rule of law. Monitors will be responsible for the *proactive* engagement of the KPS as monitors, mentors and advisors.

Monitors will remain knowledgeable of Operational Bulletin 0.66 in the most current version. All monitors will have entry access into the KMIS database system where they can submit monitoring reports including Managerial Skills Assessment Reports. Monitors must have a basic familiarisation with the Provisional Criminal Code of Kosovo, the Provisional Criminal Procedure Code, Kosovo Traffic Law and the KPS PPM.

KOSOVO MONITORING INFORMATION SYSTEM (KMIS)

The KMIS database is used by monitor staff (including all supervisors), Regional and Central Unit of Criminal Data (RUCD and CUCD) to record the assessment of KPS officer function, Managerial Skills Assessment and Non-Compliance reports.

CHAPTER SEVENTEEN
Tangible Evidence

THE INITIAL PROBLEM faced was setting up both North and South RMBS. No monitor base station accommodation had been identified and no premises, other than UNMIK police stations, were available.

It was decided between UNMIK and the KPS, the top floor of two UNMIK police stations could be used by the monitors, one at North Station, the other in South Mitrovica at the UNMIK police station in Vushtrri/Vucitrn. When both these UNMIK stations were handed over to the KPS, both RMBS remained in situ.

Initially, and over a number of weeks, many CIVPOL working in Mitrovica were interviewed and tested by a question (paper) and answer method on their suitability on becoming KPS monitors. Test questions were taken from Bulletin 0.66, 5.3. Those CIVPOL who were deemed to be suitably qualified were given the option of redeploying to an RMBS or redeploying elsewhere.

The task of interviewing and testing the potential monitors was quite interesting and, although monitoring was a serious and important programme, I found during the question paper process quite a few answers to the questions posed very amusing.

The interviews and tests took place in North Station and were conducted by me in my capacity as the TMLO, Don Evans, *Chief of the UNMIK Transition Unit Monitoring Team*, Joaquin Navarro Garrido, *Head of the Monitoring Team* and a number of SCLOs.

In order to speed up the process other CIVPOL became involved in the interviews and to be fair on those being examined, I didn't say much as my broad Glasgow accent seemed to be a bit difficult to understand. I was happy with a German colleague doing most of the talking and all but a few completely understood his good English, spoken with a very soft accent.

The questionnaire papers, used by the transition unit for patrol monitors contained five questions all compiled from Bulletin 0.66, 5.3. On asking the questions it was very obvious most of those officers being tested already knew the answers to the questions. The questions were asked after the short interview and the answers given were practically verbatim to what was written on the question paper.

Question four asked: *'What is the purpose of a monitoring report?'* The answer came in three parts. Several CIVPOL struggled with their English, however, one word they did remember was 'tangible'. That word appeared twice in the answer to question four and every CIVPOL being tested remembered it. Several of those officers being tested became so confused when they forgot the answer and instead of just saying politely, 'Sorry I don't know,' they gave it a shot all the same.

One correct answer to the question was: *To provide tangible evidence of the progress made by the KPS in becoming an independent democratic and professional police service.*

One of the ridiculous answers given was: *To provide progress in becoming an independent democratic and tangible service.*

Soon after those interviews I made a recommendation to Don Evans to have a large bank of questions compiled with five questions selected at random immediately prior to the test. That recommendation was approved and initially I was permitted to compile those questions. I think my recommendation encouraged CIVPOL officers to review Bulletin 0.66 on a more regular basis.

After a couple of weeks of deliberation an initial thirty-six CIVPOL were to be redeployed and assigned to the monitoring base stations; fifteen were deployed to North RMBS and twenty-one to South RMBS. I appointed six monitors to become team leaders, three for each RMBS; however, I was reluctant to immediately identify RMBS supervisors. Most CIVPOL officers from Zvecan and Leposavic police stations were redeployed to North RMBS, but due to officer safety and travel restrictions, Leposavic station became an unofficial monitor sub-station to North RMBS. An American CIVPOL officer Chuck Pagliuca was the monitor team leader at Leposavic sub-station and if my memory serves me correctly, he supervised around three monitors; all from Poland. I must add, due to those travel restrictions, I rarely visited Leposavic sub-station, although I met and spoke with Chuck elsewhere on numerous occasions. After a little advice and a few tweaks to the monitor reports, Chuck and his small team produced quality reports. I also met Chuck in a future mission; he is a true professional and a well respected team member and supervisor; he was a real pleasure to work with.

As each UNMIK police station was handed over to the KPS more CIVPOL would be redeployed from the stations and most would join the monitoring programme. The same applied to the local language assistants; around fifteen were redeployed initially.

Alice Holmes was impressed by the progress I was making in establishing the RMBS teams, and she gave me a lot of credit and recognition. Basically I had just followed Bulletin 0.66 guidelines and had created monitoring teams according to those guidelines.

The one major issue I had was the quality of the monitors. As most of those CIVPOL who passed the question paper test knew the answers beforehand, it was impossible to predict if they would make good monitors. I didn't know how they would perform out in the field, monitoring their KPS counterparts, or what sort of standard their monitor reports would produce.

One problem I faced was with administration and logistics, however, one LA who was redeployed from Zvecan police station became my saviour.

Miljan (Kani) Radivojevic was responsible for all administration tasks at Zvecan police station and after being redeployed to North RMBS his administrative experience and creativity was put to immediate use. Following my guidance Kani compiled monthly rosters for both CIVPOL monitors and LAs. The rosters followed the same pattern as the CIVPOL patrols had originally worked at North Station.

Kani also compiled, organised and maintained most other documentation that was relevant in managing large groups of UN employees, Warden's Charts and Evacuation Plans for example.

As far as vehicles and office equipment were concerned, I arranged with the SCLOs to have all their surplus UN equipment (previously used by CIVPOL patrols) handed over to both North and South RMBS. They, and their KPS counterparts, were overjoyed at having more office space and more parking spaces for KPS vehicles.

True to his word, Joe Schaeck did appoint me as overall supervisor to both base stations, completely against policy; needless to say I didn't complain. On hindsight Joe should've appointed me as supervisor to one or the other RMBS, that would have made a lot more sense. My recent redeployment took me from North Station duty office to Mitrovica RHQ operations and under the guise of Mitrovica TMLO. However, the redeployment order was a paper exercise, I based myself in North Station's top floor with the monitors.

Being in that supervisory role was really beginning to bother me and I again brought my concern to both Alice and Joe. Once again Joe reassured me, even though I still had doubts in my own mind. As far as the monitoring programme in Mitrovica was concerned Joe had basically given me a free role to exercise my power and authority and enforce both whenever I felt the need. Now that really bothered me.

A short time after both RMBS were up and running Alice introduced me to CIVPOL Dave King (USA) who she recommended and approved as the new RMBS South supervisor; Dave accepted that he would be answerable to me. I was embarrassed but grateful for Dave's understanding and eventual support. During his term as RMBS South supervisor Dave never once questioned my position, work ethics or any decisions I made.

After being advertised for a couple of weeks there was very little response for the vacant North RMBS supervisor's position. Eventually, two CIVPOL monitors did apply, Kaiwan (Kevin) Abbassi from Pakistan being one, and the other a female officer from Bulgaria. I knew Kevin's monitor report writing was very good and his professional attitude was excellent. Although the Bulgarian officer had similar qualities, after the interviews I recommended Kevin for the position, which was subsequently approved.

Before joining the monitoring programme Kevin spent several weeks as a North Station patrol officer, however, he believed his talents were being wasted carrying out this menial role.

During one particular shift Kevin sought out Station Commander Roger Phillips regarding a potential station investigator position although he knew the odds were stacked against him, and as Kevin told me, Roger reserved the good jobs only for 'multinationals of his liking.' Not to be put off by Roger's favouritism or 'English haughtiness' and in an attempt to 'get rid of laborious patrolling' Kevin attended Roger's office to make a personal request. This is Kevin's amusing side to the story:

'As I entered the office I noticed him sitting in his chair surrounded by all his souvenirs of English glory – English flags and pictures of the River Thames etc. I noticed he was doing nothing in particular, yet he pretended to be busy. He looked at me rather contemptuously as if I were a trespasser. "Good evening sir," I greeted him.

"Yes Kevin," he replied.

"Sir I have come to you to request an opportunity to work in the station investigation unit please?"

"Hmmm, what do you know about investigations?" he asked.

"Sir to me, it is a process through which an investigating officer

Kaiwan (Kevin) Abbassi

collects the available pieces of evidence from a crime scene and tries to attribute the crime to the accused or otherwise."

"Okay."

He looked a bit upset with my answer.

"Can you tell me about DNA as a diagnostic tool in the field of investigation?" he asked.

I replied, "Sir do you want to know about Deoxyribonucleic acid; as an agent to carry the characteristic of humans from one generation to another or its importance as an investigative tool?"

"As an investigative tool obviously," he replied.

"Sir, DNA, or Deoxyribonucleic acid, is the hereditary material in humans and almost all other organisms. All the cells in a person's body have the same DNA. As DNA is located in the cell nucleus, and regarding a crime scene, if any part of a living body for example hair, finger nails, body fluid, stool, nasal secretion etc is found and if preserved properly can help the investigator to a great extent in the detection of a crime." I explained the whole thing in a single breath leaving him speechless for a moment or so. He was stunned. However, he stuck to a previous decision, he can't take me on as an investigator. I left the office heavy heartedly, condemning myself for relying upon a wrong person for a right thing.'

I had really found my niche with the monitoring programme and used my knowledge and experience as a tutor constable to gradually improve the monitor's skills, especially monitor report writing. I spent hours every day (on the KMIS) reviewing old and current monitor reports, from all regions, and taking notes. I had daily meetings with Dave King and Kevin and eventually both supervisors knew exactly how I expected a monitor's report to be completed before being submitted through the KMIS.

Every CIVPOL attended a monitoring course which included an in-depth PowerPoint presentation on the KMIS. One flaw in the PowerPoint was not enough examples of what should be written in the front 'Cover Sheet' and 'Narrative Section' of the reports were shown. One point was emphasised regarding the contents of the narrative section and that was: 'The narrative section should not be used to explain details of a criminal case. The narrative should mainly be used to explain the professional performance of the KPS being monitored and any advice given.'

It appeared many of the monitors (mission wide) had either forgot, were lazy or just weren't sure how to complete the Cover Sheet or the Narrative Section of the report. Before completing the cover sheet a few minor details were required including the monitors name, date and time.

The Cover Sheet was a blank text box and used to give a short verbal explanation and description of the event or occurrence, which was monitored. It was not, as some monitors thought, a database for a police case. Many monitors used the Cover Sheet to write a complete police report. Copied from a KPS officer's report, I might add.

The Narrative Section, again a blank text box, was used to describe the KPS officer's actions during the monitored event or occurrence. And again monitors were wrongly describing police cases and nothing about the KPS performance.

Monitor report templates came with different headings each serving a different purpose. Most templates included a Cover Sheet, a Narrative Section and a tick box questionnaire which helped the monitor complete the report. The monitor report templates were:

- Arrest and Prisoners
- Calls for Service
- Non-Compliance
- Procedural
- Managerial Skills Assessments
- Daily Report
- Weekly Report

The most commonly used template or (blank) report was the *Procedural Report*. The purpose of the a Procedural Report was used to comment on that day's overall professional performance of a KPS patrol officer as he went about his routine (daily) duties, including mobile patrol, foot patrol and Vehicle Check Points (VCP). Procedural Reports were generally submitted near the end of the monitor's shift.

Considering a KPS patrol officer worked an eight-hour shift, as did the monitor, and routinely conducted at least one foot patrol, one VCP and carried out continuous mobile patrols, I found it completely unacceptable when I reviewed many of the Mitrovica Procedural Reports.

On several reports the Cover Sheet read: 'Today I monitored KPS officer number 1234'. The report's narrative read: 'KPS officer 1234 did a good job'.

Or the Cover Sheet read: 'I monitored KPS officer 1234'. The narrative read: 'Nothing special happened.' There was absolutely no evidence of KPS performance.

As far as I was concerned those inadequate comments typified many un-interested and lazy CIVPOL monitors. They spent an eight-hour shift shadowing a KPS patrol officer or a two-man KPS patrol unit and all they could come up with when completing the monitor report was, 'nothing special happened'. Those three words were appearing regularly in the Narrative Section of a Procedural Report.

What many monitors did was log in to a computer, open a Microsoft Word document, and write their paltry comments then save the Word document. After the 'alleged' monitoring period the monitor would open the saved Word document then copy and paste the comments into a Procedural Report's Narrative Section. What an easy life. There was rarely any mention of advice given, encouragement or feedback. It was as if the monitor presumed the KPS officer knew it all and didn't need any sort of support. Either that or the monitor was just simply not interested.

Not all monitor reports were substandard and as an example here is a perfectly acceptable Cover Sheet and Narrative Section from a genuine Procedural Report.

Cover Sheet

'At the date and time stated above I monitored one KPS officer during a vehicle checkpoint.'

Narrative Section

'The KPS officer carried out his duties in a professional manner by being courteous to all motorists and explaining the reason he had stopped them. After checking all relevant documents and without any further delay the vehicle was safely directed back in to the flow of traffic.'

That report is far better than most, however, there was room for improvement in structure, presentation and content and that is what I started to work on.

Other police related business and investigations were monitored followed by the relevant monitor report. For example, if a KPS officer responded to an emergency call the monitor would also attend, observe and then complete a *Call for Service* monitor report.

Call for Service reports (and others) included a (tick box) questionnaire which really did help the monitor. One example was, 'Did the police respond to the calls for service promptly?' There were always three options, 'yes', 'no' and 'not observed'. One box was checked and if the answer was 'no', an explanation had to be included in the Narrative Section.

I read one Call for Service report and I'm glad to say it wasn't from a Mitrovica monitor. The Cover Sheet read:

'Today I attended an apparent suicide and monitored KPS officer 2345 from the station investigation unit as he carried out initial enquiries.'

I thought, 'Good start, now let's look at the narrative for the KPS performance.' The short entry in the Narrative Section read: *'After suicide the victim died.'* That particular CIVPOL claimed to be a forensic specialist and I've no argument with that. Whatever else he may have claimed to be it certainly couldn't have been a creative writer.

Although the Mitrovica monitor reports did improve, a number of CIVPOL just didn't like putting in a day's graft. They saw monitoring as a way of skiving off for the day and a few had their colleagues cover for them. Near the end of the shift they'd return to the base station and write a bogus report or have their colleagues mention their name in a report.

I read reports where the monitor wrote: 'Today, along with CIVPOL monitor Charlie Hull, we monitored two KPS officers as they interviewed a suspect.' In reality, Charlie Hull probably spent the day shopping in Pristina, which was a popular pastime for CIVPOL officers.

On a few occasions when I attended Pristina on business I'd see on duty Mitrovica monitors having coffee in one of Pristina's café bars. The only official action I felt I was able to take was to inform their 'real' supervisor. Those monitors usually had a good story ready for Dave King or Kevin Abbassi and usually, after a slap on the wrist, no further action was taken.

In between making improvements to the Mitrovica monitoring programme I attended meetings and around April I attended a meeting chaired by Don Evans, with the transition team, who had been continuing to update Bulletin 0.66.

The Bulletin had now been updated to Bulletin 0.66 5.6, and now included a position similar to, and with the same duties and responsibilities as, the TMLO, however, with a different title. The position's title was now *The Regional Monitor Liaison Officer* (RMLO). The RMLO position was also included in a RHQ chain of command chart and stood side by side with the (post region transition) Regional Commander Liaison Officer (ROLO) which, at first glance, was a little misleading.

After I read the role of the RMLO I began to get that worried feeling again. I wasn't sure how Dave and Kevin would react to my now official and *non-supervisory* position.

After the meeting with Don Evans, I asked for a meeting with Joe, Alice and both RMBS supervisors. I made sure each had a copy of the new Bulletin and read aloud the position of the RMLO.

> 'The RMLO will serve the Regional Command staff as an information liaison officer between the RHQ and MHQ. The RMLO will answer in the chain of command to the RCLO. The RMLO will ensure that the Region follows all guidelines, directives, UNMIK PPM, OPS Bulletin 0.66, 5.6 regarding the Monitor Program. He will ensure the dissemination of all pertinent information regarding the monitoring program from MHQ and RHQ to all UNMIK police monitor personnel in the Region. The RMLO will notify MHQ (chain of command and the MHQ Transition Unit-Monitoring Team) of any issues affecting the program within the region.'

Before I read the next part I looked at Joe and Alice and said with a hint of sarcasm, 'You'll love this.'

'The position of RMLO is *not* a command position, therefore the RMLO will *not* be responsible for the supervision of any RMBS or be involved operationally in the affairs of any transitioned police station in the region.'

Joe showed no reaction. I was reassured yet again by Joe and Alice and told by Joe to let him worry about Don Evans and his monitoring team. So I just carried on as normal and continued to supervise both base stations whilst developing more productive ideas to the monitoring programme.

To complete my improvement plans I needed certain documents from my home in the UK. I also needed a break away from work. I was reading more and more monitor reports and really getting more annoyed and frustrated with the monitors and their poor attitude. I was still very reluctant to use my adopted power as at the back of my mind I knew officially I wasn't a supervisor.

I made more suggestions regarding improvements and left both Dave and Kevin to implement them. And I've got to add again, Dave and Kevin were true professionals, they really did treat me with respect and as far as they were concerned I *was* their boss.

Around June 2005 I took two weeks CTO and returned to the UK where I (temporarily) forgot about the awkward position I found myself in between Mitrovica command staff, the monitors and the transition unit.

During my time at home I paid a visit to my local barber and asked for my usual trim. As the barber was snipping away over the top of my head (at the back) he paused for a minute then asked me if the scab on the back of my head was painful. I didn't know of any scab and was a bit embarrassed. The barber held up a small mirror behind me and, looking at the mirror in front of me, I could just about see a small round reddish looking blemish on the back of my head. I pressed my index finger against the area and felt no pain. I asked the barber to continue and just be careful around that area of my head. From that day on I couldn't stop touching and prodding the small sore and eventually it started to bleed. I decided not to do anything about it, thinking 'it probably happened during a drunken night out and that I had banged my head somewhere.' I dismissed it and thought it would soon disappear.

Before returning to Kosovo I packed several folders which contained my tutor constable material and information regarding police performance management and integrated competency framework. That material became my monitor reference guide and was to play a big part in improving the overall quality and content of monitor report writing.

When I returned from CTO Marty picked me up at Pristina airport. Arriving back at his house in Mitrovica, he headed straight for the fridge and took out two Heineken. Two became four, then six, then eight. We spoke late into the night talking about the KPS transition and Marty mentioned the Regional Traffic Unit and its imminent transition.

Marty was worried about his current position as a traffic patrol officer and what would happen to him post-transition. He knew very little about the monitoring programme or Bulletin 0.66, however he *had* started to take an interest. I told him, like the KPS stations, only two CIVPOL would remain in situ in regional traffic. As far as the positions were concerned the title of Chief of Traffic and Deputy Chief would, after transition, become Traffic Unit Liaison Officer (TULO) and Traffic Operations Liaison Officer (TOLO).

I also told him about the interview and question paper and whoever the successful applicant was would also have to satisfy a selection board on his capability on becoming a TULO. If the current traffic commander and his deputy applied for the posts, there was no guarantee they would be selected.

I stayed in Marty's house for a few hours and when I was leaving he asked who I'd been fighting with. He was of course referring to my little scabby friend which was, after my hair cut, a lot more visible. I told him to get his nose stuck in to Bulletin 0.66 and never mind my scabby head.

When the interviews for the TULO and TOLO took place Marty excelled. His overall knowledge of the Mitrovica Traffic Unit and Kosovo Traffic Laws was excellent. He was the obvious choice and was later appointed as Mitrovica Traffic Unit Liaison Officer.

Traffic chaos when the traffic lights fail

CHAPTER EIGHTEEN
That's The Way To Do It

AFTER I RETURNED from CTO I wasn't due back at work for another two days and as it was during a weekend I made the most of the Saturday and Sunday. I spent both evenings in Xponto with big Alun Ferguson; Marty was busy working on some big operation regarding the smuggling of fuel from Kosovo to Serbia and the Mitrovica Regional Traffic Unit had been implicated in the crime.

On Saturday Alun and I were in Xponto a lot earlier than usual and had agreed that when it got too busy we'd head off somewhere else. We sat at a table well away from the bar and spoke about nothing in particular. At that time of the evening there was only one barman working who was known by his nickname Pero. Just about every local person I met in Kosovo is referred to by a nickname.

Pero is the vocalist in a local rock band, 'Hosenfefer,' and describes the band's music as Punk and Roll. They are actually quite good and have had reasonable success around the Balkans. I got to know Pero and most of the other band members quite well, so much so my son Jamie and his band were invited, by Pero, to play in Xponto. Jamie's band, *Someone's Sons* visited Kosovo twice and both times played to packed crowds, once in Xponto and once in a bar called Zamak.

When the bar started to get busy and quite crammed Alun and I talked of leaving, however, a small blonde sitting at the bar was keeping me from going anywhere. I'm not in the habit of ogling women, especially not women from a territory that is anti-UN. However, I found I couldn't take my eyes off her. At the UN induction course all CIVPOL were advised not to fraternise with the locals and some international contingents were warned if they did they would be repatriated; that rule did not apply to the UK contingent.

We decided to stay a little longer and as the bar started to get much busier, I lost sight of the small blonde; in fact I thought she had left the pub. As the evening wore on we decided to stay put and just grin and bear the noise, at least we had a seat and therefore avoided the bumping and banging.

Eventually I had to push my way through the crowd to reach the toilet and on my way back I spotted blondie who had decided to block the path back to my seat. She wouldn't budge from her standing position as I tried to squeeze between her and another female. I did say 'excuse me' but that request fell on deaf ears. Just as I was about to find another route, the blonde looked at me and said, 'Are you never going to speak to me?' I didn't know what to say, I was really embarrassed. Before I could say anything she moved to the side and I made a hasty retreat back to my seat.

Later in the evening blondie and a friend joined Alun and I at our table and, after introductions and an awkward conversation, I plucked up the courage to ask her if she'd like to meet me during the week for a coffee. She said yes and on the following Monday we met in a restaurant just behind North Station. After that first meeting we met quite regularly in that restaurant during working hours. During the weekends we met inside Xponto, her with her friends and me with mine.

Now I was back at work I was eager to start remedial training for the monitors and continued working on my own PowerPoint slide show that I hoped would improve monitor report writing. Dave King and Kevin Abbassi kept busy checking monitor reports and sending messages to monitors regarding the quality and quantity of those reports and how to improve them.

Both supervisors worked tirelessly to motivate and encourage the monitors, however, it seemed several continued to abuse the system.

Dave King had printed off a number of reports and brought them to my office. I spent around one hour reading those reports and was really quite appalled by what I was reading. I have taken extracts from those reports to give you an idea of what Dave, Kevin and I were up against.

The Cover Sheet on one report read:

'Today I monitored the KPS as they carried out a foot patrol.'

The narrative of the same report read:

'The KPS carried out the vehicle check point very professionally.'

Another report read:

'During the dark evening the KPS used proper illuminated lights.' The report was timed at 2 pm.

And one other report mentioned the monitoring of a KPS traffic unit which was conducting speed checks with a Laser speed gun. I received a phone call from Marty Walsh who brought the report to my attention. He told me the KPS Traffic Unit had one Laser speed gun and on the day the monitor report was

Davie Hutton, Martin Walsh and Me

submitted, the speed gun was not in use as it was being calibrated.

Reports that had already been entered were being used repeatedly by the copy and paste method. Those reports were altered very slightly and sometimes with just one word. Where the report started 'I monitored a KPS officer,' followed by the monitors observations; the report was altered to read: 'I monitored a police officer,' followed by the copied observations.

The Regional Commander (Joe Schaeck) had started to read the monitor reports and eventually sent e-mails to all monitors. If the substandard and inaccurate monitor report writing did not improve, those CIVPOL officers responsible for submitting such reports would not have any mission extension requests approved.

Joe's threats also made my position as 'supervisor' a little more difficult when I was required to complete End of Mission Performance Appraisals, which were checked before being countersigned by the Regional Commander.

I wouldn't say it was customary within UNMIK, but the performance appraisal core values and competencies of the officer being reported on were, at times, unrealistically scored very high, irrespective of the officer's actual and true performance. Many end of mission appraisals were marked with an overall performance rating of 'exceeds expectation' which was more or less what the officer being assessed expected. Those officers with such a high rating were judged to be in the top 24 per cent who produced a distinctly better performance than reasonably expected, including a consistent willingness to undertake additional work. As long as Joe Schaeck was Regional Commander I had to be very careful how I completed those end of mission appraisals. I couldn't always justify giving such a high rating as exceeds expectations. I was more prone to tick the box against 'fully satisfactory' which was a competent performance that fully met 'reasonable expectations'; that rating was in the top 55 per cent. On a few occasions I was approached by officers who told me if they did not receive a higher rating than fully satisfactory they would be looked on (by their home police force) as a bit of a failure. I must say, I did reconsider my assessments on a number of occasions, lucky for me Joe didn't question my overall (officer) rating.

I had now finished my slideshow and after presenting it to the Regional Commander it was incorporated into the Mitrovica (new) monitors welcome pack. I had created an electronic folder which contained a PowerPoint slideshow detailing the Narrative Section, monitoring report templates and one more slideshow entitled KMIS use and purpose. There were also a few more useful booklets on monitoring.

Although my PowerPoint was entitled Narrative slideshow, the PowerPoint explained, in detail, other aspects of monitoring report writing. To assist monitors when completing the narrative, I introduced four headings that relate to core policing skills and I explained how to use those headings when monitoring KPS officers. The headings were also a way of making sure the monitor knew what to look for during the monitored event and to ensure the report was properly completed with full details.

These are the four headings with guidelines:

Professional and Ethical Standards
- Self management (punctuality, lateness standard of dress/hygiene etc)
- Working relationship with colleagues
- Views on gender or ethnicity
- Compliance with KPS PPM
- International Policing Standards
- Human Rights
- Awareness of local issues
- Working relationship with colleagues
- Knowledge of Kosovo law
- Attitude and behaviour towards local citizens

Decision Making
- Judgement
- Course of action taken
- Assessment of situation
- Relies on colleagues to make the decision
- Identifies important issues
- Poor or wrong decision

Communication Skills

- Contact with local citizens
- Police report writing
- Statement taking
- Interviewing techniques
- Radio procedures
- Listening skills
- Contact with colleagues

Self Motivation

- Interest in the job
- Commitment to the KPS
- Generates own work or not
- Keeps up to date with Professional knowledge
- Keeps up to date with KPS PPM and the Kosovo law
- Keeps abreast of all other legislation
- Time management

As soon as those headings were introduced the Mitrovica monitor reports improved immediately and many monitors mentioned my slideshow helped them tremendously to better understand what was required. Many other monitors kept silent. I knew my new monitor reporting style created a lot more work and I think I was resented for making those slightly dramatic but necessary improvements. With the headings now acting as a firm guideline, this is what an improved narrative now looked like.

Professional and Ethical Standards

The KPS officers arrived at the VCP location just before the assigned time according to the daily roster. Both officers were properly dressed and carried all officially issued police equipment. They were very polite to all persons checked including the passengers of vehicles stopped.

Decision Making

The VCP was conducted in a safe area and did not interfere with other road users. A number of drivers were stopped and after being checked were given advice about the importance of wearing a seatbelt. No tickets were issued for those drivers who did not wear a seatbelt.

UK2 Contingent Commander Andy Kirkwood

Communication Skills

Both KPS officers spoke clearly and made sure all persons checked knew the reason for being checked. One KPS officer entered into an argument regarding a defective tyre on a vehicle, however, he took no action against the driver. I offered him words of advice regarding his conduct and he agreed he could have handled the situation differently.

Self Motivation

Many vehicles were stopped and checked during the sixty-minute VCP and both KPS officers remained very positive and alert even though it rained during most of the VCP.

I received a phone call from Don Evans who had noticed the sudden change and improvement in the Mitrovica monitors report writing format. I explained the slideshow and how I had implemented my own style of monitor report writing and Don thought the idea was very good. So good in fact that Don wanted all monitors to view the slideshow and follow my example.

The core competency headings started to appear in all monitor reports, mission wide, and eventually they became pretty much a permanent fixture on the KMIS database.

Not long after I made those changes, I received a phone call from Alice Holmes telling me she was ending her mission early and was returning home; she never said why and I never asked. Alice thanked me for all my effort and I never saw her again.

A short while after Alice left Kosovo I received a UN memorandum with the subject heading: 'Letter commending UK officer John Duncanson.' It was from Alice and addressed to my Contingent Commander Andy Kirkwood, Don Evans, Joe Schaeck and Jill Muncy, who was the Deputy Commissioner.

I was completely overwhelmed by the memo's contents and saddened that I never got the opportunity to thank Alice. This is the contents of the memo in its entirety:

'I would like to take the opportunity to commend an officer of the UK contingent, John Duncanson.

John Duncanson returned to the mission in December 2004. In early January 2005 the monitoring program underwent a total revision and it was necessary to designate a regional liaison on a short notice.

Because of his previous mission experience, John was asked to take on this unknown position, which had no guidelines firmly in place yet and was not fully operational; in fact, no one was exactly sure what needed to be done, and how to do it. In spite of this, John accepted the challenge and it has not been easy.

Due to the changes in the program, there was confusion on who was responsible for the logistical assets (vehicles, radios, etc), who and how the supervision of the monitors would fit into the program, obtaining the needed language assistants, how to meet the guidelines of the Operational Bulletin 0.66 and so much more.

Due to significant changes at the Regional HQ, there were sometimes other crisis situations demanding immediate attention and John often had to direct the program without additional assistance.

At a time in the mission when so many officers attempted to avoid hard work, John was a refreshing change, working long hours to create the program in Mitrovica. He still faces some obstacles in getting the program into the final stages, but he has taken it as a challenge and it is one that he is meeting every day.

I will be leaving the mission earlier than expected and I want John to know that his work was noticed and recognised. When he reaches the end of his mission the command may have changed several times and no one may be aware that he accomplished so much with so little. Therefore, I would like the UK contingent to be aware of his outstanding performance and dedication to duty.

He is an excellent representative of the UK contingent and a positive reflection of his home agency. It is a pleasure to have worked with him and I would welcome the opportunity to work with him again in a future mission.'

Mitrovica Regional Commander Gary Smith

Alice was right, the command staff did change and during June, July and August 2005, new rotations of CIVPOL joined the mission and many new monitors were redeployed to Mitrovica. I was now supervisor to just over eighty CIVPOL monitors and thirty LAs. Both North and South RMBS worked with three teams and continued on the same eight-hour shift pattern as previously worked by CIVPOL patrol teams. On average each team consisted of fifteen monitors and five LAs.

The changes in command staff did nothing to affect my position as RMLO. Joe Schaeck was still behind me as was his deputy (whose name escapes me) and the Chief of Operations (American CIVPOL) Gary Smith. One minor blip to my position was that the transition team questioned my authority as RMLO, and informed Joe Schaeck I should not have any sort of supervisory powers. During a meeting with Mariya Grozdanova from the transition monitoring unit Joe explained my contribution to the monitoring programme and basically told Mariya he would not be taking away my supervisory powers. Gary Smith agreed wholeheartedly with Joe. In fact, I remember Gary getting a little irate, and at one point speaking with a raised voice announced, 'In Mitrovica John Duncanson is monitoring.' I think I know what Gary meant. After the meeting nothing more was ever mentioned about my position. On a personal note, after that meeting my confidence had risen to an all time high.

Not long after the meeting with Mariya Grozdanova, Kevin Abbassi's mission came to an end and he returned home to Pakistan. Kaiwan (Kevin) Abbassi was a Senior Inspector of police (since promoted to Deputy Superintendent of police) in Pakistan, nevertheless my recommendation to appoint him as North RBMS supervisor did raise a few eyebrows in certain places.

If my memory serves me correctly, and during my three UN missions in Kosovo, not many CIVPOL from Asia or Africa achieved supervisory status. As far as I can remember, many Asian (with the exception of Russian) and African officers were often overlooked in favour of CIVPOL officers from Europe and North America.

Not long after Kevin ended his mission Dave King redeployed from South RMBS to a more senior position in Pristina. Dave's position was taken over by (American CIVPOL) Ed Cottrell who was an incredibly hard and dedicated worker and, I'm glad to say, was on the same wavelength as me. Kevin was replaced by (Romanian CIVPOL) Marius Cristea who resented the fact I was in overall charge of North RMBS. Marius knew Bulletin 0.66 as well as I did and often questioned my authority. The issue of my authority had long been dealt with and Marius had to live with that; he couldn't, and eventually he gave up his position and, through my recommendation, was redeployed to the Regional Crime Unit. Marius' position was taken over by (American CIVPOL) Stan Osterhoudt who was very laid back and never questioned my position or authority.

As 2005 drew to a close plans were underway to give the monitoring programme a complete revamp. As I prepared for the new changes I carried on with my job and now and again was riled by those minority monitors who were from time to time submitting those ridiculous and now inappropriate monitor reports.

During a KPS investigation into a death by drowning and after the monitor's observations, he had the audacity to include in his monitor report comments on the victim's wife and described her obvious distraught state as: 'Performing the usual Balkan's drama.' He also described the officer's duty to perform the death notification as: 'Do the dirty deed.' I was happy to allow the monitor's supervisor (Ed Cottrell) to deal with this matter and as usual words of advice were given.

I couldn't understand the attitude of the CIVPOL monitors. We (UNMIK police) had volunteered to work in Kosovo, to pass on our professional experience and knowledge to a very young police service, who *I* hoped would look up to me and remember me for all the right reasons. Too many CIVPOL were just not interested and the big shame was they were letting themselves down, their home force and of course the UN and the KPS. That said, my personal belief was, any form of disciplinary action was not, unless absolutely necessary, an option.

Although I thought many CIVPOL monitors were 'just playing at it' I didn't want to be the one who ruined their career. Like their mission, mine wouldn't last forever. At some point we would all go home and that particular mission would just be a memory. And the fact I never felt comfortable being the overall (unofficial) supervisor to both RMBS made me all the more uncomfortable when I completed those end of mission performance appraisals.

KPS officers obviously knew they were under the spotlight when CIVPOL monitors were in their presence, especially during routine tasks. Being monitored and later reported on didn't seem to bother them and they seldom asked to read the report before or after it was submitted, which is just as well.

During one very cold and bitter night, topped with heavy snowfall, I was travelling in a local taxi when it slowly passed a KPS patrol carrying out a VCP. The KPS vehicle was parked under the canopy of a nearby fuel station and was well out of the way of traffic and of course the snow. There were two KPS officers conducting the VCP and both were wearing reflective vests and were well wrapped up. The KPS officer stopping traffic carried a torch with a red illuminated cover.

Close by sat a parked UN Coca Cola 4Runner occupied by two monitors. One monitor sat in the front of the vehicle with his seat reclined, while the other sat in the back. I didn't notice if they were accompanied by an LA. I took a note of the Coca Cola's registration number and checked the time.

The following day, as usual, I checked all the previous day's monitor reports. When I read the report from the CIVPOL officers who monitored that VCP it was excellent. All headings were used and with plenty of detail. The report stated the KPS had parked the police vehicle in a safe position, the officers were properly dressed, they spoke with all vehicle occupants in a good manner, they wore reflective vests and much more. The report was basically a repeat of many other VCP procedural reports, very repetitive, however, there was not much else to say on a routine VCP.

The only problem I had with the report was there was no mention of the inclement weather conditions; don't you find that rather odd? After a little hunting, I found an identical report from two month's earlier. Copy and paste strikes again. That monitor report really typified many other monitor reports and what the minority of CIVPOL must have got up to during a shift.

During my time as Mitrovica RMLO, Sunday was always a very quiet day and I usually spent the day in my office. On one of those Sundays I was making a coffee when I heard a very faint knock on my office door. I paused for a second before a second knock came which wasn't any louder than the first. I said, 'Yes, come in,' and in came the immaculately dressed (in uniform) RMBS South monitor William Darko. William, from Ghana, took two steps into the office, came to attention and gave me a very slow salute. I remember my Boy's Brigade Captain, always telling me, 'Longest way up, shortest way down' the first time he explained how I should salute. That was exactly the way William addressed me. He never moved any further until I invited him to sit down. William wanted to thank me for helping him understand how to better his knowledge on the monitoring programme and how to improve his monitor reports. He was very interested in the United Kingdom and especially its history. He told me about Ghana and about his culture and beliefs. William really restored my flagging faith in what I was attempting to achieve with monitoring and I'll always appreciate and respect him for that.

I was usually brought back to earth during the week when the monitoring reports were submitted and checked.

NON-COMPLIANCE REPORTS
Non-Compliance Reports were prepared and submitted (to the KPS Station Commander and the SCLO) when a monitor reported non-compliance from a KPS officer; normally regarding a 'serious' breach of KPS policy and procedure, persistent breaches of rules or refusing to follow advice offered by the monitor. The Non-Compliance report was always created as an open report against the KPS officer who then became the subject of a disciplinary report.

Unless it was a serious breach of regulations, CIVPOL monitors with more commonsense than others, very rarely reported their KPS counterpart. Minor issues were discussed and normally resolved over a coffee or two.

A few monitors took non-compliance to extremes when they, without any advice given, reported KPS officers who failed to wear a seatbelt in a police vehicle or who reported for duty inappropriately dressed, for example, not wearing a hat or tie. These were the same monitors who would submit substandard Procedural Reports.

CHAPTER NINETEEN
Stringent Security

POOR PERFORMANCES OF Mitrovica CIVPOL monitors didn't only occur within the monitoring programme. Quite a few CIVPOL seemed to forget, first and foremost, they were police officers with a duty to uphold law and order. And during one particular police operation out with monitoring, their lack of commitment was once again exposed.

For a number of reasons the rioting in Kosovo during March 2004 saw major setbacks to the UN mission in Kosovo. Minority Serbian communities lost confidence in UNMIK and KFOR including a small Serbian community living in the village of *Svinjare*, which is located in the majority Albanian area of South Mitrovica.

During the March riots, over one hundred Serbian families fled their homes in Svinjare after a mob of Albanians rushed to the village. At the nearby French KFOR base, Camp Belvedere, troops did little to stop Albanian looters and arsonists.

Albanians took Serbian possessions in trucks, tractors and other vehicles and nobody stopped them. Apparently KFOR were not willing to defend the village and only evacuated the Serbians to North Mitrovica. The village was just about destroyed although that KFOR base was erected to protect the Serbian enclave.

After numerous allegations of continuing thefts and burglary from unoccupied property were reported to the KPS, an Operational Plan was implemented to deter criminal acts and to apprehend offenders. A twenty-four hour checkpoint was established on the main road running through Svinjare and it was operated by CIVPOL monitors (who were now outside their comfort zone) with support from the KPS. Both North and South RMBS were involved in that task mainly due to a lack of UNMIK operational resources in the Mitrovica region.

CIVPOL monitors working at the checkpoint in Svinjare were under instructions to carry out 100 per cent vehicle searches and take any other action deemed necessary to detect and prevent any criminal acts. A CIVPOL mobile patrol was also present in the area and also under instruction to stop and search all vehicles. That checkpoint and mobile patrol seemed to do little in the prevention of crime as thefts and burglaries were still continually reported.

Local residents *and* KPS officers claimed the CIVPOL (monitors) conducting the vehicle checkpoint (and the mobile patrol units) were not stopping all vehicles or searching all of those they did stop. Apparently monitors would sit in their Coca Colas without getting out and on several occasions pickup trucks and tractors, full of household items including baths *and* latrines, were spotted driving past the checkpoint without being stopped.

Although many of those vehicles were driven by Serbians who had recovered their personal belongings from their destroyed and burnt out homes, many more were driven by the brazen thieves who were simply taking a chance as they drove past the police checkpoint.

On occasions, when I visited Svinjare, the monitors were always out of their vehicles carrying out the stop and search. It seemed they knew I was in the area. If I wasn't in my office, where else might I be? I worked at Coulport long enough to know what to do when a supervisor left a building. Get on the phone and warn your colleagues, 'The boss is out and about.'

The Ops plan regarding Svinjare village was eventually handed over to the KPS who became solely responsible for the detection and prevention of crime. On hindsight that transfer of authority was probably a sensible move by Mitrovica (UNMIK) RHQ.

Around the end of 2005 or the beginning of 2006, the MHQ Transition Monitoring Unit came to the conclusion monitoring KPS patrol officers had run its course and should be scaled down and eventually stopped altogether. Apparently questions had been asked, from whom I do not know, about monitoring the KPS patrol officers. It was thought the reports were getting very repetitive and other than RMBS supervisors, no one on a higher level of authority was bothering to read and check them. Procedural reports were certainly very repetitive and of course they were becoming identical to previously submitted reports. The main focus of monitor attention was now to be aimed at KPS mid-level managers and above. New monitor positions and titles were introduced which created new jobs for CIVPOL. It also created problems in Mitrovica as there were around eighty-five patrol monitors and only fourteen new monitor positions available.

Those new positions did not include night shift, which most CIVPOL loathed, and when the positions became available I hoped those CIVPOL who were deserving candidates would not be overlooked. I, along with the Chief of Administration Services, American CIVPOL Van Williams, discussed the options before Van allowed me to make recommendations on who could be appointed into those new positions. Van trusted my ability to select reliable and hard working (and honest) CIVPOL, which I based on experience, professionalism, attitude, commitment (to the monitoring programme) and of course, the standard of previous monitor reports produced.

I made several selections and surprisingly no vacancy announcements were produced, completely against UN policy on advertised posts; however, that was the way it was.

Of the fourteen CIVPOL I selected, five were from Africa and three from Asia. Like Kevin Abbassi's appointment as RMBS North Supervisor, my selections, again, raised a few eyebrows, but as far as I was concerned I had made the correct decision.

The KPS police stations are categorised by the class of station, and the class depends on the number of KPS assigned to the station. Therefore, some KPS police stations were increased by two monitors, others by three. The new position titles were: Station Investigation Liaison Officer (SILO), Station Investigation Monitor (SIM) and Shift Leader Monitor (SLM).

After those fourteen positions were assigned, the remainder of CIVPOL carried on monitoring and also continued to assist in various operations being carried out in the Mitrovica region.

One other on-going operation 'Stringent Security' (implemented mission wide by the KPS in December 2005) would see many of the patrol monitors redeployed (also in the Mitrovica region) to a new unit (*Enhancement Forces*) to enhance operation Stringent Security, with the remainder of CIVPOL continuing as patrol monitors. I didn't know what was in store for me; the RMLO position was also to be phased out, along with patrol monitoring.

During early 2006 most of the talk in the region was about Operational Stringent Security and the new Enhancement Forces. The Enhancement Forces were to be created to aggressively enforce the law and identify criminals. That appendix to the Stringent Security Operational Plan was necessary due to an increase (Kosovo-wide) in serious incidents including attacks on the minorities with explosives and rocket launchers. After several inspections were made, the concept of Stringent Security was not being put into action by the KPS and therefore CIVPOL officers were utilised to enhance the Operational Plan.

I read over the orders for the new CIVPOL Mitrovica Enhancement Force and my immediate thought was, 'This is a big step backwards for UNMIK'. It looked like the monitoring programme was now *not* the main mission priority. I was also thinking about the poor performances from many monitors. If they couldn't be bothered to carry out the simple task of monitoring, there's no way they'd want to be part of what looked like a potential specialist, hands-on, police unit.

The Police Commissioner's main intention now was to change policing from low- to high-profile for twenty-four hours seven days a week with a long-term operation. Measures were necessary to achieve a safer and more secure environment. This was to be done by putting UNMIK police MHQ in the lead in all sensitive cases, adjusting Kosovo-wide policing, specifying tasks and responsibilities in detail, strengthening the control of activities on all levels by inspections and taking disciplinary measures in cases of disobedience to orders. 'Heavy duty indeed,' I thought.

Generally speaking, from the turn of the year, the security situation in Kosovo remained stable, although fragile, and was not affected by recent changes in the political leadership of Kosovo. The level of inter-ethnic incidents were low and it seemed that criminal rather than ethnical motives were the origin of several reported incidents.

With a new Enhancement Force being deployed in certain areas of Kosovo I foresaw trouble. The term 'aggressively enforce the law' annoyed me. How do you *aggressively* enforce the law?

Operation Stringent Security was to be enhanced in four identified minority areas with forty CIVPOL officers deployed in each of four towns and cities; Gracanica (Pristina region), Strpce (Ferizaj/Urosevac region), Decani (Peja/Pec region) and North Mitrovica.

The forty CIVPOL were to be deployed in a phased manner in order to avoid a perceived sudden impact of a higher security and policing situation by those local minority communities. The CIVPOL officers were to be introduced to those minority communities with an initial ten and increased by a further ten every two weeks until all forty were deployed. Their duties would include:

- Active community policing
- Intelligence gathering
- Carrying out vehicle checks
- High visibility patrolling, both by vehicle and on foot
- Executing search and arrest warrants.

And any other duty assigned by MHQ, the ROLO, and in the case of Mitrovica, the Regional Commander.

In support of the operational plan a Polish and Romanian SPU (later to be known as FPU, Forward Police Units) and a Ukrainian dog unit would be assigned and deployed in North Mitrovica.

I just couldn't think of forty CIVPOL currently working in Mitrovica who would relish the challenge of that enhancement force. I actually couldn't think of any.

By early March the command staff had, once again, changed in Mitrovica and a French CIVPOL officer, Thiery Lapenty was now the Regional Commander, Gary Smith was his Deputy and Gerard Chevrier, also French, was Chief of Operations.

CHAPTER TWENTY
Enhancement Force

AS I INITIALLY thought, the enhancement to Operation Stringent Security with its aggressive policing policy didn't go down well with most CIVPOL monitors in Mitrovica. They knew locals in the North wouldn't tolerate heavy-handed UNMIK police tactics and wouldn't hesitate to retaliate if they felt unduly done by.

It literally takes minutes for large crowds to gather in North Mitrovica and, as it has already been proved, members of the local population have no second thoughts about defending their territory and citizens against UN forces.

In the short term, my position as RMLO continued to function normally and I just got on with my job. I remained in regular contact with the MHQ transition unit and gave assistance and advice to the CIVPOL mid-level manager monitors; they would often ask for my assistance with various issues regarding monitor reports. I was now spending less time in my office and more time travelling around the region meeting the SCLOs and OLOs and also Marty Walsh in his position as TULO.

One morning, before heading off to the Regional Traffic Unit, I was having a shower and washing my hair. As I put both my hands on the back of my head to rub in some shampoo I felt a small indent on the back of my head. The indent was in the same area as that small blemish (scab) which had developed on my head. When my head was wet, the affected area felt soft and reminded me of a small rounded moon crater. When my hair was dry the scab reformed and became hard. I was starting to get slightly worried about this unidentified little menace. Added to my worry was another small scab which was now developing on my chest and every week looked to be getting a little bigger. By now it was obvious, whatever the blemish on my head was, I didn't get it from any bump or fall. Like most big men I did the obvious thing – nothing. I continued to think; no hope, both would disappear.

Like Mitrovica RHQ, the Regional Traffic Unit was based in South Mitrovica and when I arrived Marty was busy writing up a Managerial Skills Assessment which had to be completed every three months. The assessment was carried out on the monitor's KPS counterpart and, like all monitor reports, it was entered into the KMIS.

After Marty finished his skills assessment he checked his e-mails and one interesting message from the UK Contingent Commander included the names of the next MDP rotation and to which region they were being deployed in. Marty read out aloud: 'Deployment to Mitrovica Region, Constable David Letsche, Constable William Crawford, Constable Glyn Smith, Constable David Hutton and Sergeant Roy Beresford.' Marty and I didn't know any of those officers. I suspected they'd probably be deployed to the new Enhancement Force.

After work Marty, Alun and I met in Xponto and later that evening we were joined by my (blonde) friend, who I had now been dating for several months. My friend, Vesela, spoke reasonably good English and during our short time together we had become extremely close.

A couple of days after the night out in Xponto I was summoned to the Regional Commander's office and asked to bring the monthly rosters for both North and South RMBS. Between both RMBS there were around seventy monitors and thirty LAs.

On my arrival I was greeted by the Regional Commander and Gary Smith. Thiery Lapenty was a good Regional Commander; he let me get on with my job as RMLO without question, just like Joe Schaeck before him.

Gary took both rosters from me and placed them on a large table that sat in the corner of the office. The three of us sat down at the table and for a few minutes Gary and Thiery kept silent as they studied both rosters. I sat patiently looking around the office until my eyes became focused on a rocket launcher and AK47 assault rifle that were both displayed on one of the walls. Although the AK47 was displayed on the wall for ornamental purposes it was fully functional. During a future mission I would see the weapon in the hands of the Mitrovica Regional Commander (who is an MDP constable) as he crouched behind a large concrete lamp post taking cover in a street and offering alternative armed protection to a convoy of windowless and battered UNMIK police vehicles and ambulances as they were driven at frantic speeds to escape a city in turmoil.

Thiery spoke first and with his very thick French accent said, 'John, eeteez like zees.' Well, maybe not quite like that. Thiery went on to explain he and Gary had been discussing Operation Stringent Security and and also the CIVPOL qualities, 'motivated and experienced' expressed in the operational plan. Thiery wanted the initial ten CIVPOL to be selected from particular continents and nationalities and who were 'more suited', better equipped and better qualified than other nationalities to carry out the duties detailed in the ops plan. Thiery asked me to select those ten (qualified) CIVPOL officers to be redeployed to the new enhancement force, which funnily enough would be named Mitrovica Enhancement Force (E-Force). Selecting the first ten qualified CIVPOL according to Thiery's criterion was relatively easy; however, selecting the next thirty proved to be a little more difficult.

E-Force officers Zoran Kurz, Guenter Rundel and Scott Brown

A meeting to discuss the Enhancement Forces was scheduled to take place in UNMIK MHQ Pristina within the next few weeks and Thiery wanted me to attend with him. The reason for my attendance left me motionless and temporarily speechless; I must have looked like a waxwork model from Madame Tussauds. Thiery told me before attending the meeting in MHQ, he was to identify one CIVPOL officer who could establish and lead Mitrovica E-Force and bring that person along to the meeting; apparently I was the obvious choice, a choice backed up by Gary Smith. I was overwhelmed they held me in such high regard, however, I was also very sceptical.

'Oh, no, no, no,' I eventually told them both; I couldn't possibly accept the supervisor's position. Although I didn't particularly agree with the curious officer selection process, I didn't mind helping with identifying those officers who were, in Thiery's eyes, qualified. I felt I barely had the experience to be considered for an E-Force patrol officer's position, never mind be its supervisor.

My previous mission supervisory roles as Deputy Chief of Communications and the RMLO might have improved my communication and creative skills; however, in my opinion E-Force was going to need a supervisor with proven experience in planning, leadership, negotiation, strategic planning and most definitely achieving result. Although I had passed the first stage of the constable to sergeant promotion exam, I didn't feel comfortable or confident enough to take on what I knew would be a huge amount of responsibility.

I would compare the E-Force supervisor's position to a very experienced UK police Chief Inspector, possibly a Superintendent (three and four ranks above a police constable). The new E-Force supervisor's position was definitely not for me.

I looked at Thiery and Gary and asked if they knew my police rank with the MDP and did they know what my day-to-day routine entailed back in the UK? 'Yes,' they did know I was a constable with the Ministry of Defence Police; however, their minds seemed to be made up, especially Thiery's.

And two valuable skills Gary Smith has are negotiation and influence and, after a further twenty-minute discussion with both Gary and Thiery, I, with some reservation, accepted the task and was willing to be the E-Force supervisor. I had thought about the small number of CIVPOL and that managing forty wouldn't be too bad. Even with the conditions given, I had managed to select the initial ten CIVPOL who I knew well and I knew they would give me their support.

One other important factor in making my decision was, most operational directives came directly from UNMIK MHQ, specifically the Police Commissioner, his deputy and the Director of Operations. I would be following their orders and, at a regional level, I'd be following the orders of the Regional Commander, how can I possibly go wrong?

After having coffee I was on my way with Thiery and Gary to look at premises which had been identified as a possible base for the new E-Force. On the way to the building I was told by Thiery to inform the ten selected CIVPOL they would be redeployed in the near future and let them know about *my* redeployment and anything else I felt they should know.

When we arrived at the potential E-Force HQ, the building looked too small and was too near the main bridge. It had insufficient electrical appliances, no female toilet and, amongst other issues, had no protective grounds for parking and keeping the thirteen UNMIK police vehicles that were to be assigned to the new unit secure.

I suggested accommodating the initial ten CIVPOL at North Station; I could use up one of the offices vacated by the redeployed monitors. I later spoke with the KPS Station Commander, who I got along well with, and he allowed me to use the entire top floor of the station if required.

The following day I was on a bit of a high with lots of ideas, a bit of *déjà vu* I suppose. Thiery paid me a visit in my office and led me out to the corridor. He wanted to know how many offices there were and what computer equipment was in each office. As well as plenty of office space there was a relatively large room which I used for monitoring briefings and meetings. Along with the briefing room there were at least four good size offices which could easily accommodate a small team of forty CIVPOL, especially as they would be working on the three shift system.

Thiery inspected all the offices before telling me there would probably be more than forty E-Force CIVPOL officers in North Mitrovica; more like 140 he announced, probably more. And when you add the LAs to that list, you're looking at close to 200 staff. Once again I was left speechless. Supervisor to nearly 200 UN personnel; I was in for a bumpy ride. However, my trump card would be, 'If you don't like any orders or decisions, complain to the Commissioner, he made the rules, I'm just the messenger.'

The reason for Thiery's startling revelation was the now imminent demise of patrol monitoring. In a matter of weeks there would be no patrol monitors and therefore no jobs for the CIVPOL officers, other than E-Force. Thiery wasn't happy about that situation; he wouldn't get that quality of CIVPOL officer he thought E-Force really required. That issue was, however, out of his hands and a decision had been made at MHQ level. And to add to *my* dilemma, many of the new CIVPOL deployed to the mission would be deployed from PTC to Mitrovica E-Force. I wouldn't know what experience or what skills they had, not until after they were already deployed into the unit.

CHAPTER TWENTY-ONE
April Fool

TWO DAYS AFTER Thiery's visit to North station the mood in both North and South RMBS was very sombre to say the least. By now every CIVPOL working in Mitrovica knew, unless they redeployed from the region, there was a chance they'd be redeployed to E-Force. I'd already explained I was to be the new E-Force supervisor and I'd be following all directives from UNMIK MHQ and Mitrovica RHQ.

The first ten E-Force CIVPOL had now been informed they would soon be redeployed and they were not happy. I'd selected three American CIVPOL officers, four German, two Russian and one French officer. Three of those officers were already team leaders with North RMBS and I assured them they would join E-Force as team leaders. As for the others I couldn't promise anything, I just asked for their continued support.

I told those ten CIVPOL officers to carry on with their monitor duties and I would give them plenty of notice regarding their redeployment. When all was said and done it goes back to what I said earlier, we were in Kosovo to uphold the law. Patrol monitoring to some was a holiday, now it was time to do some of that real police work. I had a big challenge ahead and I was very nervous.

There was a mad scramble to find alternative jobs and many monitors did manage to secure other (office) jobs in the region and a few were very lucky to escape Mitrovica altogether. A small minority of the CIVPOL were actually looking forward to joining the new unit and had no problem with whatever challenges lay ahead.

Very soon after Thiery's visit I received a phone call from him to say we were to attend a meeting with MHQ Director of Operation, Colin Aitken (MDP). The plans for E-Force had been brought forward and the new unit would be operational from tomorrow, which happened to be April Fool's Day. However, that phone call from Thiery was no prank; E-Force was to be implemented weeks ahead of schedule.

The meeting with Colin Aitken was a bit chaotic. There was no way E-Force could operate properly at such short notice. I was told to inform the initial ten CIVPOL to report to North Station at 9am the following day and get the operation started; 'aye right'. I did meet with those officers, however we had a lot of work to do before any patrolling in the minority areas would commence. The first task was to have them redeployed which took about one hour. I was also redeployed although I also retained my position as the regions RMLO. I was now officially Mitrovica RMLO/Enhancement Force Supervisor.

APRIL AND MAY

I want to mention now, my time as E-Force Supervisor was short-lived, lasting from April to September, and I'm telling you this now so you can follow my short reign whilst making your mind up – villain or victim. I knew I was up against it from the off, especially as I was supervisor to most of the monitors I had chastised during the monitoring programme.

During that first week in April the RMBS admin clerk Kani was also redeployed to E-Force and after his first day of work he had created monthly rosters for the new 'Enhancement Force.' In the short term Kani worked between North RMBS and E-Force. Fifteen other LAs were also redeployed to the new unit.

As promised, the three former RMBS team leaders kept their position and, as a paper exercise, the three E-Force teams were made up of four CIVPOL in one team and three in the other two. Until I was a bit more organised I had all officers work day shifts. They assisted me with a few admin and logistical issues. Team leader Zoran Kurz is a bit of a computer buff and he created a daily roster, which was amended and improved upon as the unit grew.

Over the next few weeks I was still juggling with two positions. The RMLO position continued to take up some of my time and the E-Force supervisor's position was taking up more. Before the end of April a deputy supervisor, Guenter Rundel (German CIVPOL), had been appointed (by the Regional Commander and I appointed LA, Aleksandar Markovic, as my personal assistant. During April and May I followed the operational directive and increased E-Force by ten officers (and a little more) every two weeks. By the middle of May E-Force resources stood at around sixty CIVPOL (not forty) and forty LAs. Not all of those CIVPOL fitted Thiery's criterion and although many were experienced, they certainly weren't motivated; nevertheless, UNMIK police were now back 'on the beat' and carrying out general police duties in 'areas of interest' whilst maintaining a high profile.

Guenter and I worked well together and during the first few weeks E-Force functioned well. I wasn't aware of any major problems and all officers were carrying out instructions, which changed daily, without complaint and I did appreciate that.

Aleksandar Markovic joined me on the recommendation of Marty Walsh who worked with Aleksandar at Mitrovica Regional Traffic Unit. Aleksandar was a *Del Boy Trotter* type of character and I mean that in the nicest way. He knew many people and if you needed anything Aleksandar was the man who knew a man. Both Kani and Aleksandar became my close friends and to this day continue to be so. I also became good friends with other LAs, too many to mention.

As directed by the original appendix to operation Stringent Security, the initial E-Force duties included mobile and foot patrols and mandatory static duties (including VCPs) in high risk minority areas around Mitrovica city centre.

Although the daily roster did not include the words 'meal break' I expected the mobile and foot patrols, which lasted two hours each, to use common sense and take coffee breaks and meal breaks as and when required during the patrol hours. During a routine shift, mobile and foot patrols took up most of the eight hour shift; plenty of time for organising breaks.When operational requirements dictated, breaks would have to be taken whenever and wherever possible; again it's common sense.

A few confused and probably conscientious team members followed the daily roster as it was compiled and decided meal breaks were not permitted. I put that down to a lack of common sense and communication. Foot patrols were the perfect opportunity to enter a café and have a coffee whist chatting to the locals. In other words that was the foot patrols' opportunity for Intelligence Gathering.

Mobile patrol was another opportunity to have a break and do whatever took your fancy. When I realised what was going on I distributed memos explaining how flexible the daily roster was and when breaks could be taken. Ridiculous I know, but that's what I had to do.

May was the first month when Mitrovica Regional Operations produced an order whereby mobile and foot patrols were extended from Mitrovica city centre, to include the towns of Zvecan, Zubin Potok and Leposavic. Zubin Potok and Leposavic are about a forty-minute drive from Mitrovica and whenever possible, the journey to Leposavic was made with two patrol teams.

In August 2003, an Indian CIVPOL officer was tragically murdered as he drove a UN vehicle on the main road from Zvecan to Leposavic. Along with a UK colleague (an MDP constable), they were attacked from the rural and densely populated (high ground) forests that grow high above most of that road. A person or persons unknown opened fire from the high ground on the vehicle with an automatic weapon with several bullets penetrating the soft-skinned Toyota 4Runner. The Indian officer was hit and suffered fatal injuries; incredibly the

UK CIVPOL officer was uninjured. Travel restrictions for all UN personnel were put into force and lasted for over a year. That tragic incident was the main reason for Leposavic KPS station becoming an RMBS sub-station. When the Leposavic monitors moved between Leposavic and Mitrovica they always travelled in a RG32, which could only be driven after completing a training course. At my request, several other RMBS monitors and E-Force patrol officers were trained to drive that armoured vehicle and used it when travelling in or patrolling high risk areas. I tried as much as I possibly could to have two patrols travelling together on that road, to back up each other in the event of any serious incidents. Other than the protection of an armoured vehicle, many E-Force officers didn't have adequate protective or tactical equipment to deal with most firearms incidents and I didn't agree with the orders to travel and patrol in Leposavic. The UN did supply body armour and ballistic helmets, however, E-Force had more officers than I had protective equipment. Like me, most other European CIVPOL officers were lucky to have their own personally issued equipment. It was the African and Asian officers who had limited protective clothing.

One order I argued fiercely against, on a daily basis, was a static duty which took place within the home of a Serbian family whose lives had been threatened. The UN offered the householder, his wife and two children protection by both North and South Mitrovica RMBS, while discussions were held on what, if any, level of specialist protection the family should receive. It was alleged the owner of the house (a former Serbian policeman) was an informant and certain factions were out to kill him and his family.

Many of the monitors were not qualified or equipped for that type of operation and during RHQ morning briefings I made sure the Chief of Operations (MDP Constable Gary Forster) was aware of the fact. I wouldn't let the matter lie and continuously complained it may not be just the family who could lose their lives. I also spent lots of time in that home trying to reassure some very nervous 'people'; it was unlikely an attempt on the family's life would occur with a UN police vehicle parked outside the house. I obviously had no idea if an attempt on that family's life would take place, irrespective of who was protecting them.

Although the order was to provide protection whilst inside the home, as a deterrent, I had one Coca Cola with two CIVPOL, park in the family's garden. One of the E-Force mobiles also patrolled every hour in that area. Eventually, E-Force took over that dangerous role from the monitors and not long afterwards a decision was made to move the family, who then became part of a witness protection programme.

CHAPTER TWENTY-TWO
He's Behind You

DURING MY TIME as E-Force supervisor I was approached by a Shift Leader Monitor (Indian CIVPOL officer) Amod Kumar (remember the name) who was to be redeployed from North Station to Bravo Control. He was told by the station SCLO he was no good at his job so he must be redeployed immediately. The SCLO had not previously advised this officer of his apparent incompetence to do the job or offered any corrective action, which was against the UN PPM.

Amod was seeking advice from me and wanted to know how to redress the matter. I told him to look at the UN PPM (Officer Behaviour) and read it carefully. If he felt procedure had not been properly followed and if he thought he had a good case, he should proceed with his redress through his chain of command. A short while later I received a memo from Gerard Chevrier regarding the redress and his conclusion was the SCLO had not followed proper procedure. Amod Kumar was not redeployed and kept his SLM position. Gerard Chevrier has double standards and you will find out why later on.

When patrol monitoring officially ended and all my efforts were focused on E-Force, I received a letter of appreciation from Ed Cottrell, who managed to find a position as a Station Investigation Officer at Skenderaj/Srbica police station. This is the complete letter, counter-signed by Gary Smith who was now the Mitrovica Regional Commander. Gary's deputy was (German CIVPOL) Thomas Urny and Gerard Chevrier was still Chief of Operations.

'We wish to commend and formally recognise your professionalism and leadership skills during your assignment as the Regional Monitor Liaison Officer for RMBS Mitrovica. Your dedication to the unit was evident in the performance of your officers under your guidance as you put in countless hours of overtime without compensation.

During your service as our supervisor, you guided us through every phase of the monitoring program up to its finale. You coordinated all the program taxed to both North and South RMBS units and ensured they were carried out to the letter. And, it should be noted the higher *standards you developed in monitoring reports is what led our unit to be at the top of the list for other monitoring units to gauge their selves against.*

From myself and the other members from RMBS South we wish to thank you for the time you put into planning and coordinating of operations, the reading of countless reports and representing us as our liaison officer.

Your professionalism, dedication, high level of management has not gone unnoticed as we present our appreciation for the contribution you made to the unit.

You are a valued member of UNMIK police and we wish you much success in the future.'

Once again I was overwhelmed with those kind words and, unlike Alice Holmes, I was able to meet both Ed and Gary to thank them. It was great to see that at least a few people did appreciate what I was trying to achieve and for Ed to express his opinions the way he did made me feel extremely proud.

JUNE

I'm struggling for a word here, however June was probably the month when my, let's call it *dependability* was 'first' questioned, when I came up against a group of newly deployed (from PTC) CIVPOL officers. Around ten German and thirty American CIVPOL officers joined Mitrovica E-Force straight from the UN induction week and were not at all happy with their new assignment. Several of them had prior (Kosovo) mission experience, however, I don't think many of them were prepared for E-Force and its operational policies within Mitrovica.

June was also the month the UK rotated its CIVPOL contingent and the five officers Marty Walsh had mentioned to me were also deployed from PTC to Mitrovica and E-Force. With my position as the RMLO now gone my sole responsibility lay with E-Force, which was expanding rapidly.

During that huge influx of CIVPOL, all major decisions regarding or affecting E-Force and its duties and responsibilities were still being made slightly easier for me as I continued to follow all directives as instructed by Operational Order 'Stringent Security', MHQ and RHQ. Any new amendments to Operation Stringent Security or other instructions from MHQ and RHQ were normally read by me before being forwarded to my deputy and all team leaders. I didn't always agree with my new orders, but I always complied with them.

During June, and for the third time, more changes (by MHQ) were made to Operation Stringent Security. The order now was to increase high visibility police patrols and perform pro-active vehicle and pedestrian checks. The E-Force area of responsibility was extended again and included the vast South Mitrovica. Intelligence efforts were to be strengthened and closer relationships with KPS, FPUs and KFOR were to be formed. Extending patrols to include South Mitrovica was a killer blow for quite a few CIVPOL.

That new area of responsibility was now covering the whole of Mitrovica (140 square miles) and it really did take its toll on many E-Force officers. Just about all the CIVPOL wanted to redeploy elsewhere, from E-Force, and several officers managed to find positions in other regions; mainly in Pristina.

By the middle of June E-Force had around 130 CIVPOL and somewhere in the region of fifty LAs. Each patrol consisted of three (at times four) CIVPOL officers and one or no LA. I started to get reports (from LAs) of minor squabbles between CIVPOL regarding crammed vehicles and who should drive or sit in the front passenger seat. Travelling in crowded vehicles would surely make temperatures rise with squabbles and minor arguments inevitable. I started to consider having more teams with less patrol officers in a patrol team.

Static duties were becoming very repetitive with the same local people and vehicles being stopped and checked every day and night. It came to the point where the locals were complaining about police harassment. Another problem was when four CIVPOL were on patrol together. Complaints were being made by the same officers who claimed they always seemed to be the ones conducting a VCP whilst their 'lazy' colleagues remained in the patrol vehicle.

VCPs were continually carried out with all driver and passenger personal details logged (at the time) then, at the end of each shift, all VCP log sheets were collated before the information was entered (by an LA) into a database (created by me).

LAs started to complain that CIVPOL officers were doing next to nothing at the VCPs; it was the LAs who were checking the vehicle occupants before completing the VCP log sheets. The amount of vehicle and people checks during a busy week ran well into the hundreds. The complaints I received from both the CIVPOL and LAs were never official. I suppose I should say they moaned a lot, rather than complained.

I must have personally known around 95 per cent of the LAs, some a lot more than others. Many LAs were also called upon to assist UNMIK police officers in an unofficial capacity and were really taken for granted.

Notwithstanding the hard work done by the LAs and the potentially dangerous situations they faced on a daily basis, many were wrongly relied upon to carry out personal errands (for UNMIK police) and on occasions found themselves shopping for bargains and bartering at the local markets just to get a one Euro reduction on a three Euros pair of house slippers. Some were even asked to escort officers to the local barbers to explain how he should trim the officer's hair. I know one CIVPOL officer who ordered food in a restaurant by way of a phone call to an LA. He told the LA what he wanted to order before handing the menu and phone to a confused waiter, who then spoke with the embarrassed LA before taking the order. An unusual way to order food, but it worked.

On one occasion I had to rely on my personal assistant Aleksandar Markovic literally digging me out of a hole. I was travelling (in a 4Runner) with Aleksandar in a very rural and dense forest area near Zvecan when I managed to get the vehicle stuck in a very muddy and wet track. All four wheels were stuck fast and the weight of the vehicle didn't help as we started to sink into the mud.

Aleksandar fetched a few pieces of tree branches which we both placed under the vehicle. I did tell Aleksandar I would manage alone, however, he was having none of it and got stuck in.

After around one hour of pushing and shoving (with very little movement) and slipping and sliding I managed to get a bit of traction. By the time I got us moving again we were soaking wet and our clothes were thick with mud. I really don't think I could have got out of that situation without the assistance of someone who was under no obligation to help.

During my short spell as E-Force supervisor I assisted regional and station investigation units by supplying officers to assist with various criminal investigations. E-Force became involved in two major investigations, the first being an attempted robbery at a petrol station on the main Pristina Mitrovica Highway. Two Serbian petrol station attendants were shot by two suspects who opened fire with AK47s which resulted in serious injury to both attendants. The other incident involved the murder of a young Serbian man, shot in his vehicle by persons unknown.

Additional E-Force mobile patrols and VCPs were carried out at random and identified areas in order to gather information from the local communities in an attempt to identify and locate the suspects and suspected vehicles used in both crimes.

With so many CIVPOL now attached to E-Force and the area of coverage now extended, I made a request for more vehicles which was approved. The unit now had more than enough vehicles and so I made a conscious decision to increase the E-Force unit from three to six teams. That move reduced the amount of officers in a patrol team and created more space in a vehicle. Having three additional teams also meant each patrol unit spent less time travelling to and patrolling in remote areas.

I appointed Guenter Rundel as the responsible supervisor for the new Team 1A, B and C and introduced another CIVPOL officer, Sanjay Dattatra Yenpure from India, who became a second deputy supervisor and responsible for Team 2A, B and C. I maintained overall responsibility for both teams. The expansion of the E-Force unit was explained through a memo to all team leaders. That drastic change to the original creation of the Enhancement Forces was my first decision without prior approval from RHQ or MHQ.

JULY

At some point during the mission, the UN decided to rename the job title given to local staff and they became known as Administrative Assistants (AA), so I received a written complaint from a Serbian AA regarding two E-Force patrol officers who, just after the start of an afternoon shift, drove to South Mitrovica and parked the vehicle just behind RHQ.

Both officers left the vehicle and went shopping, while the AA was left alone. As she was in South Mitrovica she became uncomfortable. 'There were too many people on the street at the time, and I just did not feel comfortable at all,' wrote the AA. I assumed the 'people on the streets' were Albanian.

After around five minutes the AA called an RHQ operations officer, Anthony Allen, to tell him she had been left alone in the vehicle and didn't know what to do. Anthony told the AA, who incidentally was a close friend of his, that he would report the matter to her team leader. A short while later both E-Force patrol officers returned to the vehicle. After driving to their accommodation in Zvecan, where they dropped off several shopping items, they headed for Leposavic; which was their patrol area.

Initially I found out about that incident from Anthony Allen who was far from happy. After the AA sent me her memo of complaint Anthony wanted to know what I intended to do about it. The first thing I did was to tell Anthony whatever I decided to do had nothing to do with him. I don't think he was impressed. I gave both CIVPOL an opportunity to explain their unacceptable behaviour before reminding them they have a duty of care towards all AAs and should never leave any AA in a vulnerable or uncomfortable position. Those two officers just picked the wrong time and the wrong occasion to pick up their weekly groceries. I suppose the AA's predicament was my perfect opportunity to inflict some form of minor disciplinary action. Unlike my iffy role as RMBS supervisor, I 'was' in an official position and did have the power to take action. However, and as I've already explained, I would not apply disciplinary action unless absolutely necessary. On this occasion, once again, I felt it was not necessary. Words of advice was the better option.

After that minor incident Anthony Allen became a pest as far as E-Force was concerned. The duties of UNMIK RHQ operations officers included taking responsibility for ensuring operational plans were carried out as per the operational plan directives. I don't know if Anthony Allen was officially responsible for overseeing the appendix to Operational Order Stringent Security, but he was usually skulking around North Mitrovica with one other operations officer, American CIVPOL officer Ronald Clancey and picking faults with E-Force patrols.

Whilst Anthony Allen had me now constantly looking over my shoulder and irritating me at the same time, I started to get complaints about the monthly rosters and the three-day shift pattern which I had adopted and implemented (to both RMBS and E-Force) from the North Station patrol team rosters. Several CIVPOL, mainly from the German and American contingent (deployed to E-Force weeks earlier from PTC) asked me if the shift pattern could be reviewed with a view to making it 'better' and with fewer night shifts worked per calendar month. I agreed to the request and made 'every' team member aware of the situation. I sent out a general memo stating if any officer felt the current shift pattern could be improved in any way, staying reasonably within the UN PPM directives on Duty Hours, I'd like to hear from them and discuss any alternative and acceptable shift patterns they may have in mind.

The decision for E-Force to stay with that original shift pattern was solely mine with no influence from MHQ or RHQ. I also sought advice from the Director of Personnel and Administration who just happened to be another MDP constable, Mark Cunningham, who also found himself in a senior managerial position. Mark reminded me of the PPM on working hours and apart from telling me I was bending the rules as it stood, didn't want to interfere.

Hours of work for UNMIK personnel are divided into two categories and E-Force fell into the Operational Duty Hours (ODH) category. I could have created a roster with seven days worked on the same shift, however, I decided three days on one shift was long enough. Now, after working for more than a year with a perfectly good shift pattern I was getting earache and it was mainly about the amount of nights shifts worked. Officially UN working directives on an operational unit state: 'A shift shall not be less than eight hours in any twenty-hour period, unless authorised.'

After an early shift, all Mitrovica E-Force officers had thirty-two hours off before they commenced a night shift. One team in particular loved the shift pattern. Between their last early and first night shift, they always met and partied the night away. That particular team gelled well together and I put it down to their camaraderie and social life. Davie Hutton, who was a much respected deputy team leader, usually arranged the nights out.

When the new suggestions and roster proposals started to appear on my desk they were all put in the bin before the officer delivering them could close the office door behind him. A few of the rosters did show less night shifts per month, however, when I took a closer look, some days only included morning and afternoon shifts with no team on night shift. Some rosters included weekends off. UNMIK police worked every day of the week, no days off. A few rosters were completely incomprehensible. My final decision was, 'the original roster stays.'

Several of the American E-Force officers couldn't accept my decision and initially went over my head to the Regional Commander. They obviously put pressure on Gary Smith as he really started to get on my back about coming up with a better roster. I told Gary the situation with UN rules and explained the only way to create a better roster was to bend the rules until they snapped. Gary was adamant, he wanted that roster changed, and for the better. I couldn't do it and eventually the American (E-Force) contingent called a meeting in the E-Force briefing room; star guest was Gary Smith; I was not invited. Was that the beginning of my E-Force downfall, probably?

The Deputy Regional Commander, Thomas Urny, got involved in the roster-gate fiasco and said he would try and come up with an acceptable solution. During that period of time I was thinking, 'would these characters cause as much irritation in their home force?'

On a Saturday afternoon in July the Police Commissioner travelled through Mitrovica on his way to meet the mayor of Zvecan. As his vehicle travelled through King Peter Street the Commissioner expected to see the Mitrovica E-Force patrols. He neither saw any mobile or foot patrols which wasn't unusual.

Later that evening, during a night out in Xponto, I received a phone call from Thomas Urny who explained the Commissioner's observations and asked me for an explanation. When I established the time of the Commissioner's visit I told Thomas I could fax him a copy of the daily roster which would explain where all the E-Force patrols were during the course of the day.

At around eleven o'clock that evening I was in my office faxing Thomas both that day's and the monthly roster for July. I assumed Thomas would fax both to the Commissioner's office.

The following Monday I received another phone call from Thomas and he informed me the Commissioner was satisfied with the daily roster and now realised how varied Mitrovica E-Force duties were and how far and wide their area of responsibility extended. There was a mobile patrol assigned to Mitrovica city centre, however, its area also extended to Little Bosnia and Suvi Do. The city centre foot patrol could have just been out of sight, mingling with all the Saturday afternoon city centre shoppers.

The daily rosters also came in handy when the Security Monitoring Team was on the prowl. As part of the appendix to Operation Stringent Security, an UNMIK police security monitoring team was created to check on and monitor E-Force patrols in order to make sure they were where they should be and conducting their duties according to the current plan. When the security team visited Mitrovica I always supplied its CIVPOL officers with a copy of that day's roster which helped them find all the patrols. As far as I'm aware the Security Monitoring Team never had any issues or complaints regarding Mitrovica E-Force.

One issue I had with the E-Force officers was the inability or unwillingness to issue traffic tickets for motoring offences. On a number of occasions during VCPs the E-Force officers detained motorists for various motoring offences then expected the KPS to attend with a ticket book and issue a ticket. When a KPS officer refused, stating he did not witness the offence, the E-Force officer was left with the decision, issue the ticket himself or release the offender. The offender was usually released. More serious crimes committed by offenders and detained by E-Force officers were always handed over to the KPS, but only after the initial paperwork was reluctantly generated by the E-Force officer concerned.

Guenter suggested and devised a small training package for all E-Force officers that included the Kosovo law and the Kosovo Traffic Laws, including the procedure for completing a traffic ticket. A good idea from Guenter, but it was ridiculous to think experienced police officers were in need of such training. It took literally five minutes to work out how to complete a traffic ticket (which were printed in English). As far as I was concerned, E-Force patrol officers, many of whom were former monitors, were and I'll say it again, playing at it.

CHAPTER TWENTY-THREE
Give Us A Break

THE INCREASE IN E-Force vehicles and less time spent patrolling in far off remote areas of South Mitrovica did nothing to reduce the in-house squabbling and although the Security Monitoring Team seemed happy with the way E-Force was operating, it did, however, continue to chase up the patrol teams. I really could sympathise with the E-Force unit. Now the CIVPOL patrols were being monitored instead of the KPS patrols. Absolutely crazy.

I was so grateful to have two excellent deputies who kept me sane. Guenter and Sanjay were getting on with supervising their teams and always kept me informed on any internal issues needing my attention or approval. At the end of the day I was ultimately in charge of E-Force and didn't want my deputies taking the flack that I was getting from a minority of CIVPOL, including those two officers from RHQ operations, Anthony Allen and Ronald Clancey. Anthony's main issue was officers patrolling out with the assigned area and officers sitting in their vehicle when they should be conducting a VCP. Other officers were also reported as being too casual during a VCP which could compromise officer safety. Those issues had been discussed and addressed by me and my deputies, long before Anthony Allen stuck his neck in. Obviously our advice had made no difference.

I got to the stage where all I wanted to do after work was relax and forget personal issues and E-Force. I started spending quite a lot of my spare time socialising, mainly in Xponto. I also liked to join, and at times keep a close eye on, a few of the E-Force officers who also liked to socialise in the pub. I didn't want anyone getting into bother with other internationals or the locals and more often than not I would leave Xponto, along with the rest of the guys, at closing time, which was around 3am. The E-Force officers I socialised with were well behaved, and never caused any trouble. They may have been a little boisterous, but nothing more.

I must also say that by July 2006 I was spending more time going out with and being distracted by Vesela and usually met the E-Force guys and Marty and Alun later in the evening in Xponto. Vesela liked to go out after eleven o'clock (pm) when Xponto was beginning to get busy.

Incidentally, Vesela always picked me up in her unregistered Vauxhall Nova which she had no insurance for, nor did the vehicle have registration plates. At that time in North Mitrovica there was no requirement to register vehicles of a certain age (UN agreement). Many vehicles were driven without registration and insurance and many of those vehicle owners did not possess a valid driving licence. This unusual practice continues today, however, efforts are being made to rectify the issue.

Davie Hutton was also a regular in Xponto and was now my good friend. Davie had found accommodation with Dave Letsche. Willie Crawford, Glyn Smith and Roy Beresford found accommodation in South Mitrovica. Although Roy was an MDP sergeant and I, Constable Duncanson, was his mission supervisor, Roy always respected my position and accepted the somewhat odd situation we found ourselves in. During the Kosovo mission, similar circumstances of MDP constables managing MDP sergeants and above did occur.

Now, with Anthony Allen and Ronald Clancey still on my case, I thought it a good idea to pay more frequent visits to the E-Force patrols out on the ground. During one early morning drive around Mitrovica I paid a number of visits to the night shift (static points) not long before they were due to be relieved from duty. My first stop was the static patrol near the main bridge. When I pulled up alongside the Coca Cola, both officers appeared to be sleeping. I beeped the horn twice and quickly got their attention. After I parked my vehicle I got out and very slowly walked towards the Coca Cola. What I was actually trying to do was give both officers enough time to come up with a reasonable excuse as to why their eyes were closed; however, it would appear they were not as smart as my quick thinking MDP colleague Mike Harris. Both officers immediately admitted to falling asleep and apologised.

I found two other static patrols in similar positions with the exception of one Bulgarian officer, who was awake. However, I gave him a ticking off for not giving his sleepy colleague a dig in the ribs when I turned up. I gave all officers the talk about officer safety, being spotted by the public, the KPS or the Regional Commander who was an early riser. I also mentioned repatriation as a punishment, which would have been the most likely outcome had I reported them.

I really was trying my best at being the considerate (and probably out of my depth) supervisor and I did ask for advice from other police officers who I knew were more experienced at supervising large groups of people than I was.

Complaints about the monthly roster continued and Thomas Urny continued to look at the alternatives for a more acceptable roster. I was starting to get a little concerned, and every time I now made a decision or change, not influenced or directed by MHQ or RHQ, that affected E-Force and its staff, I made sure the information was e-mailed to all team leaders with a hard copy hand delivered to all team leader trays *and* one posted on the E-Force information board. I left nothing to chance, hence the reason for making almost every memo in triplicate.

Near the beginning of July, and after a morning briefing, I received an (eight-page, photocopy) stapled document from the Chief of Operations Gerard Chevrier. With his big smarmy smile, Gerard handed me the document and asked if I'd read it; I hadn't seen the document before it was handed to me. Gerard also took pleasure in telling me a copy had also been delivered to the Regional Commander.

The front cover of the document donned the UN insignia and below it read: *Proposed Enhancement Force Mitrovica North.* The name Teddy Crouch was written in the top right corner of the document. When I opened the document and read the first two paragraphs I became concerned, then angry. Here are those paragraphs, taken straight from the document, which I've kept since it was handed to me.

> 'With the creation of Enhancement Forces in Mitrovica many officers were redeployed with the purpose of covering potentially high areas of violence. As the teams (and overall force) have grown, more and more duties have been placed on the shoulders of the officers while at the same time their freedoms have been decreased. Officers are no longer allowed to take lunch breaks and daily activities have become frustrating and cluttered. Morale is at an all time low in a group that used to accept and enjoy their duties openly.
>
> In order to operate at the appropriate level, the Enhancement Forces should run like a police department, because that is what they are. They are unique in the Kosovo Mission and should be treated as such. This team may eventually play a major part in the transition of the region and the final status of the future country. To make this work it must be prepared and focused on the goal of accomplishing whatever task it is faced with. Currently this is NOT realistic. The current team consists of many very good officers from all over the world. These officers are more than capable but due to the current operation, they are very confused and extremely agitated.'

When American CIVPOL officer Teddy Crouch produced his 'proposal' he was an E-Force team leader and he was correct, more and more duties *were* being placed on the shoulders of the officers. Those additional duties were due to the ever changing ops plan and, of course, it's no surprise morale may have been low. Teddy's remarks regarding lunch breaks threw me and I hadn't a clue why he thought officers were no longer allowed to take a lunch break. I was very angry and took that remark quite personally. So to make *my* concerns known, I sent a memo (through the Chief of Operations) to the Regional Commander. I also wanted to clear up the issue of lunch breaks by quoting from previous memos which I had sent to all E-Force team leaders. Here are two of Teddy's comments regarding lunch breaks followed by extracts from my previously sent memos.

> TC: *'Officers are no longer allowed to take lunch breaks.'*
> TC: *'Everyone in Kosovo is allowed a lunch break with the exception of the Mitrovica E-Force.'*
> JD: *'These rosters will enable each individual officer to make plans regarding their next tour of duty (pick-ups, meal breaks, etc.)'*
> JD: *'When on mobile/foot patrols, meal/coffee breaks can be taken within a reasonable time and distance from the assigned activity.'*
> JD: *'The rosters can be viewed as quite flexible. For example, although most activities cover a two-hour period there is no requirement to spend two hours on mobile patrol or two hours on foot patrol.'*

Teddy's document proposal also contained the following headings:

- Complete Ranking Structure
- Reassignment of vehicles
- Zone Assignments
- Morale
- Shifts
- Scheduling
- Team Reformation
- Kosovo wide Re-structure
- Conclusion

Amongst other proposed plans, concerns and criticisms, Teddy had drawn up a new rank structure and their duties and responsibilities. On the subject of shifts Teddy felt officers should start at 8am and not 7am. His reason for this was to do with the water supply. If officers started at 8am, they could take a shower before work. Apparently the local utility system did not allow many officers 'the luxury of showering before a shift.' What happened to showering or having a bath the night before work? Or is that just a Scottish thing? I can remember Pat Kearney one morning, during a power cut in Dragodan, standing in an empty bath scooping water from a 300 litre water tank before pouring large buckets of freezing cold water over his shrivelled bits. And were we (UNMIK police) not supposed to be prepared for hardships and such, 'expected' events?

There was also a new name for the unit, Mitrovica Enhancement Force Bravo Platoon which was made up of a supervisor and squad leaders. Oh! ... and the new look daily roster had 'one' assigned lunch break per patrol per day.

In amongst Teddy's proposal for the restructuring of E-Force, some of his comments were rather scathing. Here are just a few of those comments.

> 'A single weak link in command can cause chaos that inadvertently makes the entire team breakdown.'

> 'It feels like a punishment to be part of such an unorganized and disrespected group.'

> 'Morale is always an important aspect and is almost overlooked or just ignored. Keeping officers happy and treating them like human beings are the most important things that can be done. Everyone in Kosovo is allowed a lunch break with the exception of the Mitrovica E-Force. This is ludicrous.'

This next comment, by no means Teddy's last, made me laugh; however, the last part made me very angry. I don't think Teddy realised what he was writing at the time, or is it just my twisted sense of humour?

> 'Many officers refuse to take bathroom breaks because of being told they must stay in their assigned areas until relieved. This is not only not acceptable but inexcusable supervision.'

Seriously though, is Teddy saying grown men and women sat or stood with their legs crossed and bottoms clenched refusing to go to the bathroom because the supervisor told them to wait for a 'relief' to arrive before they could make a frantic dash to the nearest toilet? Maybe the daily roster should have mentioned a lunch break and a toilet break.

The document ended with:

'The content of this proposal are simply ideas of an individual. But due to first hand, in the field, knowledge of the operations and daily functions, I can honestly say it does not work and it feels like a punishment to be part of such an unorganised and disrespected group.'

As Teddy's proposal was not submitted through his chain of command (E-Force Supervisor, Chief of Operations, Regional Commander) my memo to the Regional Commander, as well as addressing the issue of lunch breaks and the other criticisms, was also a petty complaint; Teddy did break the chain of command. After a meeting with Gary Smith, his advice to me was remove Teddy from his position as team leader (my decision) or redeployment. I told Gary I'd like to speak with Teddy and sort things out if we could. I also wanted Teddy to tell me face to face why he decided to make his concerns and criticisms so public. When Teddy and I did meet I was shocked at his answer. Teddy told me the document wasn't aimed at me (who then?) and then in the same breath he told me he would be redeploying from E-Force to the KPS station in Vushtrri/Vucitrn. That was basically the end of the conversation. Sure enough, nine days later on the 15 July 2006 Teddy was redeployed to Vushtrri/Vucitrn police station. I'm sure he became a mid-level manager monitor. I still don't know if Teddy asked to be redeployed or if Gary Smith gave him a little encouragement.

As I sit here and write this chapter I'm just thinking about the reasons for the creation of Enhancement Forces with its aggressive enforcement of the law and its executive policing role. Why did the powers that be allow an increase in the original (ops plan) resources of forty to just fewer than 150 CIVPOL officers? Was it because the area of responsibility was extended to include the vast Mitrovica south; was it because patrol monitoring had finished and there was no place else for the CIVPOL to go? And why was 'someone like me,' with very little supervisory experience allowed to be its supervisor?

Teddy Crouch certainly put a lot of thought into his eight page 'proposal'; however, I have nothing more to say on why he may have decided to write what he did in the way he did or who, if not me, it was aimed at.

What I will say is I think Teddy's timing of the proposal's production just days before his redeployment was rather clever. And I also think it was a contributing factor to my imminent removal from E-Force. Oh! By the way; the proposal was not approved.

CHAPTER TWENTY-FOUR
Lucky Escape

AUGUST

For various reasons, August was not a good month for several CIVPOL officers working with Mitrovica E-Force. On a personal note I was pretty much down for a number of reasons and my days with E-Force were well and truly numbered.

Monday 3 August was my first day back at work. I had taken a week off and travelled to Montenegro with Vesela for a week's holiday. I also tried, and failed miserably, to forget about Teddy Crouch and his so called proposals.

On that Monday morning and just before entering the conference room at RHQ, where the morning briefings were held, I met Thomas Urny. In my absence Thomas had introduced the new E-Force roster which now saw officers finishing their third and last early shift at 3 pm only to return at 11 pm for the first of three night shifts. I don't intend to blab on about shift patterns any longer, however, that's what Thomas came up with and the matter was closed.

That morning briefing was just as busy as every morning briefing and in attendance were the usual command staff, which included the Regional Commander, his deputy, the Chief of Operations and all KPS SCLOs. CIVPOL officers from other units also attended and various representatives from KFOR and non-government organisations.

After the routine business and usual trivial matters were discussed and dealt with the Regional Commander (Gary Smith) turned to look at me with an unusual and slightly awkward-looking expression. Gary told me, with the others listening intently, E-Force would lose thirty of its CIVPOL officers who would be redeployed to a number of the borders and boundaries surrounding Kosovo.If there was another job, apart from E-Force, to avoid with UNMIK it was the BBP. Hours of checking a continuous line of vehicles as they slowly passed through the very busy borders and boundaries did not appeal to most CIVPOL.

To keep in line with the UN's policy on national balance Gary mentioned three specific nationalities which must be selected: American (seven), British (two) and Greek (four). The seventeen other CIVPOL could be selected at random. Gary then told me he'd select the seven American officers and I must select the others.

The conference room then burst into life with a plethora of voices each trying to out-shout the other as they put their arguments forward to the Regional Commander why certain members of their contingent should and should not be selected. Gary Smith was unfazed. I was making the selections and no one else would be getting involved in any influencing.

Those morning briefings tended to be rather lively and petty arguments were pretty much par for the course. I think it was the fact Mitrovica region was always simmering and the CIVPOL present at the meetings just wanted to let off steam.

Before the meeting finished Gary asked me to go directly to the Chief of Admin and give him my selections; he wanted those officers selected immediately and redeployed within a week. I must say I was a bit shocked and I knew my failing popularity would take a further knock. I was glad though Gary gave me that news in the presence of other CIVPOL, who in a roundabout way tried to get me off the hook. When the meeting was over I headed down the corridor to the admin office chased by a number of SCLOs, who were desperate to shaft or save members of their contingent.

Once inside the admin office I phoned Kani and had him fax me a full list of the E-Force resources which was 150. Before I set about my unenviable task, the Admin Chief, Van Williams, had to physically remove one of my pursuers from his office. I did speak with some of those SCLOs and agreed to help, where I could.

It didn't take long to come up with names. My big problem was selecting two British CIVPOL officers. With Van's approval I wrote down five names and placed five pieces of folded paper in a UN beret. Van did the honours and took out two names; Roy Beresford and Willie Crawford. Davie Hutton, Glyn Smith and Dave Letsche were saved.

After that morning's briefing news had spread quickly about the redeployments and when I returned to North Station, there were a few anxious faces waiting for me in the briefing room. I explained the situation to those present and again later that day to other team members. Before the end of the following day, all E-Force CIVPOL knew who was staying and who was going; a few were happy to escape E-Force, a few were not so happy. During August around forty CIVPOL ended their nightmare with E-Force, either by redeployment or by ending their mission.

I spoke with Roy Beresford and Willie Crawford and could only apologise for my actions. After their redeployment to the BBP I never saw much of Roy and Willie and I'm not too sure when they ended their mission. I think Roy may have gone home after completing just six months.

Almost five months after the inception of E-Force, Mitrovica Region remained calm. I think the amount and high profile of E-Force officers really did help to deter would-be criminals. The new shift pattern was beginning to cause anxiety amongst the recently deployed CIVPOL (I'm not surprised), however, Thomas Urny assured me the majority of CIVPOL did not have any objections to working it. Apparently Thomas had successfully introduced the same shift pattern in another region. Come on, can you imagine a UK police officer returning home after a busy eight-hour early shift, only to get prepared for an eight-hour night shift?

E-Force team members continued to find fault with and argue with each other. The main arguments came during the shift changeover. Some teams were later reporting for duty than others and other team members were taking their time relieving their colleagues out in the field. A few static points required officers to stay in situ until relieved by the on-coming shift and those officers being relieved were sometimes kept waiting fifteen to twenty minutes after the shift started.

It was the team leader's responsibility to make sure his team members reported on time for the daily briefing and be out on the ground with as little delay as possible. One team had perfected that practice using common sense. Prior to reporting for duty, that oncoming team leader and his deputy picked up all other team members and reported to North Station in time to get ready and briefed on that day's activities. In other words the team leader made a decision to pick his team up early. Those officers waiting to finish their shift were sometimes relieved a little early and were seldom left waiting more than five minutes after the following shift started. Other team leaders refused to arrive at North Station one minute before their start time.

E-Force had around twenty-five different nationalities and with such a large and diverse group of officers, tempers often flared with race and culture being the apparent cause of the arguments. One Nigerian officer being picked up for duty was told by a Spanish colleague the vehicle was full and he'd need to jump in the boot of the 4Runner as there was no other space. The Nigerian officer became very irate and told the Spanish officer, 'Maybe that's common practice in your country. In my country not even a dog would get in that filthy space, I'll get a taxi to work.' And he did. Those two officers were also seen having a shouting match in full view of the Mitrovica city centre daily shoppers. Eventually the Spanish officer, who was an acting team leader, handed me a set of car keys and said, 'I've had enough, I don't want to pick up any more officers or have any sort of responsibility.' That Spanish officer had volunteered to be an acting team leader to cover for a shortfall in resources, due to officers being off on

CTO. Davie Hutton stepped in and took over the acting team leader role. Davie later became a permanent team leader and loved the challenges he faced. Not surprisingly, Davie's team became one of the more cooperative and I would put that down to Davie's common sense approach and probably his positive MDP mentality. Incidentally, two other team leaders who had different but effective ways of keeping their respective teams happy (at their work) were singled out to me (I don't want to say by whom) and I was advised to 'get rid of them' as team leaders. One reason was that one was useless while the other dressed like a hobo. I refused to remove either from their positions. Within days of me refusing that 'request' the powers that be redeployed one officer to the BBP, the other lost his position as E-Force team leader and became an E-Force team member. Both CIVPOL were American.

The behaviour of certain team members was getting to the rest of the E-Force officers and more and more arguments started occurring between team members; arguments that were nothing more than people just nit-picking. I was really up against it, but what could I do?

In the middle of August I took more days off just to give myself a break from the crumbling E-Force. When I returned to my office on 20 August Guenter was waiting for me. I learned that during my time off Sanjay drafted a memo, proposing a few changes within E-Force team two. After the proposals were explained by a team leader during a morning briefing, one CIVPOL officer asked, 'What monkey wrote that?' The comment caused that CIVPOL officer to be reported to the Regional Commander and his Contingent Commander.

After a very quick investigation the officer was repatriated. I didn't have time to speak with him before his repatriation and cannot comment on his apparent *ethnic slur.* I was surprised to hear who the officer was and just wondered if the comment was brought on by the pressures of working in E-Force and having to deal with the constant changes brought about by RHQ and MHQ. Or was it down to the changes I made, or was the officer usually outspoken? I will never know.

26 August 2006

I left my office a little early on Saturday 26 August. I had arranged to meet Davie Hutton in Xponto and I wanted to relax before a long night out. After having a shower I checked my mobile phone and saw a missed call, just after 7 pm, from Jelena Mitkovic, one of the E-Force AAs. Before I called Jelena back, I turned on my UN Motorola radio. I just instinctively knew something was wrong. My radio should never have been switched off, especially in my position as a supervisor. It was also a UN rule.

When I called Jelena back she obviously recognised my mobile number. Her first words were: 'John, a bomb has exploded in Dolce Vita café bar, Davie Hutton has been blown up.'

I immediately felt a strange rush throughout my body and before my legs gave way I sat down. Before I had time to think about body parts splattered all over the bomb-blitzed café Jelena quickly went on to say although Davie was badly injured he was conscious and talking and had been transported to Mitrovica North hospital by a local taxi driver.

Jelena went on to tell me she had walked past Dolce Vita on her way home just minutes before the blast and ran back when she heard the loud explosion. Not a sensible move I thought, there could have been more explosions. However, Jelena saw Davie, along with a number of other injured and bloody people. Like those injured people, Davie was sprawled on the ground between a number of upturned tables and chairs; his uniform was in shreds and blood poured from his head, body and legs. He was attempting to get to his feet but couldn't. Before Jelena had a chance to help Davie, a number of UNMIK and KPS vehicles arrived and immediately tended to the injured.

Jelena was ordered from the area by a KPS officer and at that point she called me. As I was getting ready to head off to Mitrovica I recognised the Regional Commander's voice bellowing through the radio, he was at the scene of the incident transmitting messages to Bravo control.

When I arrived in the city I parked my vehicle at the T-junction, near the main bridge, and noticed crime scene tape all around the outside area of Dolce Vita's summer (beer) garden. The area was swarming with UNMIK police, KFOR, KPS and many local people. The main bridge was blocked at both the North and South end with an SPU unit and KFOR controlling movement.

Gary Smith and Chief of Operations Gerard Chevrier were at the north end of the bridge and I could see both were busy on their radio and mobile phones. At that point the situation was pretty much under control, but I was angry with myself for not being more alert and having my radio switched off.

When the situation was a little calmer I explained to Gary I was having a shower when the incident occurred and 'got here as soon as I could'. First thing Gary told me was Davie Hutton was one of several people injured, none of whom had life-threatening injuries. One person (an Albanian) was arrested immediately after the explosion and it appeared he acted alone when he crossed the main bridge from the south side before throwing one hand grenade towards the Dolce Vita.

Gary gave me instructions to increase security around the bottom end of the city by setting up more static points and increasing mobile and foot patrols in the inter-ethnic areas of the city. I contacted Guenter and Sanjay and we met at the scene. I briefed them both and handed over responsibility to them for organising the extra patrols and contacting every E-Force team leader (and later team members) and arranged an emergency briefing in North Station. Guenter and Sanjay set about their work and I just prayed all team members would realise the next few days would be very busy and hoped I would get their full cooperation and support.

After around thirty minutes with Guenter and Sanjay I headed to North Mitrovica hospital. When I arrived the hospital car park was full of press, many concerned family members and of course the KPS and UNMIK police. Once inside the hospital I was directed up three flights of stairs and along a busy corridor. Near the end of the corridor and standing outside a closed door were two E-Force officers. I greeted both before one opened the door to allow me entry. When I entered the two-bed ward I was greeted by a smiling, but bloody, Davie Hutton. I couldn't believe his cheerfulness. Although he was smiling and chatting to two nurses Davie's wincing showed me he was obviously in a lot of pain. He assured me, however, that he was fine. Believe me, he wasn't fine.

Davie's injuries were caused when a young Albanian youth walked over the main bridge and from around fifty yards, threw a hand grenade towards Dolce Vita. Davie told me, 'I was waiting on my coffee arriving and then for some reason I looked down at the ground between my legs. Next thing I noticed was a grenade and I remembered stupidly saying to myself, "that shouldn't be there", then bang!! I actually thought the blast hadn't injured me, I felt no pain; blood then started seeping through my shirt. I then thought, "what if there's a second one, move!" I then realised I couldn't move, my legs felt paralysed. When I arrived at the hospital so much blood was pouring out of me, one nurse thought I'd been shot in the head. When I was taken to a side room a doctor started to pull at my combat trousers and was attempting to pull them off over my boots. As he tugged and pulled the pain in my legs started to increase and I was screaming in agony. The doctor ignored my outburst and didn't stop pulling my trousers until he got them off.'

The blast caused injuries to Davie's forehead, his torso, arms and legs. Hundreds of small ball bearings from the blast were now embedded in Davie's body and left him covered in blood. Nurses were busy cleaning Davie's wounds and were discarding used and blooded medical swabs in a plastic trash bucket next to Davie's bed. Blood from a badly inserted intravenous drip was seeping from his arm and the needle inserted in his arm was causing more discomfort than his injuries. There was also blood on Davie's bed cover and on the floor. I wasn't impressed by the hospital's cleanliness.

I made two trips to Davie's accommodation to pick up a few personal items and in between those journeys I contacted the UK Contingent Commander. I also completed all necessary paperwork required after such an incident and injury to a member of UN staff before delivering it to the Chief of Admin office. I also gave the Regional Commander an update on Davie's condition. I did as much as I was required to do before getting back to the hospital and giving Davie some company. During the evening two UN doctors attended the hospital and after speaking with a local doctor it was decided Davie would be moved to a French KFOR hospital for further treatment. I left the hospital at exactly 11.08 pm; I know that because my mobile phone started to ring and I noticed the time.

When I answered the phone, it was Anthony Allen. He wanted to know why the E-Force evening shift officers on the main bridge had not been relieved. I was absolutely livid. He went on to tell me an E-Force officer had contacted him and was concerned no one from the night shift had turned up to relieve him. I asked Anthony the concerned officer's name and low and behold he was an American officer.

I didn't think I needed to explain myself to Anthony, however, I reminded him about the earlier incident and told him the night shift were probably delayed as some officers may not have been briefed about the day's events. I also told him Davie was fine and not to worry too much.

After my phone conversation with Anthony Allen I drove to the main bridge. The nightshift officers had arrived and sure enough had been delayed due to an extended and full briefing. Guenter and Sanjay had worked hard that day and evening and all the new (temporary) posts were up and running, without too many complaints.

Davie Hutton spent three days in the French KFOR hospital before being released. He returned home to the UK where he spent a number of weeks convalescing and picking ball bearings from his head, body and legs. After his doctor pronounced him fit for duty Davie returned to the mission and North Mitrovica.

As far as I'm aware all other people injured in that grenade attack made a full recovery. I have no idea of what punishment was issued to the apprehended suspect.

CHAPTER TWENTY-FIVE
Temporary Reinforcements

WITHIN TWO DAYS of the attack on Dolce Vita an operational order from Mitrovica RHQ operations was published and entitled *Temporary Reinforcement of RHQ Mitrovica*. Access over the main bridge was restricted and policed 24/7 by CIVPOL and KPS. The increase in static, mobile and foot patrols called for reinforcements from Pristina and Peja/Pec E-Force personnel. Twenty-four E-Force CIVPOL officers were utilised to cover nine additional (temporary) duties.

Six officers each from Pristina and Peja/Pec regions travelled to Mitrovica every day and the journey time from Peja/Pec took around two hours. I spoke with both Regional Commanders of Pristina and Peja/Pec who were initially under the impression travel time would be included in the number of hours worked.

The Pristina Regional Commander, Kevin Craddock, was also my Contingent Commander and he didn't appear to be very happy about the additional hours his officers would have to work. I reminded Kevin of the UN PPM:

> 'Officers may be directed by their respective chain of command to work irregular or longer hours than normally scheduled in the event of special or unusual mission requirements.'

Although the reinforcements were detailed to start duty at the same time as Mitrovica E-Force, they seldom did. They arrived late and left early. They should've waited at their post until relieved by their colleagues, they didn't.

My problems were also increased by the Mitrovica E-Force officers who could not, or did not, follow instructions and who neglected to properly assist and relieve their reinforcement colleagues. The reinforcement officers were being left at static points longer than the allocated time and a few were not being relieved for meal breaks. On other occasions the reinforcement officers were also being left to carry out mobile patrols, in unfamiliar areas, without being accompanied by at least one Mitrovica E-Force colleague.

I had a meeting with all team leaders and reminded them about the temporary order and its contents and insisted they check up on all their team members at regular intervals during the shift. If need be the team leader should relieve officers for breaks. I would probably have got more cooperation from a lame, domesticated donkey.

The temporary operational order included a detailed map showing the new patrol areas with the number of officers required for each patrol. It also differentiated between Mitrovica E-Force officers and the reinforcement officers. The instructions could not have been made any simpler.

After just two days, word got back to the Pristina and Peja/Pec Regional Commander; their E-Force officers were being treated very badly and were being refused a meal break. That old chestnut rears its ugly head again. A copy of an e-mail was copied to me that had originated from Gary Smith and originally sent to Mike Shanks (American CIVPOL), Peja/Pec Regional Commander. The e-mail is Gary's reply to an earlier e-mail, sent by Mr Shanks, which, unfortunately, I never saw. I was never given the opportunity to defend myself. Here's Gary's reply.

'Mike, I agree with everything you say and will forward your message to my Ops Chief and to John. We absolutely have to be more appreciative for the help we're getting and it is my personal belief that EVERYONE gets a meal break. I will talk to you in more detail tomorrow at the Ops meeting.'

From the inception of the temporary reinforcement order the Dangerous Brothers (Anthony Allen and Ronald Clancey) from RHQ operations had been out and about with pen and paper at the ready, finding more faults with the E-Force patrols. Mobile and foot patrols were not patrolling in their assigned area. Patrol officers continued to sit in their vehicles and others were conducting VCPs in an incorrect and dangerous manner. And of course it was all my fault. And all the time I thought I was supervising an experienced and motivated unit – not! In five short days my world had begun to collapse and I knew it wouldn't be long before I was summoned to the Regional Commander's office. To be honest, I didn't have the energy in me to fight my corner. I felt the whole of RHQ operations and E-Force was against me. I also had personal issues which needed sorting.

Vesela and I had now been together well over a year and I had fallen deeply in love with her; soon I'd have to make a life-changing decision. My two-year mission had three more months to run before I returned to the UK and I didn't know if I could cope with a long distance relationship. Too many personal thoughts were now rushing around my mind and maybe I just didn't see how bad the situation with E-Force was getting. My health issues had also started to really worry me.

The blemish on my head just wouldn't heal and, although it wasn't any bigger, it was now burrowing itself deeper into my scalp. Vesela had spotted the sore and I told her not to worry, 'I'd been to a UK doctor and it was nothing to worry about. It would clear up through time.' Complete lies, of course, I hadn't been anywhere near a doctor. The scab on my chest was steadily spreading and was double its original size. I managed to hide my scabby chest from Vesela for a few months and she hadn't seen it grow. When I did reveal it to her she was quite shocked. I told her both blemishes were similar and again nothing to worry about. At that point in time she accepted my nonchalant explanation and kept quiet; she didn't make a fuss. I decided to do a little internet research to try and discover what was growing on my body.

SEPTEMBER

On 1 September, during a morning shift, Guenter and I were conducting inspections of the E-Force patrols in the lower half of North Mitrovica. After being in the area for about twenty minutes I heard a radio message from Anthony Allen 'asking' one of the morning shift E-Force team leaders to meet him at the main bridge.

I made a transmission to Anthony and asked him if there was anything I should know and he then asked me if I could also attend the main bridge.

When Guenter and I arrived at the bridge we were met by E-Force team leader Ralf Ossarek (German CIVPOL), Anthony and his sidekick Ronald Clancey. Anthony expressed his concerns to me regarding several E-Force officers who were 'once again' not following the temporary reinforcement orders. Anthony was repeating himself again regarding officers sitting in vehicles and conducting dangerous VCPs. I told Guenter I had also noticed Anthony's observations and would make sure it didn't happen again. Ronald Clancey kept quiet, I thought by his big, round, red face he may have been a tiny bit embarrassed by Anthony's school teacher telling off antics.

Anthony was really doing my head in. He was giving me exact distances from street corners to where a VCP should be set up, and telling me where my officers should place themselves whilst conducting the vehicle stop. He was once again explaining to me the dangers of conducting a VCP and the potential dangers. I was actually fed up of reminding my officers of the correct procedures (and potential dangers) during any vehicle stop. I may not have had as much police experience as Anthony as far as vehicle stops were concerned, however, the correct procedures were hammered into me during my pre-deployment training and I lost count of the various VCP (potentially dangerous and dangerous) scenarios which I was trained to deal with. I did try to pass on my training techniques to several E-Force officers, however, it would appear my advice was falling on deaf ears. After around ten minutes of being scolded by Anthony, Guenter, Ralf and I went for a coffee. During our coffee I announced an emergency team leader meeting was necessary later in the day. Several E-Force officers *were indeed* disobeying orders and it had to be stopped. Unfortunately for me, that particular meeting came too late.

Next day I received a phone call from the personnel department; Gary Smith wanted to see me in his office immediately and could I inform Guenter that his presence was also required. On the way to Gary's office I told Guenter not to worry about his position. I knew it was me who should be doing all the worrying and I should probably be congratulating Guenter on his imminent promotion to E-Force Supervisor.

I stood outside Gary's office with Guenter and waited five long minutes. When Gary appeared from his office he told me to come in and for Guenter to wait outside. I was surprised to see RHQ operations officer Michael Pufahl and his chief Gerard Chevrier sitting at that corner table in the Regional Commander's office and wondered what else lay in store for me apart from Gary's big elbow knocking me off my perch.

Gary sat behind his desk and motioned me to sit down alongside Michael and Gerard. Big Gary never minced his words and that day was no exception. As soon as I sat down I looked at Gary and he said, 'John I'm letting you go from E-Force, but I'm gonna look after you.' There was a slight pause as if Gary was waiting for a reaction or reply; it never came. I sat and said nothing; I just turned to look at Gerard, who looked back at me a bit mystified.

I wanted to say, speak up Gerard, you know Gary can't do this; he hasn't followed UN Policy and Procedure (Officer Behaviour). If you remember I previously mentioned Amod Kumar, the Indian officer who Gerard said could not be redeployed as UN Policy and Procedure had not been followed. So why then was Gerard not speaking up now? I'd never had any previous verbal or written warnings.

To be honest I was glad Gerard sat and said nothing. And of course I didn't expect him to say anything, my thoughts were miles away from E-Force and its motley crew of incompetent skivers.

As Gary continued to speak, I just about heard the words, captain and sinking ship before I became oblivious to the big man's American drawl. My mind was more occupied, thinking about an unfamiliar name which I had discovered during my internet browsing – *Basal Cell Carcinoma (BCC)* – my head blemish was almost certainly a form of skin cancer. I thought I was going to die.

I found one website which described my head blemish in detail and also showed other various types and forms of skin cancer. I didn't like what I read: 'Basil Cell Carcinomas are easily treated in their early stages.' The larger the tumour has grown, however, the more extensive the treatment needed. Although the skin cancer seldom spreads, or metastasises, to vital organs, it can damage surrounding tissue, sometimes causing considerable destruction and disfigurement and some BCCs are more aggressive than others.'

I'd ignored that blemish for months and started to think the cancer had got into my bloodstream. I was really scared and confused and it made no difference what I was reading, I convinced myself I was very ill. I thought of my dad and his short battle with cancer.

I gradually started to focus on Gary as he continued to speak. He went on to tell me he had heard stories of me, 'Burning the candle at both ends in Xponto.' Staying out until three and four in the morning and then driving to work smelling of alcohol.

Gary said I had a huge responsibility as E-Force Supervisor and my behaviour would not be tolerated. I also heard later that Gary was told when Davie Hutton was suffering in hospital; I was more interested in being in Xponto than visiting my friend in hospital. The knives were definitely out and there was nothing I wanted to do or say to defend myself. I had enough on my plate. Apart from my health scare, I had one other dilemma to consider: do I want to continue my relationship with Vesela after my mission ends?

Gary Smith kept his word and he did look after me. The reason Michael Pufahl and Gerard Chevrier were invited to Gary's office was for me to be introduced to my new supervisors. Gary redeployed me to RHQ operations, where I replaced Anthony Allen, who became the new E-Force Deputy Supervisor, surprise surprise, in place of Guenter Rundel who became the new E-Force Supervisor.

One day after Anthony's appointment he issued a memo to the team leaders. To, I assume, emphasise his authority, Anthony used bold text and underlined part of the memo. The point of the memo was for team leaders to reduce the time of their daily briefings and get the teams out on the ground as soon as briefings were finished. Anthony didn't refer to himself as Deputy Supervisor, oh no,

Anthony was the Deputy 'Chief' of Enhancement Forces.

And also, days after Anthony's appointment, the monthly roster was amended to show Anthony as the sole Deputy Supervisor with a call sign BS2. That call sign was originally assigned to E-Force (and second) Deputy Sanjay Yenpure, who lost his position and title when he became the E-Force admin officer/MTO officer. A bit of a blow for Sanya's self-esteem I would imagine.

I was happy to be relieved of my E-Force supervisory responsibilities. I could now relax and plan my last three months in mission, free of any work pressure. I think I was redeployed to RHQ operations so Gerard Chevrier could keep an eye on me and make sure I arrived at work at 8 am prompt, not smelling of alcohol.

When I was redeployed from E-Force there was around 112 CIVPOL and an average of 18 team members in six teams. The unit fluctuated between 100 and 150 CIVPOL and just over 50 AAs. A handful for any mug to deal with.

My job as operations officer was to oversee the operational running of two UNMIK boundary gates, one near Leposavic (Gate 1) and one near Zubin Potok (Gate 31). Both those gates are the exit and entry routes to and from Serbia. One UNMIK police Gate Commander was employed at each gate and I failed to see what I could really do other than be a hindrance to both commanders.

After just two weeks, basically twiddling my thumbs, I told Gary my job was boring and I had nothing to do. I'll give the big man his due, he redeployed me to Zvecan police station as the KPS OLO, no interview, no test, just start on Monday type of a deal. There were a few angry faces. Stuff them.

I worked with American CIVPOL officer Ron Henderson who was the KPS SCLO and a true gentleman. Ron and I worked a little system where we basically broke UN regulations and job shared; Gary Smith was a good friend of Ron's and must have known what we were up to. Each day I barely worked half a shift. The KPS Station Commander and his deputy (Ron's and my counterpart) were more than capable of doing their job and my last few months in mission were quite relaxing with little mentoring or advising necessary. As far as the Managerial Skills Assessments were concerned I only needed to complete one.

During a morning in October I finished work earlier than usual to join Vesela and her family who were preparing for an annual Serbian Orthodox religious celebration, known as Slava.

Slava is the celebration of the patron saint for each family in Serbia. Different families have different saints, handed down through the generations. Vesela's family patron saint is Saint Paraskeva of the Balkans, also known as Sveta Petka.

To be honest I was a bit overwhelmed by the whole occasion which is a day of ritual and feasting. Before the meal begins, there are certain rituals that are celebrated. First, a tall candle is lit and remains burning throughout the day. This reminds everyone of the significance of the event and, in particular, symbolises that 'Christ is the light of the world'.

The family attends Church in the morning and breaks *slavski kolac* (sweet bread decorated with the dove of peace and the sign of the cross) and *zito* (boiled wheat), both of which are blessed by the priest. Slavski kolac is a symbol of the real presence of Jesus Christ, while zito represents their faith in the resurrection of the dead. Red wine, symbolic of the blood of Christ, is also part of the ceremony.

I was very grateful to Vesela's brother who made sure I was never hungry, or dry. Tradition states that the host stands until the end of the evening and makes sure the guests are looked after. The celebration began when trays were served with prosciutto (cured ham), cornichons (sour French pickle), goat's cheese and pita (paper-thin pastry rolled with a cheese filling) followed by smoked pork ribs and spit-roasted suckling pig. There were also various salads prepared by Vesela's younger sister, including Russian salad which I couldn't get enough of.

A selection of desserts, including *kiflice* (pastry rolled with sweet fillings) and *oblande* (a cake made from large wafer sheets and chocolate cream) was then served followed by copious amounts of alcohol. The following day at work was spent behind a desk, with my feet up, drinking gallons of water and lots of very milky tea with heaps of sugar.

When Davie Hutton returned to the mission area, after his injury, he continued where he left off at E-Force. He was soon appointed team leader and in November when Ron Henderson's mission ended Davie took over Ron's position as Zvecan station KPS SCLO.

Guenter and Anthony Allen didn't get along at all and Guenter found it very difficult to work with him. Whatever the reason for Guenter and Anthony's grievances, Anthony lasted just fifty-eight days with E-Force before his short reign as Deputy Supervisor came to an end. He was redeployed to South Station as the KPS SCLO, although maybe he preferred to be called Chief SCLO.

In November Guenter's mission came to an end and he was replaced by a CIVPOL officer from France. That French officer immediately appointed a French colleague as a third MTO officer. The position was a day job with an office, computer and access to a vehicle.

Days before my mission came to an end on 6 December I still hadn't reached a decision regarding my relationship and future with Vesela. First of all I needed to see a specialist about my 'condition' and take things from there.

Where as on my first mission I checked out from the mission in five minutes, it took me around five days to check out on the second mission.

As E-Force Supervisor I was required to sign for over 100 items of UN equipment. Those items included: computers and accessories, office furniture, body armour, riot shields and helmets, mag lites and somewhere in the region of 30 Toyota 4Runners. My hasty exit from E-Force did not allow me to do an immediate handover of the equipment and by the time I got round to doing it, the French CIVPOL officer had already taken over from Guenter. One of the reasons it took so long to hand over the equipment was, each 4Runner was transported (one at a time) to the busy UN workshop and checked for recent and unreported damage. I asked my French colleague, 'Why only one at a time, you have enough MTOs to transport three at a time, your process will take forever?' His reply was a shrug of the shoulders. I think that may have been his pay back from our time working together during the mission. I think he was one of the many CIVPOL who didn't like the way I worked.

I managed to check out the day before my flight back to the UK.

Before I returned to the UK I received a performance appraisal from Gary Smith and this is what he had to say:

> 'During the time that John Duncanson has been under my command, I have found him to be one of the most professional individuals in mission. His work ethic is second to none and his dedication to duty is of the highest order. He accepts challenges without complaint and always strives to succeed.
>
> He was given the challenge of forming a new unit consisting of a diverse group of officers from numerous different nations. The work was difficult and challenging and the unit was one of the most important assignments in the mission.
>
> John gave 150 per cent at all times and is to be commended for the manner in which he approached his duties. Even when faced with difficulties related to scheduling, working conditions, and the demands placed on the unit, John continued to perform his duties without complaint.
>
> Officer John Duncanson has earned my respect as a man and as a professional. His contingent and his home country can be proud of the manner in which he has represented them.
>
> I would be proud to work alongside him in any future mission.'

I was very moved by Gary's comments and I believe his words were straight from the heart. I have kept in touch with Gary through social media; however, I've never really broached the subject of my removal from E-Force. I remember what Gary told me at the time, but I think he may have listened to and protected others who may have stuck the proverbial knife in my back.

CHAPTER TWENTY-SIX
Back Home

WHEN I RETURNED to the UK I once again reported to PTC Wethersfield for a one week reintegration course and a post-mission medical, which was now being offered to returning seconded MDP officers. During the medical the doctor measured my blood pressure; it was 'extraordinarily high.' It should have been around 120/70 and it was 150/110, not good. I also showed both my blemishes to the doc, who told me I should see a dermatologist. I never mentioned anything about cancer, neither did the doc.

Apart from the worry of maybe having cancer, my head was all over the place during that week at Wethersfield and I'm not sure it was my new health scare that was contributing to the way I was feeling. Apparently high blood pressure doesn't have any obvious symptoms, so I couldn't explain the cause of my sudden panic attacks or why my heart was rapidly pounding against the inside walls of my chest.

Although I was also suffering with personal issues I didn't put my 'funny turns' down to them. If the offer of post-mission counselling had been presented to me maybe I would have opened up and shared my personal dilemmas. As it was, once again, I was not offered any sort of counselling and I made the decision not to approach anyone either. I just suffered in silence until I returned home to Glasgow.

When I got back home from the reintegration course I moved in with my mother before returning to work at Coulport. I didn't want to worry my mum so I didn't immediately tell her about the blemishes. She found out when she inadvertently opened a letter addressed to me from Glasgow Royal Infirmary.

I started back at work in January 2007 and due to a shortfall in staff I was rostered to work with a different section (four section) of coppers from the section (one section) I had spent seventeen years with. On a personal level I barely knew anyone in four section. Unlike one section, I had no real friends to speak of on four section, and some of the senior staff with whom I tried to speak and explain my difficult time were less than useless.

After explaining to one inspector how I was feeling and how I was finding certain situations difficult to cope with, I mentioned to him that I felt I needed help. His response to my cry for help was that he ushered me out his office saying, 'Let me know how you get on then.' I can laugh now, but that inspector was a complete and utter tool.

A few weeks after joining four section I felt confident enough to approach and speak with a sergeant, Davie Murty. Davie arranged for me to see a MOD welfare officer who was fantastic and who spent time listening to me and helping me to get my head back together. I settled down in four section and, thanks to a few understanding coppers from both one and four section, I gradually got my life back on track.

During an examination of my head at the Royal's dermatology department a consultant asked me if I had any other blemishes anywhere else on my body. I pulled up my T-Shirt to reveal my other friend. The consultant told me he wanted a second opinion, alarm bells were now ringing when he left the examination room to seek a colleague. When the consultant returned his colleague examined my head first and confirmed my fears, I had skin cancer; he also told me the condition was not life threatening and that I wasn't going to die. He obviously knew the thought would have crossed my mind. As for my chest, a biopsy was recommended, however, there was no apparent rush to deal with that.

The blemish on my head was a bit different. When the procedure was explained to me I wasn't happy. 'After administering a general anaesthetic, we'll dig the tumour out from your scalp, take skin from behind an ear or a thigh and graft it over the treated area,' the consultant explained.

To prevent any permanent bald patch, I was told tiny balloons would be inserted under the grafted skin and inflated to stretch my skin. When my skin had stretched sufficiently, the balloons would be deflated and removed. The loose skin would then be pulled together cut and stitched which would, eventually, result in a bald patch free head.

When the day of the operation arrived I was very nervous, however, Vesela had arrived from Kosovo and was now with me at the hospital. She had also met my mother and sons.

After the successful operation I realised I'd been one very lucky chappy. The doctor who performed the operation used 'brute force' to pull my skin together (and inserted eleven stitches) without the need for skin grafts. I felt like the skin from the back of my neck was sitting on my forehead. My neck was completely immobile for a week. Today my hair covers a very small dent and scar.

Also during that year between missions I paid a visit to my GP who monitored my blood pressure for one month. It didn't return to normal and I now take medication to keep it under control. Later in the year I had the blemish on my chest removed (by local anaesthetic) and the biopsy results were negative. Coincidently, I also received eleven stitches after the minor surgery.

When I initially reapplied to go back to Kosovo I was worried my scare with skin cancer and my high blood pressure may void my application, luckily it didn't. During the pre-deployment medical the doctor asked me to supply a letter from my GP stating I was fit for duty and to travel. I was one step ahead of him in that respect. A glutton for punishment? Maybe, but once again I was Kosovo-bound and heading back to Mitrovica.

During the pre-deployment course all officers were told about a handover from UNMIK to the European Union. By the end of 2008, the EU would take over the rule of law in Kosovo and the mission would be known as the *European Union Rule of Law Mission in Kosovo* (EULEX). In December 2008, EULEX was deployed throughout the territory of Kosovo, assuming responsibilities in the areas of police, customs and the judiciary.

All officers who were interested in being seconded to the EULEX mission were required to apply for specific jobs which they felt they were qualified to do. The EU application process required all applicants to select three advertised posts. I tried to be smart and my first choice was a position which had 78 vacancies Kosovo wide; the more vacancies, the more chance of getting the job, I thought. I didn't really consider the position itself. I was applying for a post which was advisor to a KPS Captain. If my application was unsuccessful, I'd be home in time for Christmas 2008.

I went into the mission with no expectations. If I got a year out of it I'd be happy. Those twelve months in mission would also give me a chance to plan my future with Vesela.

PART FOUR

MITROVICA

DECEMBER 2007 TO
NOVEMBER 2008

DECEMBER 2007 TO NOVEMBER 2008

I WAS HOME for exactly one year before returning to Kosovo (6 December 2007) and one last UN mission. I had made a couple of social visits in between missions and any doubts I had regarding my relationship with Vesela were now gone.

Nothing much had changed in the mission area except a substantial downsize in the number of UNMIK police personnel and an increase in the KPS. The total amount of UNMIK police stood at around 2,000, against just over 7,000 KPS officers. As far as the UK police were concerned around sixty continued to work in mission.

I returned to the mission along with two other prior mission colleagues from Coulport, Marty Walsh and Davy Rodden. Marty would join me in Mitrovica and Davy would go back to Pristina airport. In total nineteen MDP (thirteen constables) were seconded to UNMIK during that rotation and most officers had previous mission experience.

A few familiar faces were still around Mitrovica and the mission area in general. Davie Hutton was still the KPS SCLO at Zvecan police station and Mitrovica RHQ had still not transitioned. A MDP constable (and good friend) Davie McLean (*left*) was the Mitrovica Regional Commander which was no real surprise to some as during a previous Kosovo deployment Davie achieved the position of Regional Commander in the Peja/Pec Region. I had known the 'wee man' for years.

The monitoring programme was now fully concentrated on KPS mid-level managers and a few job titles had changed once again. CIVPOL monitors were now expected to monitor their KPS counterpart for 80 per cent of their daily shift.

One significant point to make is during this, my shortest and last UN mission, Kosovo declared its independence from Serbia and a risk assessment for unlawful action and riots was considered to be high.

Although over the years the conditions at Coulport and the MDP in general had changed dramatically, for the better I might add, I was desperate to return to Kosovo. I spent my first six weeks in mission working as a patrol officer before securing a position with Mitrovica Regional Crime Unit which saw me through to the end of that UN mission. Thankfully I never came up against any more people or groups who disagreed with or questioned my working practices.

CHAPTER TWENTY-SEVEN
Beat Bobby

MY FIRST POSITION during my final mission with UNMIK was with a familiar unit; Enhancement Force. I was now an E-Force patrol officer and finding out what is was like from the other side of an office desk. Marty Walsh and I were appointed to Team C, which was the third of four teams. Our team leader was Mariyan Dimitrov, a very quiet young man from Bulgaria. Two American CIVPOL colleagues who I previously worked with in Mitrovica, Van Williams (former Chief of Admin Services) and Ron Henderson (former SCLO at Zvecan police station), had also returned to the mission and like Marty and me were working on patrol with E-Force.

Here was another case where those former (mission) big bosses found themselves reduced to being Officer Nobody. If you wanted to climb back up that chain of command and get off patrolling and shifts, you had to wait for a higher position to be advertised and then hope for the best.

The E-Force supervisor was an American CIVPOL officer, Travis Hawkinson. During our first shift Travis met Marty and I and said he didn't expect we'd be working with him for very long and he was quite correct.

Our friend and colleague, the Regional Commander, Davie McLean had already mentioned two positions to Marty and I that would soon be advertised, Traffic Unit Liaison Officer and Deputy Regional Commander Investigation Monitor with the Mitrovica Regional Crime Unit. I thought Marty was a cert to walk into the TULO position but, as for the job with Regional Crime I wasn't qualified. My only hope, if I did apply, was my prior mission and monitoring experience.

Travis Hawkinson looked quite embarrassed that first day we met, he knew a lot about me and the fact it was me who initially created E-Force before becoming its first supervisor. I told Travis it was a new mission and a new start for me, from the bottom. He would get my full cooperation and commitment; I obviously knew how hard a supervisor's job can be.

E-Force officers

The E-Force shift pattern had now changed and once more the UN PPM was being slightly bent. Shifts were now divided into four, with two 'day shifts' worked in between an evening and early shift. The day shifts were a later start than an early shift and basically were used for training and 'special duties.' Day shifts were really two days rest from patrolling, and I had to hand it to Travis for accommodating his officers with those easy days. He also reduced the number of night shifts worked, however, he was putting his job on the line. Nonetheless, he got away with it.

The daily roster did not include a meal break and patrols were continuous and changed every hour. By that time most CIVPOL had sussed out the 'meal break' times, not like my former colleague Teddy Crouch, remember his comment – *'Everyone in Kosovo is allowed a lunch break with the exception of the Mitrovica E-Force.'*

Travis' daily roster consisted of eight separate patrol duties and, like my original roster, it was full of opportunities to have a break, in fact five breaks, the same as my roster.

E-Force had 155 CIVPOL and, incidentally, eight of those officers could not pass the UN driving test; nevertheless they were permitted to remain in the mission without possessing a UN driving licence.

For our first few shifts Mariyan teamed Marty and I up with a Ghanaian CIVPOL officer, Kobina Ampah Korsah. Kobina was a big man with a big smile, loved his job and loved to drive on every shift; that arrangement suited me and Marty fine. The day-to-day duties hadn't changed much with the original VCP and static points still in place. One interesting observation I did make was every patrol seemed to be more alert and even although it was bitterly cold I didn't see many CIVPOL neglecting their duties. VCPs were being conducted with all officers out of the police vehicle and doing their bit, so to speak. During night

shift when we were on mobile patrol, Kobina drove around the whole time and never once stopped for a break (that's not a complaint) or asked me or Marty to drive; we did offer, but he always refused.

During one morning shift when Marty and I were having a coffee in between a foot patrol we were joined by Davie McLean and I happened

Mariyan Dimitrov

Big Kobina

to mention how 'keen' the E-Force officers seemed to be; Davie just smiled and said, 'Keen! They're not keen they're just committed to keeping themselves from being sent packing.'

Davie then spoke about when he came back into the mission, six months before Marty and I, and how he too spent a few weeks on patrol with E-Force. When Davie ended his first Mission as Peja/Pec Regional Commander he made such an impression with UNMIK that he was contacted in the UK and asked if he could be redeployed back to the mission and take up the position as Regional Commander in Mitrovica.

Davie had no plans to seek another overseas mission, however, after the unusual and unexpected request by the UN he said he was so honoured to be asked back into the mission, he could not refuse such an incredible offer. 'For an MDP constable to be asked back into the mission and be trusted to take control of such a sensitive territory as Mitrovica was the biggest compliment the UN could have given me. I was quite shocked, nevertheless, I knew I would not let anyone down.'

When Davie arrived in Mitrovica RHQ the out-going Regional Commander still had ten days left in mission which suited the wee man fine. In the interim period Davie was deployed to E-Force and made sure no one in Mitrovica, other than the Regional Commander and the Chief of Admin, knew he was to become the new Regional Commander. Davie knew all about E-Force from his previous mission in Peja/Pec and wanted to see for himself how the Mitrovica E-Force operated.

During his first night shift Davie sat in a Coca Cola the whole night. His two patrol colleagues never once left the vehicle to carry out a VCP, a foot patrol or to check any locals who were out on the streets at odd hours during the night. On his first morning shift at the static point on the main bridge, again no one left the vehicle. There was absolutely no interaction with the local citizens or the KPS.

After a few shifts Davie realised his team leader was never present during the shift, only at the start and the end of the shift and that was when he could be found in his office. Davie said, 'After a couple of days I visited my team leader and asked why we don't get out of the vehicle and check cars crossing over the main bridge and did he think we could improve on anything whilst working in the mission?' The team leader's answer didn't impress Davie: 'The UN will never change anything and why should we do any work when the local police don't?'

Davie replied to the team leader, 'It's the UN who takes the lead in Mitrovica. The KPS hasn't transitioned here and we should be leading the way and helping to improve the new police service.' The team leader just laughed and said no one is going to make any difference here.

Davie then said, 'I hope I can, I'll be appointed the new Regional Commander on Friday. I'll see you then at the morning briefing'. At that point Davie departed the team leader's office.

That Friday the outgoing Regional Commander introduced Davie who immediately made a few changes to E-Force including the dismissal of one or two team leaders.

During one morning shift Davie sent for me and Marty and had some good news. The jobs he had previously mentioned were now up for grabs and if we wanted a day job it was time to start studying for the job interviews and tests. I just realised then, I'd never been interviewed for any of the previous positions I'd held with UNMIK which made me feel rather nervous. What made me more nervous was, unlike the questions for the TULO's position, I'd never had access to any of the questions for Regional Crime positions. During our 'meeting' with Davie I couldn't stop laughing when he said, 'Too many people have the answers to the question papers, so I've set my own bank of questions.'

Davie assured me and Marty, unless we were completely stupid, we wouldn't have any problems scoring high during our questionnaire test paper. Our success really depended on how well we conducted ourselves during the interview. I'd heard that two other CIVPOL officers were also to be interviewed and I was told both were detective inspectors with their home force.

The day of my interview came days after Davie's wee pep talk. I can honestly say I got a grilling from a panel of three supervisory CIVPOL officers. I can also say I impressed myself with my answers to a few of those questions, which were a little different to the questions I thought I was going to be asked. After the interviews, recommendations were made to Davie McLean on who was more suited to the positions applied for. Lucky for me Davie had the final say.

On 20 January 2008 I was redeployed to Mitrovica Regional Crime Unit as the new Deputy Regional Commander Investigation Monitor (DRCIM) and third in command in the Mitrovica region. Oh, Marty was also redeployed. He got the TULO job.

Martin Walsh, Mariyan Dimitrov, Alaksander Markovic, Me and Kani

CHAPTER TWENTY-EIGHT
Finding My Feet

MY FIRST COUPLE of days at Regional Crime were spent in the company of my predecessor, an American CIVPOL officer, Harold Walker, whose end of mission was days away. Harold introduced me to five AAs who worked in the same office as he did and who were also kept extremely busy. Four of the AAs were Albanian and the other told me he was Yugoslavian. I was also introduced to a Danish CIVPOL officer Jan Ravnholt (General Crime Monitor) who also worked in that office and at times shared my workload. Jan was a very experienced detective in his home country and after previously working alongside an MDP sergeant, Dave Mitchell, he knew a little about the MDP and how it functioned. Jan also knew I was a constable who worked on a nuclear base, nevertheless, he never questioned my appointment or my supervisory position.

I also met my KPS counterparts who were a female Serbian Major (Olga Stefanovic) and a Albanian Captain (Arsim Krasniqi). I completed quarterly Managerial Skills Assessments on both officers and submitted my reports through the KMIS.

Incidentally, I was very surprised, yet proud, to see my five police competency headings now incorporated into the KMIS and used mission-wide by every monitor.

Regional Crime had around forty KPS officers, including just seven Serbian and several supervisory ranks (heads of departments) that were monitored by four other CIVPOL officers. Those CIVPOL monitors were mentors to KPS supervisors from Regional Intelligence, Forensics, Specialised Crime and General Crime. The CIVPOL monitors were under my command and I'm glad to say, after a little coaching, they submitted quality monitor reports and never complained about anything. In contrast to my previous mission, I was now working in a department where the majority of police officers were KPS. The attitude of KPS officers and the CIVPOL officers was superb. No in-house squabbles or complainers.

As I had absolutely no experience in serious criminal investigations I was happy just to observe and learn how each department worked and tried to look like I knew what was going on. I visited various crime departments and introduced myself to the CIVPOL monitors and as many KPS investigators and supervisors as I could.

Although I was very confident about monitoring my counterparts and submitting monitoring reports on their performance, I was a bit wary of what I may be faced with during any major incidents. In other words I wasn't looking forward to attending bloody crime scenes where I might be confronted with dead and quite possibly mutilated bodies. It was usually Arsim who I monitored as he went about his business at the scene of a crime. Olga was more of a delegator than an investigator.

AA Jelena and Mariyan

It was just days after I became the DRCIM when, for the first time, I, along with Arsim, attended a crime scene (in North Mitrovica) where a body had been found after an apparent suicide; an elderly Serbian farmer was found dead by his daughter. When I arrived at the farm the farmer's wife, daughter and her two children were standing outside the farmhouse. The daughter had found her father, in a barn, with a noose around his neck and hanging from a wooden beam.

I didn't go into the barn. I felt if I did the family would think I was gloating; ridiculous really. I was part of a criminal investigation unit. It was part of the job to examine crime scenes along with my counterpart, however, that day I chose not to. It was probably the humane side of me coming out rather than my criminal investigative police skills, which I obviously didn't have much of. I observed from a distance and monitored Arsim and the KPS specialists, as they went about their job.

Arsim, who speaks good English and Serbian, asked the deceased's wife if he could see the farmer's everyday footwear, as he had been found bare foot, which I thought was a bit odd. I followed the woman and Arsim to the porch of the farmhouse and found numerous pairs of boots and shoes neatly stacked in a plastic shoe rack. I immediately thought of Pat Kearney and his encounter with that 'wee granny'. One pair of muddy boots and one pair of shoes belonging to the farmer were found which seemed to satisfy Arsim.

Arsim then asked to see the farmer's Serbian identity card and, after removing our footwear, the farmer's wife led us to a bedroom. The bedroom was extremely small with one single bed and one small wardrobe. Hanging outside the wardrobe was a neatly pressed two-piece black suit and on the floor, below the suit, was a pair of polished black brogue shoes.

The farmer's wife took the identity card from the wardrobe drawer and handed it to Arsim. The woman then left the room and stood with me by the bedroom door. Arsim was now looking around the room; I never asked why. I kept quiet and the woman cried quietly by my side.

To be honest I could have quite easily shared a tear in the woman's sorrow. I had to learn to control those emotional thoughts and get on with my job.

Around one hour later the crime unit had finished its investigation and were satisfied the death was indeed a suicide and reported it as such.

After that tragic suicide I attended many other serious incidents where I experienced distressing and upsetting situations; nevertheless, I also had a job to do.

CHAPTER TWENTY-NINE
The Wee Man

IN BETWEEN ATTENDING gruesome crime scenes and pursuing baddies I always found time to visit Davie McLean. My office in RHQ was directly below the Regional Commanders and when he wasn't busy I usually paid Davie a visit for a coffee and to listen to his amusing tales.

He may have been an MDP police constable with probably not that much more experience than me, however, the laid back Davie McLean was extremely confident and was never scared to tackle any situation or take full responsibility for and stand by any decisions he made.

I knew Davie had that prior mission experience in the Peja/Pec region, however, it wasn't until we met in Mitrovica in 2007 that I really got the chance to speak to him about that period of time.

Davie was deployed to Peja/Pec Region in June 2004 and was assigned as a patrol officer. From patrol he was redeployed to Peja Regional Operations and later became Chief of Operations. His hard work earned him the position as Peja Deputy Regional Commander and ultimately Regional Commander. MDP Constable Davie McLean's huge leap from CIVPOL patrol officer to Peja/Pec Regional Commander occurred within his two short years and first Kosovo secondment. Weeks after his second Kosovo secondment, he was appointed Mitrovica Regional Commander. Agree or Disagree, that was the UN's non-ranking mission (and unusual system) for you.

Davie told me one amusing story when he was a patrol office in Peja/Pec that had a rather stinking ending.

> 'On one night shift I and a KPS Sergeant Javid Muccli, were conducting a VCP and I told Javid I would stop and check the next vehicle. It wasn't long before a vehicle, a small Yugo, approached the VCP and I could see sparks coming from the underside of the car as it crossed over the railway line just ahead of us. I signalled for the car to pull in and to my surprise and shock there was a cow with its legs tied together lying inside the car. Cow dung was splattered all over the inside of the car and as it stopped I quickly stepped to one side and moved the car on.

Javid knew the driver and told me he was a farmer and that's how he moved his cattle around. You learn something new every day.'

As the Regional Commander of Mitrovica, Davie seemed to have created a more ambient atmosphere than I remembered from my last mission in Mitrovica. No arguments at the morning briefings and plenty of one liner jokes from Davie. Once he took his position at the end of that very long conference room table, there was complete silence from a respectful audience. Davie was very much a hands-on Regional Commander and during February and March 2008, he was a very busy man.

On 17 February 2008, the Assembly of Kosovo held a session during which it adopted a 'declaration of independence', declaring Kosovo an independent and Sovereign State. The declaration stated that Kosovo fully accepted the obligations of the Comprehensive Proposal for the Kosovo Status Settlement.

Prime Minister Hashim Thaci stated that there would be equal opportunities for all of Kosovo's inhabitants and that discrimination against members of minority communities would be eliminated. The declaration also pledged that Kosovo would adhere to UN resolution 1244 and would commit itself to working constructively with the United Nations. One hundred and nine out of 120 Assembly members present voted in favour of the declaration. The ten Serbian deputies of the Kosovo Assembly did not attend the session.

The authorities in Belgrade and Serbians condemned the declaration of independence. On 18 February, Boris Tadic, President of Serbia, informed the Secretary-General of the United Nations that Serbia had adopted a decision stating that the declaration of independence by Kosovo represents a forceful and unilateral secession of a part of the territory of Serbia, and does not produce any legal effect either in Serbia or in the international legal order.

The Serbians reacted to the declaration of independence by holding daily, largely peaceful protests in several areas in Kosovo where Serbians live, including North Mitrovica; however some protests turned violent, particularly in the north part of Kosovo. On 19 February the two boundaries at Gate 1 and Gate 31 were attacked and destroyed by a small group of violent demonstrators.

During the protests, which took place at exactly 12:44 pm (in reference to UN resolution 1244), at the Mitrovica main bridge, Davie McLean summoned CIVPOL officers from Regional Crime (me included) and Regional Traffic (Marty Walsh) to reinforce the security of the bridge.

The first day I stood waiting for those protesters I thought back to the Poll Tax riots in the UK during the 1990s when the demonstrators went on the rampage and gave several police officers a good hiding. At 12:44, and before they reached the bridge, I could hear the noise from the masses around 200 yards away and I could see the tops of many Serbian flags as they appeared over a hill. As the protestors marched down the hill towards the bridge I couldn't see the end of the procession. I could see the end of my life; I was scared; I was very scared. Not even the number of UNMIK police and KFOR (over one hundred) was making me feel any better. I just had to get on with my job and try to remain focused. There was no time for panicking.

The 1244 demo

I wore as much protection as I was able to acquire and shook behind a shield which, when grounded, protected my legs and nothing else. When more than a thousand screaming protesters were no more than a few yards from the line of CIVPOL and KPS standing on the bridge the rocks and fireworks started to fly towards us. I held my shield up and luckily most missiles were easily deflected. One small rock was thrown directly at my face, however, my ballistic helmet's visor came to my rescue. I was hit a few times during those daily protests which I attended for a week and thankfully the crowds never became more violent than throwing a few rocks and setting off fireworks.

One significant change brought about by Kosovo's declaration of independence was a 'walk out' by the Serbian KPS officers who worked in the south part of

Kosovo. The Serbian KPS officers working in Mitrovica RHQ refused to work on the South side of Mitrovica and after 17 February 2008, reported for duty in North Mitrovica. My Serbian counterpart Major Stefanovic set up an office in North Station and never returned to RHQ. She was later transferred to the KPS training school.

In the South part of Kosovo several hundred Serbian KPS officers who refused to cooperate or report for duty were suspended.

On 14 March, after staging (daily) peaceful demonstrations outside the court in North Mitrovica that prevented ethnic Albanian court employees from entering the court, numerous Serbians broke into the building and started a four day sit-in. Negotiations by UN officials, to end the sit-in protest failed and on 17 March, exactly four years after the March 2004 riots, UNMIK police with the assistance of KFOR entered the courthouse in a pre-dawn raid.

Whilst that operation was taking place I was sound asleep and once again my radio was switched off. I was awoken at 7 am by a phone call from Marty Walsh. All Marty said was, 'It's kicked off big time at the court, meet me in ten minutes at Zvecan station.'

Riot cops

Less than ten minutes later I was with Marty and a number of other nervous looking CIVPOL officers. On my way to Zvecan station I'd been catching bits of a three-way conversation on my radio between officers from MHQ, Davie McLean and Ground Commander (American CIVPOL and Regional Intelligence monitor) Randy Darty. Randy was yelling that police officers were being bombarded with rocks and Molotov cocktails and now hand grenades were being thrown and exploding around the exposed police and KFOR units.

From Randy's transmissions it was obvious UN personnel were being severely injured by the lethal projectiles. Randy asked for permission to use lethal force and it was granted immediately; I was shocked. When radio transmissions were being made to MHQ control I could hear bursts from automatic gun fire. I could also hear the whistling sounds and explosions from the missiles as they landed. I learned later the automatic gun fire came from KFOR and the attacking demonstrators.

Not long after my arrival at Zvecan, a Coca Cola vehicle came hammering towards the station with four CIVPOL inside. They were part of the prisoner escort unit form Pristina and had fled Mitrovica chased by a number of people with firearms. Luckily they found their way to the relative safety of Zvecan police station.

A decision was then made (don't know who by) to get out of North Mitrovica. With all windows open in my 4Runner and my pistol drawn (like all my colleagues) we set off in convoy to the UN log base in South Mitrovica. We used the back road out of North Mitrovica to avoid the mayhem taking place at the courthouse. Once at the log base we were given instructions, passed on from MHQ to remain in South Mitrovica.

Stand-off

The situation at the courthouse got out of hand when hundreds of Serbians obstructed the Prisoner Escort convey as they attempted to leave the area of the court with the detainees. Before UN reinforcements were brought to the court the arresting officers were attacked by the ever-growing crowd of protesters, who had amassed outside both the front and back entrances to the court. About half of the court demonstrators who had been arrested were freed by protesters during the clashes, with the rest being transported to the detention centre in Pristina for questioning.

Both entrances to the court building (which is adjacent to North Station) had been blocked by hundreds of protesters, civilian vehicles and also, inadvertently I might add, by KFOR armoured vehicles when they arrived at the scene. Those blockades resulted in emergency vehicles being stranded at the court with seriously injured casualties.

Eventually the situation was brought under control when most of the crowd of demonstrators dispersed and retreated further down King Peter Street. Small factions remained in nearby areas and became observers.

Once a passage from the courthouse was cleared, with assistance from KFOR and their heavy armoured vehicles an evacuation route leading to South Mitrovica was identified. Although it was the shortest way back to the south side it was the most dangerous route to take. With small crowds continuing to loiter around the area, the fleet of emergency vehicles would have to face a gauntlet of missile-

Someone's sons on the north side of the main bridge

throwing demonstrators. To assist with the evacuation one main street had to be kept clear and secured whilst the emergency vehicles escaped from the north.

Back at the log base Marty and I had teamed up together and decided to have a drive around South Mitrovica. I drove to the main bridge and parked at the South end. About ten minutes after arriving at the bridge we heard Davie McLean on the radio, he was asking MHQ control for another back-up unit as his, the Italian Carabinieri, had just driven off and left him and one colleague exposed, in the middle of a street which they were trying to keep clear for casualty evacuation.

Davie had taken it upon himself to assist in his injured colleagues' evacuation by attending and securing that main street backed up by the Carabinieri. Travis Hawkinson also accompanied Davie and now, for reasons unknown, both CIVOL officers had been abandoned.

I didn't hesitate or wait for MHQ to reply to Davie's request. I was already on my way with Marty to Davie's location which was located in the lower part of Little Bosnia. Just before a crossroads in Little Bosnia I spotted Davie's White 4Runner – every window had been smashed or shattered. I parked my vehicle behind Davie's and when Marty and I approached the vehicle we saw hundreds of live rounds from an AK47 scattered around the driver and passenger footwell.

Pistols drawn, we carefully stepped into the street where we knew Davie was, and across the road, kneeling behind a concrete street lamp, looking through the sights of an AK47 which was trained on the street up ahead, was the wee man.

The result of a petrol bomb

Travis, also with an AK47, was taking cover inside a disused building on the opposite side of the road from Davie.

Davie shouted across at us to stay under cover as he thought he spotted snipers on a high rise building about 100 yards up the road. Although Davie's cover was concrete it didn't give him full cover from sight. He really was quite exposed. Five minutes after our arrival three other CIVPOL arrived, Van Williams, Ron Henderson and a Turkish CIVPOL officer Halit Bulanikli.

Although we were also exposed with no cover at all, it was necessary to stop and search a number of passing civilian vehicles. Reports had reached us, civilian vehicles were being used to transport weapons around North Mitrovica. As we conducted those vehicle searches we relied on Davie and Travis to warn us of any other suspicious activity around that area. It wasn't a nice feeling knowing that a sniper or anyone else for that matter could take a pop at me or my colleagues. We were in fact sitting ducks but we had a job to do.

Finally those emergency vehicles appeared and roared past us towards the crossroads. Most of the windows in the half dozen or so vehicles had been smashed and I could see many officers with bandages covering their heads and arms. Due to a long wait, blood had started to seep through most of their dressings. All the vehicles made it safely back to the log base.

It later transpired, the Carabinieri left Davie and Travis to assist an Italian colleague who had apparently been threatened in his accommodation by a crowd of angry Serbians.

The violence had ended around early afternoon and tragically one Ukrainian police officer was killed when his femoral artery was severed by a grenade blast. Later reports suggested one Serbian citizen was also killed and around 70 Serbians and 61 UNMIK police and KFOR personnel wounded. Unconfirmed reports also claimed KFOR snipers and Serbian snipers were responsible for the sporadic bursts of automatic gun fire.

I read one report which claimed one UN vehicle and one NATO truck were set ablaze. I would argue with that statement. I would say a lot more people were injured. And I saw more than one UN vehicle ablaze, along with one civilian car and one civilian coach. Among the wounded UNMIK police and military personnel were officers from Poland and Ukraine and French KFOR soldiers. On the same day as the riots UNMIK police withdrew from North Mitrovica, leaving the area under the temporary control of KFOR.

In the weeks that followed the courthouse incident I viewed a video (and not for public viewing), which showed just what the UNMIK police units and KFOR were up against as they tried to prevent the screaming crowds breaching the security of the entrance gates leading to North Station and the court building.

Groups of UNMIK FPUs led by KFOR stood their ground at those main gates as missile after missile rained down on them. As the officers fell down injured they were dragged to safety by colleagues and replaced by other colleagues who faced the same fate. It was impossible to distinguish between a rock and a grenade. The flying missiles bounced off FPU riot shields only to land and explode in the middle of other FPU lines.

A nearby gas station supplied the fuel for the Molotov cocktails which were never in short supply. Other weapons used by the demonstrators were highly powerful slingshots which were fired off multiple missiles.

Watching those UNMIK police officers taking a pounding I couldn't understand why an order wasn't given to allow them to retreat back to a safer area, which was less than fifty yards from those main gates and which would have afforded them better cover and protection.

On a personal note I think the timing of the courthouse (arrest) operation was all wrong. To organise the operation and have it carried out exactly four years to the day of the 17 March riots in 2004 was just rubbing the Serbians up the wrong way.

CHAPTER THIRTY
The Three Musketeers

AS SOON AS those emergency vehicles passed, Davie thanked those officers present for their support and at that point Van, Ron and Halit headed to the log base. Davie swept the glass from his vehicle, gathered up the loose AK47 rounds and then drove back to his office, closely followed by me, Marty and Travis. Once back inside his office Davie hung the AK47 back on the wall from where he had taken it. The AK47 Travis carried was returned to the Regional Crime evidence locker. Scenes like those could only happen in Kosovo. No more was ever mentioned about two CIVPOL officers armed with AK47 assault rifles.

We sat in Davie's office reflecting on the day's events and wondering when we'd be allowed to return to our accommodation in the north. Davie's phone rang constantly with concerned officers asking for information on injured colleagues and others asking when it would be safe to return to their accommodation. One person who never contacted 'me' (I can't speak for anyone else) on that day was the UK Contingent Commander. I thought he may have been a little concerned for my welfare.

One of the phone calls Davie received was from MHQ; the arrested demonstrators were to be released and transported back to Mitrovica. A drop-off point was established and it was to be at the crossroads in Little Bosnia. We were very surprised. That crossroads is like a boundary line where South Mitrovica ends and the North begins. Davie expected trouble from the Albania community.

The constant ringing of Davie's phones caused Marty and I to let the wee man get on with his business and we headed to Marty's office. Later that day we heard messages on the radio regarding a number of UN vehicles approaching the Mitrovica region and thought it must be the Serbian detainees being returned to the north.

Marty's office was very close to Little Bosnia and we decided to drive down to the crossroads just to monitor the situation. When we arrived in Little Bosnia Davie was there with Randy Darty.

Crowds had gathered on the streets on either side of the crossroads and the Albanians were beginning to surround and jostle Davie and Randy. Apparently the Albanians didn't want the returning Serbian court official to be dropped off in Little Bosnia and the UNMIK police presence wasn't welcome either. The crowd continued to jostle Davie and Randy, and Marty and I pushed our way through the crowd to join and assist our colleagues. The Serbians standing on the other side of the crossroads stood in silence waiting on their 'heroes' and just watched what was going on in front of them.

The Albanians started to shout at us and one in particular, a young boy, was really stirring things up. He was ready for a fight and challenged Randy. Randy stayed cool and tried to calm the boy down. More Albanians appeared and crowded round us; by now we were completely surrounded and massively outnumbered. I knew it would only take one crazed person to start swinging punches and the rest would follow.

We had no chance of fighting our way out of that situation and any thought of using any sort of force was out of the question. Drawing batons or a firearm would have been ludicrous; we'd have been dead in seconds if that crowd saw that type of force.

I don't mind saying, I was petrified; I really did think I was going to be beaten to death. This wasn't some peaceful demonstration at Coulport by members of the CND, where they just lie down and become noncompliant if arrested. This crowd was savage and baying for our blood. For a second I thought about the movie *Zombie Flesh Eaters* and started to realise we were easy picking for that blood-seeking crowd. We were a few scared and anxious cops and that crowd knew it.

Randy was still trying to calm people down when I noticed a man, dressed in a suit, charging towards the crowd. He was punching and knocking down everyone that stood in his way and when others noticed him the circle of people broke away and quickly dispersed, making his passage to us clear. The young boy who challenged Randy stood his ground looking at the man; however, the man grabbed him and dragged him behind a building. Five minutes later the man reappeared, alone.

He then walked towards Randy and shook his hand. He was one of Randy's KPS colleagues from the Mitrovica Regional Intelligence Unit. Apparently he's a KPS officer who is not to be messed with. I got the feeling it wasn't just the fact he was a KPS officer that had the crowd fleeing from his unconventional crowd dispersal methods.

When the transport started to arrive with the released court officials they were greeted by a crowd of cheering Serbians. The KPS officer remained with us until all the court officials returned and had been transported back to the north. The remainder of that day passed without incident.

Davie, Marty and I spent the next few hours in Davie's office, drinking mint vodka and downing cans of cider. I've never enjoyed an alcoholic drink so much.

That same night I waited in Davie's office until dark and then returned to the north. After only one day UNMIK police resumed its patrols in North Mitrovica. The courthouse reopened on 3 October 2008.

Not long after the court building incident Davie McLean was contacted by ITV Four, from the UK, which asked for his permission to film in Mitrovica as part of their highly acclaimed TV series *Toughest Cops*, presented by ex-footballer and actor Vinnie Jones.

Davie was filmed over a couple of days and featured in the TV show describing what it was like to command in one of Europe's most violent cities. Davie described Mitrovica as 'a modern day Northern Ireland'. He also said his job is a hobby and to be in it is a buzz.

At the UK medal parade held not long after the court building incident I was presented with a 'Letter of Appreciation' signed by Joachim Rucker, *Special Representative to the Secretary General*, and Iver Frigaard, *Acting Police Commissioner*. I was also presented with a 'Letter of Commendation' signed by Davie McLean and the Ground Commander Randal Darty.

Here is what was written in the letter of appreciation:

> 'In recognition of valuable contributions to the people of Kosovo, their fellow International Police Officers and the United Nations Mission in Kosovo.
>
> To the United Kingdom Police Officers who gave above and beyond the call of duty for the safety and security of all on March 17, 2008 in North Mitrovica and for their courageous performance in the most difficult circumstances and the sacrifices they made.
>
> You have honoured all by your presence and shown your dedication to duty, honour and the respect for all life regardless of race, ethnicity, religion or gender. We give to you our heartfelt thanks and respect for the sacrifices made by all of the officers of this unit in order to ensure law and order during this time of need.'

These are the words from the letter of commendation:

> 'On March 17, 2008, the UNMIK – Police initiated an operation to retake the Mitrovica Courthouse from Serbian activists who had stormed the courthouse four days earlier.

Within minutes of securing the courthouse and making arrests, a hostile crowd began to gather and attacks on UNMIK and KFOR personal began. The officers assigned to the courthouse operation were targeted by subjects firing automatic weapons and throwing hand grenades and Molotov cocktails.

During the attack on UNMIK – P and KFOR – there were numerous injuries, most of which were caused by shrapnel from exploding hand grenades. The Ground Commander advised that there 20–30 injured Officers and Soldiers in the courthouse who urgently needed evacuation to medical facilities. Before the evacuation could begin, a key intersection that had been subjected to Kalashnikov and hand grenade fire, had to be secured.

After waiting an inordinate amount of time for KFOR assistance at that intersection, Mitrovica Regional Commander requested back up assistance to provide a safe passage for the injured colleagues. Shortly thereafter, a convoy containing nearly 30 injured UN personnel was able to move thru the intersection and evacuate to medical facilities in the south.

The action taken by Officer John Duncanson assisting in securing one of the intersections was above and beyond the call of duty and directly facilitated the removal of seriously wounded Officers and Soldiers. Conduct exemplified what being a Police Officer is all about. The courage he displayed is admirable and is an example for others to follow. I am proud to commend him for display of valour and leadership.'

CHAPTER THIRTY-ONE
Coping

NOW GETTING BACK to my day job: over those eleven short months with Regional Crime I attended a number of appalling crime scenes with Captain Krasniqi which included five murders, two attempted murders, three suicides, two deaths from natural causes and numerous grenade attacks on official buildings and private homes; more than enough serious and fatal incidents during my short reign as Deputy Regional Commander Investigations Monitor.

I don't want to go into detail about every incident I attended or how I was affected, however, I have chosen a few which will give you an idea of what I, 'The glorified security guard' from Coulport, faced and from a personal and emotional point of view, had to deal with.

One sudden death involved a thirty-year-old woman who was found dead in her bed by her estranged husband. When I arrived at the woman's home I was met by Randy Darty and directed to the bedroom. For some reason Randy usually joined me at crime scenes. What I saw next really did shake me; the woman (who died of natural causes) was nine months pregnant. My immediate thought was 'Could the unborn child be saved?' I didn't want to appear to be naive or stupid so I kept quiet and said nothing.

When I was researching for the book I read a story where, after being killed in a car accident, an eight months pregnant woman's body was taken to hospital where the staff delivered the unborn child. The child survived.

I attended another suicide where a young teenager's body was found wedged inside a ground level (circular) water well, which was about the same circumference as an old dustbin lid. The body, which was around twelve feet below ground level, was found by a family member submerged just below the water level.

When I arrived at the scene the water level had dropped and I could see the young boy's head. His arms were by his side and he was well and truly wedged in the well. It looked like the boy entered the well with his arms at his side knowing he would be wedged under water with little chance of freeing his arms had he changed his mind about ending his life.

SAME PLANET, DIFFERENT WORLDS

On a personal note, I thought it could have been more sinister than a suicide, however, the family told the KPS officers present the lad tried three times to join his girlfriend in Germany but was always refused a visa by the German authorities. The KPS officer in charge of the investigation, who was not Arsim Krasniqi, came to the conclusion and was satisfied that the lad was depressed and wanted to end his life. I followed up that investigation and nothing came back from the autopsy report to indicate foul play.

An off-duty KPS officer came to Mitrovica South Station and reported her husband, also a KPS officer, had committed suicide by shooting himself in the head with his service pistol. During extensive enquiries the female KPS officer was suspected of murdering her husband but it was never proved. I sat in on two interviews with that KPS officer and couldn't make up my mind whether she was innocent or guilty; she never showed any type of emotion during those interviews. One incident which disturbed me more than the others and still does today occurred during a Saturday evening.

I was on call 24/7 and during the evening, with my radio switched on, I received a message to attend a fatal shooting incident which had taken place in a built up area on a minor highway. One person had been shot and killed while he drove his private vehicle and one suspect was in custody. The body of the victim had not yet been removed.

When I attended a serious incident I was rarely accompanied by an AA, I didn't want to subject them to any bloody and traumatic crime scene. Arsim's English was good enough, so he was usually my interpreter.

I arrived at a police cordon around one hundred yards from the incident and had to pass a number of vehicles that were queuing and waiting to pass. I parked my vehicle just outside the cordon and was met by Arsim who'd been waiting for me. Before I went anywhere near the vehicle Arsim explained what had allegedly happened.

The suspect who did not leave the crime scene after the shooting, and waited for the police to arrive, claimed responsibility for the murder by firing and emptying one full magazine of rounds (thirty) from an AK47 into the vehicle, a black BMW. No reason was given for the suspect's actions.

When I approached the vehicle I noticed most of the bullets had penetrated the front passenger window and door. It appeared the suspect had opened fire as he hid behind some bushes on the opposite side of the road. I shone a torch inside the front of the vehicle and saw the victim; a man in his forties. He sat upright in his driving position but both blooded hands were resting on his thighs.

He wore a denim jacket and jeans and thick blood seeped out slowly from both his jacket sleeves and dripped from the bottom of his jeans. His denim jacket was beginning to seep blood and the footwell on the driver's side was thick with very dark blood. His greying hair showed specks of blood and, although he had been hit on the forehead, I don't remember seeing a lot of blood around his head or face.

As I stared at the unfamiliar and gruesome scene I was oblivious to the KPS officers and people around me, including the inquisitive householders who the KPS were failing to usher back to their homes. I had no idea what anyone expected of me; Arsim seemed to be letting me take the lead. I was clueless. I've never managed such a crime scene like that one. I continued to shine my torch in the vehicle searching for inspiration then thinking, 'What do I do now?' I could only think of a forensic examination and then suddenly I realised there was no prosecutor at the crime scene which is normal practice under Kosovo law. I asked Arsim if the prosecutor had been notified and he had, he was on his way. I then said, 'Let's wait on the prosecutor.' I couldn't think of anything else to say.

I remained at the scene with Arsim until the prosecutor arrived and he was happy for the case to proceed. Arsim was happy to take over after the prosecutor left and I was happy to do what I thought I did best, monitor!

When I went home and got into bed I couldn't get the dead man out of my mind. He had been shot to pieces and most of the AK47 rounds appeared to have found their target. His still and lifeless body and the dripping blood still haunt me today.

I attended other crime scenes where bodies lay where they were murdered and I never got used to that part of my job. Arsim took his job in his stride and never showed any type of emotion; me, I became a good actor.

Apart from the gory sights, I did enjoy my job with Regional Crime, it was a good learning curve. I also worked in a good unit with good people and didn't have to deal with the pressures or aggravation of supervising a large group of uncooperative CIVPOL officers.

My last couple of months with Regional Crime were relatively busy when I attended and monitored the situation during an incident in North Mitrovica between a group of Serbians and Albanians when (on 27 August), around 100 Serbians and 70 Albanians clashed in the ethnically-mixed Three Towers area. Although there were large numbers, the incident passed quickly and no arrests were made. Only minor injuries were sustained.

On 30 October, in the Kroi Vitaku area of North Mitrovica an attempt by a group of Albanians to initiate preparations for the reconstruction of their homes without UNMIK authorisation led to clashes with a group of Serbians. UNMIK police and subsequently KFOR, intervened to restore order. In con-nection with this incident, gunshots were exchanged in the vicinity between groups of Albanians and Serbians. No injuries were reported. I was in the area when the shootings occurred and had to take cover in a disused building for around thirty minutes before the shooting stopped. No arrests were made during or after that incident.

Not long before the end of that UN mission I received a letter from the European Union explaining my application for a secondment to EULEX was successful and I had secured a position as Advisor to KPS station Operations, which was advisor to the KPS Deputy Station Commander. That position was not one of my three EULEX choices, but it made me think my previous UN experience may have influenced the EU's decision in offering me the secondment. I was extremely lucky, a few of my contingent were not successful at that time, including Mel Goudie, who was an MDP Chief Inspector and the UK Contingent Commander. I'm sure one of the positions Mel applied for was offered to an MDP constable, how ironic.

Before I started my UN checkout and EULEX check in, I was sitting in Davie's office having a coffee with him and Marty. I remember that day vividly. I sat in that office looking at the table in the corner where, not so long ago, I sat like a sheepish wee school boy being punished by the school headmaster. I had been the supervisor to over 200 UN staff and in a matter of seconds my senior status had been swiped from beneath me.

Thanks to Davie McLean I spent eleven months in a good unit and enjoyed every minute of it. I started thinking, we are three MOD police constables mainly responsible for protecting Britain's nuclear deterrent; a job which brings no real pressure to speak of, little decision-making skills required and no screaming crowds of angry mobs who want our blood. Now here we are, big chiefs in a post-war Kosovo; Davie McLean, a Regional Commander, responsible for the supervision and welfare of hundreds of UN staff in one of Europe's most volatile cities; John Duncanson, a deputy Regional Commander (monitor) of a Regional Investigation Crime unit responsible for over forty KPS officers and CIVPOL monitors; and Martin Walsh, the responsible monitor for the Mitrovica Regional Traffic Unit with over fifty traffic officers. And not forgetting Davie Hutton who was Zvecan KPS Station Commander Liaison Officer. Although we were all, apart from Davie McLean, monitors, our counterparts considered us their senior supervisor who made – well should I say 'most' – of the important decisions. I'm sure it was our Scottish braun that helped us achieve so much with that UN mission.

One position which I agreed to fill on a temporary basis was Mitrovica Temporary Deputy Regional Commander. That temporary post came about by certain events which left several senior CIVPOL officers with shiny red faces and that's all you're getting on that issue.

Due to officers taking CTO I actually found myself in the terrifying position (my opinion) as Mitrovica Acting Regional Commander. The first day I sat in the Regional Commander's chair my mind was racing. I was responsible for the whole region, all the UNMIK police officers, all the KPS officers and all the Administrative Assistants. I was King of the castle. Not bad for a former shipyard welder from Drumchapel. Luckily the week passed without serious incident.

On 23 November 2009, I started my first day of a one-week induction course with EULEX. After that week I was deployed to Peja/Pec region and became advisor to the KPS station Operations/Deputy Station Commander at Istog/Istok police station. What should have been a one-year secondment to EULEX, was cut short (apparently due to financial constraints) and in April 2009 I returned to the UK and my big cage. In 2010 I managed to escape from Coulport after being transferred to a small MDP unit based in Bacton (Norfolk). My new job title was Authorised Firearms Officer. In June 2012 I retired from the force after serving twenty-two years and two months.

Taking a break

PART FIVE

THE MINISTRY OF DEFENCE POLICE CHIEF CONSTABLES

THE MINISTRY OF DEFENCE POLICE CHIEF CONSTABLES

WHATEVER THE REASONS and expectations for individual MDP constables (and of course other ranks) volunteering for the UN overseas mission to Kosovo, I'm sure many of us never expected to be supervising and managing UNMIK departments including, police teams, police stations and of course like Davie McLean, police regions.

This last section of the book looks at a few of my former colleagues (some already mentioned) who achieved supervisory status and who helped make this book possible by telling me about their mission experiences and who, like me, worked at an MOD establishment where their day to day job is or was repetitive and boring.

PAT KEARNEY
Mission Dates:
June 2001 – December 2002
June 2004 – June 2006
June 2007 – June 2009

I have already mentioned Pat during our first mission and during that eighteen month period with UNMIK Pat's professionalism and dedication to the KPS and all round hard work didn't go unnoticed. By the end of the mission Pat was a well-respected Station Commander of Station Four.

At the start of his second mission in June 2004, Pat was immediately headhunted by an MDP Colleague, John Kane, who was Regional Commander in the city of Gjilan/Gnjilane. After another compulsory UN induction week Pat was, at John's request, deployed from the UN training centre to the municipality of Ferizaj/Urosevac, very close to Gjilan.

Ferizaj is 24 miles south of Pristina and the third most populous city in Kosovo after Pristina and Prizren. The municipality covers an area of 133 square miles, including the city of Ferizaj and has forty-five villages. Its population is estimated at 108,690 mainly Albanian. Following the Kosovo war, the city had seen serious inter-communal unrest which resulted in almost all of the Serbian and non-Albanian inhabitants being expelled or fleeing. On Pat's arrival in Ferizaj he was immediately installed at Ferizaj police station as Station Commander. The appointment into Station Command directly from the UN initial induction week was relatively unique, but there again so was Pat Kearney.

It was only after Pat completed that second UN mission and one more after that when I caught up with him for more of his exploits and he didn't disappoint.

During a two-year deployment from 2004 to 2006, all of which was spent in Ferizaj, Pat went from Station Commander to Station Commander Liaison Officer. Again hard work and recognition saw him achieve Deputy Regional Commander Operations and finally Regional Commander Liaison Officer.

When Pat came back into the mission he was still an MDP police constable and I chose to write about an occurrence which saw Pat attend and supervise a car bomb incident.

This is Pat's recollection of events:

'I received a call from Shpend Maxhuni (now KPS Director General) who was Ferizaj KPS Station Commander at the time. Shpend told me a car had been driven through the main glass doors of the new Ben-Af shopping centre, which had only been open a few months. The car was wedged between two checkout counters and, fortunately, no one had been injured.

Initially I thought it was yet another case of idiotic Kosovo driving and almost decided not to attend, however, Shpend's explanation of events didn't sound like the actions of an irresponsible or careless motorist.

I knew Shpend from my first mission, from when he was a patrol officer and followed his rapid rise through the KPS promotion system. I appreciated the fact he listened to my advice and was also a keen and regular participant in my station exercises. I knew he had expectations to succeed in his career.

I was always proud of him and knew he would go far, didn't realise just how far though! Anyhow, I decided to return to Ferizaj and I was near the Bull Ring when I received another call from Shpend's deputy telling me they had received a call that the car was loaded with explosives; obviously this could not be confirmed in anyway but as you know, John, we treat it as such until we know otherwise.

On receiving that call it was blues 'n two's all the way. I think I set a new speed record that night, from Pristina to Ferizaj took me all of 16 mins exactly, normally it was 35 mins. Anyhow I arrived at Ben-Af which is located on the main Pristina highway just past the first turn-off for Ferizaj. I was both pleased and proud to find that Shpend and Qazim (his deputy), both very professional, had the highway shut down from both ends and had routed traffic off the highway and through Ferizaj. They had also established a 500 mtr cordon (which I later extended to 700 mtrs when we later established the vehicle was in fact packed with explosives). They had evacuated local shops and residents also, honestly John, when I say I was proud of the job they had done it is an understatement. I remember briefly thinking to myself that all the hard work, effort and time spent just talking to these guys explaining why we do things and showing them how to do it, well you know yourself mate they were like sponges taking it all in.

Anyhow, when I arrived I made contact with KFOR at Camp Bondsteel and requested the Explosive Ordnance Disposal (EOD) team which arrived within 30 minutes, I established the Forward Control Point (FCP) at the Kacanik (south) side of Pristina highway, my deputy Chad Henson (American) also arrived around this time, I instructed him to organise the CIVPOL officers and have them assist the KPS in cordon security and with the on-going evacuation of local residents.

I was at this time in constant contact with John Kane who was Gnjilane Regional Commander at this time, I remember months after the incident I told him I was surprised that he had not attended that night, his reply kind of surprised me at the time when he said, "You were there Pat and I had every confidence in you."

Anyhow I digress, after the EOD team arrived their wireless-controlled remote robot was put into action, however 150 yards from the shop entrance it stopped functioning. It was recovered and a back-up robot, operated by wire, was utilised.

The second unit was sent in and as it approached the car (red Ford Escort MKII) the windows were shattered, we could see from the remote cam that there appeared to be wires sticking out of the dashboard around where the stereo should have been. A short dialogue ensued as to whether it was a stolen vehicle when suddenly a tiny hint of smoke appeared from the console and within 30 seconds the car was on fire. Ferizaj (Trumpton) fire brigade had been on the scene since almost the beginning and I spoke with their Chief (Hugh, or was it Barney McGrew) and discovered they didn't actually have water in the tender. I couldn't believe it, well I could really. KFOR was contacted again and a Fire Tender was dispatched.

By this time the car and the store were really starting to burn. Shpend actually arrested the Ben-Af General Manager for his own safety. All the manager could see was his store burning and no one doing anything about it. He tried to make his way back to the store and was arrested and taken away from the scene.

By this point the store was fully ablaze and I could hear aerosols going off like roman candles; tins of food were popping and banging like crazy, the flames were licking through the roof and at one point I thought two newly-built stores either side of the Ben-Af would also go up.

One of the store managers, who was also at the FCP, heard me ask the question, "It's a brand new store did they not fit a sprinkler system?" He came forward and said there was but, get this, it was manually operated. Anyhow, the controls for it were housed on the outside wall somewhere on the front of the building. At this point my phone rings, it's John Kane for an update. As I finished briefing John I turned to Chad who had that look on his face, I said "What!" I then noticed about 150 yards over Chad's shoulder, one of the EOD team running towards the store with this guy (a civilian) who was wearing some sort of ballistic head protection. The guy knew where the sprinkler system was and had volunteered to show one of the EOD team where it was. I shouted for him to get back, but he continued towards the store. I was angry when I heard Chad and the EOD team agreed to let the guy help.

As they both approached the main entrance, I'd say about 100 to 120 yards from the front door, BOOOOOOOOOOOM! What an explosion. John, I kid you not, I felt the blast wave hit me full in the chest, almost took me off my feet. Windows shattered in nearby houses and shops, the fireball lit up the night sky for miles. John Kane later told me he heard the blast in Gnjilane.

Within seconds I thought, "Oh no, the EOD guy and the civvy are they dead?" The fire unit from Bondsteel started to tackle the blaze and I ran forward with Chad to find the civvy. He was slightly disorientated by the blast and the EOD guy was unconscious in the middle of the highway. The blast had thrown both of them almost 150 yards away.

The EOD guy, as I said, was unconscious with a broken arm and shrapnel sticking out of his neck. Chad and I started first aid on this guy; I knew that Chad had been a paramedic in the states prior to *joining the police, so I left him to it along with the ambulance crew. I carried on basically coordinating the aftermath etc. But boy what a night that was. We later learned from EOD that they believed it had been a remote detonation more than likely from a mobile phone.*

In the meetings and discussions which took place over the next few days we learned that the Ben-Af store had received several threats since opening, possibly from surrounding businesses who were going to be impacted by its opening.

I have always believed though, as the EOD had mentioned a remote detonation by mobile phone, that the perpetrator was among the crowds that had gathered outside the cordon and when he saw the EOD guy along with the civvy running towards the store, he pressed dial to achieve the result of blowing the car up causing further damage to the store. And also did he spare both lives by pressing dial when they were still over 100 yards from the store? Food for thought.'

During his mission life Pat studied an Open University Course, International Policing and Peace Support Operations through Stirling University and, as a result of his studies, he was invited by a university mentor, Dr Paul Rutherford, to Stirling University to talk with students about his overseas experiences in International Policing.

Pat has been visiting the university for the past three years and has increased his talks to include a PowerPoint presentation followed by a questions and answers session.

I recently found a newspaper article and wasn't surprised to read about Pat Kearney. The article was published by the Kosovo Press and I have taken a snippet from it. The headline read:

Gratitude for a distinguished officer

'On Friday Chairman of Ferizaj, Bajrush Xhemajli, presented Patrick Kearney, former commander of the UNMIK police in Ferizaj with a certificate of gratitude, as a sign of respect for his contribution in the developing processes, with particular emphasis on consolidation, of the local police.'

DAVID RODDEN
Mission Dates:
December 2002 – June 2003
December 2004 – December 2006
December 2007 – December 2008

When Davy Rodden started working at Pristina airport he was assigned to the CIVPOL airport security team and although he had no prior experience in border policing, his general police knowledge and common sense quickly saw him appointed the position of Chief of Airport Security. Davy became responsible for the supervision and administration of around thirty UNMIK police.

The security team's responsibilities were wide and varied, from dealing with pickpockets, traffic management and traffic offences, to detecting and preventing passengers *and* CIVPOL in attempting to carry concealed firearms and contraband through passport control. The team assisted the Traffic and Prostitution Investigation Unit (TPIU) with the return of victims and it provided support for the forced returnees from neighbouring European countries.

The security team also supported customs officers in joint operations and provided close protection for any dignitaries disembarking through the airport VIP area.

After arrests and or detentions, the security team facilitated the transport to the detention centre in Pristina.

It was also the security team's responsibility to patrol the airport's un-fenced perimeter fence lines and ensure no farm, or other stray animals (or people) wandered onto the runways, an occurrence which did often happen and interfered with aircraft taking off and landing.

All operational plans were devised by the security team in tandem with the special operations cell and put to force when home or foreign dignitaries travelled to and from the airport. Amongst the famous VIPs who relied on CIVPOL officers like Davy for their securities were: US President Bill Clinton, UN Secretary General Kofi Annan, former Secretary of State Hillary Clinton and UN Goodwill Ambassador and actress Angelina Jolie.

After one year of hard work, dedication and commitment Davy was appointed as Deputy Airport Commander and became responsible for the supervision of 85 UNMIK police, 250 KPS and 30 LAs.

Finding himself in this position Davy was pivotal in helping UNMIK implement proper immigration legislation to Kosovo, liaising with organisations and institutions such as the (Department of Justice) DOJ, UNHCR, OSCE, SRSG and IOM. The fact that part of this legislation meant that Kosovo legally had to accept asylum seekers meant that Davy had to mentor the KPS in human rights issues and advise accordingly as there had been no previous experience in dealing with such situations.

KPS officers deployed from their initial recruits course to Davy's unit did not receive a very comprehensive Border and Boundary training package and, with the KPS transition date looming, it was Davy's responsibility to ensure further training was scheduled and carried out in a timely manner. The courses included: Airport Security, Passport Control, Immigration, Documentation Advisor, Airport Investigation Officers and Intelligence Gathering.

To make matters more complicated and difficult for Davy his newly-appointed KPS middle managers required more intense training on how to actually manage *their* officers. This training, again Davy's responsibility, involved roster management, firearms requalification, officer welfare and Human Rights.

Through sheer determination and his new managerial and organisational skills to meet deadlines, the airport was one of the flagship stations the UN managed to handover responsibility to the Kosovo Police ahead of schedule. The successful handover was actually used as encouragement to other stations to do likewise.

Davy summarised a number of other issues and events that took place during his busy term with UNMIK working at Pristina airport; and in his own words:

> 'The airport became a very lucrative place to work for the KPS as the organised crime offered some of them serious money to allow illegal activities to take place. This was very difficult to prove and even when we had officers removed from their post they were protected by their hierarchy and in fact sent to another border location to continue the "good work". The corruption at all levels of the Kosovo Border Police was substantial and ignored, unfortunately much to my frustration.
>
> I was promoted to Airport Commander which basically was the same role as the deputy, however, I was authorised to make all command decisions and implement my own changes. I also enjoyed a great relationship with the military helping with intelligence and security details for their many visitors and training exercises. Simply put any event happening in Kosovo inevitably involved the airport in some capacity.
>
> I remember sitting in a restaurant when I received a call from the

control tower to let me know that there had been an aircraft crash and then hung up on me. I immediately was thinking the worst when I tried to call them back to get more information but the phone was engaged. When I finally got someone they told me to head to the accident scene in one of the local villages and fortunately confirmed it was only a small military aircraft. When I arrived on scene it was unbelievable as senior KPS officers were already there taking pictures as souvenirs and there were lots of people walking through the crash site. I immediately set up cordons and removed non-essential personnel. There was fuel spillage everywhere and the fire service were sitting at the vehicle smoking. Fortunately the pilot and his passenger only sustained broken legs.

Another aircraft incident was when an aircraft overshot the runway by some 100 metres during blizzard conditions and again fortunately there were no injuries just shocked passengers. I was trained in emergency management by the Icelandic people who are the leading experts in aircraft incidents and therefore it was good to put my training into practice. I helped the local accident investigation team to complete their reports and the aircraft was later recovered, serviced and cleared to fly.

Another incident involved the dog unit and saw one of the dogs (trained to detect explosives) "indicate" on a passenger's bag, which was on the airport apron. On landing, the aircraft had to be redirected to other parts of the runway and at a safe distance from the suspect bag. The airport was subsequently closed whilst this incident was on-going and eventually the EOD team arrived and dealt with the situation. The end result was the explosive dog had reacted to dog shampoo which was in the passenger's bag. A big sigh of relief that day.

On another occasion I received a call from the control tower (Albanian staff) informing me there was a hijacking of the Swiss aircraft. I immediately declared a serious incident and was just about to inform MHQ when I happened to notice the aircraft was already parked on our apron and passengers were freely disembarking.

I asked for confirmation from the tower and again they reconfirmed there was a hijacking of the Swiss aircraft. One of the controllers told me he received a phone call from Switzerland regarding the highjack.

I then asked a Swiss colleague to call Zurich to find out what's happening. The reality was there was a Swiss passenger flying that day *on the return flight who claimed that he had been kidnapped whilst in Kosovo. He intended to fly back to Switzerland and then return immediately to Kosovo with the ransom money. Apparently the Swiss authorities had asked that he receive an unhindered passage to their aircraft. When I asked the airport operations centre why I was told a hijacking was taking place I was informed that there isn't a word in Albanian that translates kidnapping so the next best appropriate translation is hijacking.'* – Comedy gold, you couldn't make it up.

During the beginning of 2008 UNMIK was preparing to handover the mission to the EU. In the next few months there would be approximately sixty UNMIK police left in mission and most, including MDP, would join the EU Rule of Law Mission in Kosovo (EULEX).

At a time when most UNMIK police were probably thinking about heading back home, winding down or just biding their time until their move to EULEX, Davy Rodden was as busy (at Pristina airport) as ever and his diligence and intuition would assist an investigation into one criminal case which later made world headlines.

Davy became involved and perhaps had a big part in the discovery of an international organ-trafficking network based in Kosovo that sold kidneys and other organs from impoverished victims. The case was one of the biggest in the discovery of organ theft, trafficking of organs and illegal transplants in Kosovo.

On the case Davy said:

'I was heavily involved in the discovery of illegal organ trafficking that was instigated through the airport. The KPS had been sending intelligence (intel) reports through their chain of command for months but nothing was done. I then sent my own intel reports via the international channels. I decided that it was time I took decisive action even although the KPS were officially in charge. In order to intervene and take over the case, UNMIK sought permission from the office in New York.

I decided that the next potential patient who arrived in Kosovo to attend the suspect Medicus private clinic would be interviewed by myself. A young man arrived from Turkey for treatment at the clinic and when I interviewed him he was nervous and couldn't give a satisfactory reason regarding his visit or which type of medical care *he would be receiving from the clinic. He also seemed quite poor and therefore my instinct led me to believe that he couldn't afford **any** type of private medical care nor the expensive return flight to Turkey.*

A joint decision was made; he would be refused entry to Kosovo and immediately returned to Turkey. The airport "mafia" called their boss in Pristina and then a high ranking KPS officer from their Border HQ called to say, "Allow him to enter as there is a surveillance team outside who will watch his every move."

This decision seemed reasonable and I agreed not to interfere with their police operation. I did, however, insist that, before his return journey to Turkey the young man should be brought to me; I wanted to interview him again. When he returned he looked quite ill and it soon became clear he had attended the Medicus clinic He admitted he had donated a kidney and thought he would receive 15,000 Euros on his return to Istanbul. He was told to keep quiet and not to speak with anyone about the operation.

After further investigations it was discovered the KPS had tipped off the Turkish doctor who was carrying out illegal transplants at the Medicus clinic and he had fled Kosovo illegally before any search of the premises could be completed.

A patient was found in recovery at the Medicus when the hospital was raided and all the remaining doctors present were arrested and placed in detention. When this patient was transported to Pristina hospital they refused to treat him due to medical liability. This then unbelievably forced UNMIK to release these doctors and put the patient back in this clinic until they sought a proper solution. The young man who donated his kidney and the recipient could not be traced in order to give evidence in the trial.'

In June 2011 an article written by author and feature writer Ed Caesar, a contributor to *The New York Times*, was published in *The Sunday Times Magazine*.

This is an extract from the report which obviously makes reference to Davy Rodden:

'Long before Yilman Altun, a 23-year-old Turk, fainted in Pristina airport, the British policeman at passport control knew something

wasn't right. Throughout the summer of 2008, this policeman (in Kosovo as part of an international deployment) had noticed an influx of two distinct types of short-stay tourist, neither of whom seemed likely candidates for a mini-break in a rocky, recently war-torn Balkan state. One group consisted of young, healthy men and women from the poorest sections of Eastern Europe and Turkey; the other of rich, sick old men from Israel and North America. Altun fell into the first category, and the officer had "flagged" his name as suspicious on arrival.

It was only when Altun collapsed before his flight from Pristina to Istanbul, however, that the full horror of the young man's brief interlude in Kosovo became apparent. He was taken by passport officials into a private room where a medic examined him. Altun showed the doctor a fresh scar on his abdomen, still sutured and raw, and said his kidney had been "stolen" at the Medicus Clinic on the outskirts of the capital. Despite promises of around $20,000, Altun said he had yet to receive payment for the illegal operation. Within hours, police raided the clinic, where they found the 74-year-old Israeli recipient of Altun's kidney, Bezalel Shafran, still recovering. Shafran said he had paid $9,000 for the organ. In fact, it cost him almost 10 times that sum.

Altun's testimony started a fire. Not only was a local and inter-national criminal investigation launched, but the allegations also fed into a sensational human-rights report by the Swiss politician Dick Marty, directed at the centre of power in this troubled corner of the Balkans.'

Like me, copper Davy Rodden completed three UN missions in Kosovo. All Davy's mission experience was gained working at Pristina airport.

JOHN PEARSON
Mission Dates:
December 2001 – June 2003

Like me John wanted to apply for the first mission, however his wife had other ideas. 'Pat had refused to even consider it stating it was too dangerous, but listening to the stories I knew this is what I wanted to do.' During the next twelve months and after speaking with colleagues who were in mission, John's desire to work overseas grew stronger, but with reservations. 'The idea both appealed to and frightened me, but the challenge of not only working but also living in the community really excited me; plus I wanted to know if I could hack it outside the fence. To leave the security of a fenced-in base and give up my home comforts also terrified me.' During a visit home from working in Kosovo, an acquaintance, Angela Curry, met the Pearsons and after a long talk managed to convince John's wife Pat the danger was minimal. I don't know if I agree with that.

Although Pat did relent, John didn't make any final decisions until a few weeks later. At work, and during a break from (Faslane south gate) being battered by the torrential rain (where have you heard that before!) John joined a few more coppers in the computer room and completed a Foreign & Commonwealth Office International Policing application. A few long working months later, enduring the Scottish weather, John was on his way to Kosovo.

I was surprised to hear John had taken up a position with the Regional Protection Unit (RPU) and was in training to become a bodyguard. His previous experience of being a bodyguard was when he wore waterproof clothing to protect his own body against the rain falling at Faslane's south gate.

The RPU and its maverick CIVPOL didn't impress John or its mandatory assessment course. The RPU shooting assessment was held in a busy public park. When John arrived at the park he, and a number of other potential body-guards, were taken to a square, caged area where faded and broken markings on the ground suggested it may once have been a tennis court. Various shooting practices were carried out in front of an audience of passing local families and their children. Those being assessed were given instructions and commands by instructors from the RPU.

I'm reluctant to use the title 'firearms instructors'. In all my years as an armed UK police officer, I never heard the command, 'Make that gun hot'. Apparently, at least one RPU American instructor used that term as an alternative to saying the more acceptable and recognisable command 'Make ready'. Make ready informs the firearms officer under training or test conditions to cock the weapon, making it ready for firing. John fired a number of rounds from a standing, kneeling and prone position all aimed at pre-positioned targets and successfully completed the firearms assessment.

The weather had changed pretty dramatically since the new rotations arrival and Pristina was now a complete white out. Snow had been falling constantly for a few days with temperatures dropping as low as –18° Celsius. The weather was so cold John wore his thermals, including socks and hat, to bed. He even climbed into a sleeping bag before negotiating the freezing cold bed. His thermal clothing made no difference; he still shivered through the night. Being located on top of a hill and more exposed to the freezing elements, the house John had rented at the top of Dragodan just didn't get warm enough; and the daily power cuts only added to the bitterness of the sub-zero conditions.

In the dark mornings John would rise from bed, already half-dressed and prepare for the mini trek down Dragodan hill. The RPU compound was just outside Pristina and John waited for his transport, in the freezing cold, at the bottom of the hill. At that time of year the RPU was very quiet, most of the people under the protection of the unit (Principles) were on holiday and out of Kosovo.

Although John had passed the shooting assessment he hadn't completed the RPU course which took place after the holiday period. That issue restricted, or rather stopped him doing any sort of close protection work. Usually after an hour in work watching colleagues play shoot 'em up games or waiting in vain to check his e-mails, John would be told 'just go'. The first time he was told to go, he thought 'go where?' He would ask to be dropped off in Pristina then spent time alone walking around the city and stopping off at the Kukri, drinking coffee, until he thought it was a reasonable time to climb up Dragodan hill.

The last time John made an appearance in the RPU compound was less than a month after arriving in mission. He *had* been feeling pretty down from the start and was missing his family. He didn't have a lot in common with most of the CIVPOL officers he worked with and was fed up doing nothing every day; John needed a change.

John applied for a patrol position at Station Four and a short while later he was working alongside Pat Kearney. John said, 'What a difference the change of job made; the minute I started on patrol I knew this was what I wanted to do. I had an area to patrol and we drove round responding to calls on the radio and dealing with anything that came up.' John was now dealing with burglaries,

268

road traffic accidents and, on occasions when the power was off, traffic control at busy junctions. Motorists in Kosovo don't used common sense when it comes to road traffic safety. When the traffic lights are out, it's every man for himself. The downside to the patrol job, and unlike the RPU, John was working shifts, however he loved it.

After two or three weeks John became a Primary Field Training Officer (PFTO) which saw him supported by a language assistant, involved in being a role model to three new KPS recruits, fresh from the KPS training school. He was also responsible for their training and evaluation and completed monthly reports. Ultimately, the PFTO was responsible for making sure KPS duties were performed properly in compliance with human rights.

After a few months John was approached by a CIVPOL colleague who asked if he would be interested in a move to join the PFTO team in Station One. John considered the move and eventually redeployed to Station One. Such was John's commitment and dedication he was offered a position as Team Leader. He accepted that offer and was then responsible for the administration and operational tasks of a small team of CIVPOL and language assistants.

During regular visits to his team, on the ground, John experienced a number of situations where his officers were putting themselves in danger during routine vehicle stop and check.

John organised training for *all* his officers where he explained and demonstrated a vehicle stop and how to approach the vehicle in a manner that promoted officer safety, the motorist's safety and the safety of all other road users. He also explained the role of the contact and cover officer, who is basically the contact officer's back-up and responsible for radio communication and note taking.

During an afternoon shift and after an explosion in the power plant Kosovo B, in Obilic, John received a radio message saying that thirty people were injured. He again proved his commitment when he volunteered to work through the night to assist with the evacuation and search for missing power plant employees. It was reported that several small explosions were caused by a lightning bolt.

Like many other MDP constables, John's commitment saw him achieve the role of Station Commander when he took up the position at Station One.

Pat Pearson joined her husband in Kosovo and after a few months, she became bar manager of the Kukri. Pat also became the chef on a Sunday when she served up Sunday roast dinners. She also took over the karaoke during the weekends. John's only UNMIK deployment lasted eighteen months.

CHRISTIAN LINETTY
Mission Dates:
December 2001 – December 2002
July 2005 – July 2006

I mentioned Christian earlier when he and his team of Regional Protection officers were attacked by a crowd in North Mitrovica. This is what Christian had to say regarding his time in mission.

'I joined the Regional Protection Unit (later to become the Close Protection Unit (CPU) directly from the UN PTC and was trained to use long-barrelled firearms. This training was necessary due to high risk operations.

It took me two months to become the RPU Team Leader and I was responsible for 13 bodyguards from a variety of nations including the RUC from Northern Ireland, Russia, Italy, Canada, USA, France, Germany and Jordan.

The rewards of carrying out the role of RPU Team Leader gave me my first ever ambitions in relation to promotion at home within the MDP. Upon returning to the UK I registered for the promotion process and passed every stage at the first attempt even going back to the UK, during my second mission, to attend the assessment centre and ultimately my final HQ structured interview.

It was an MDP Inspector, Paul Jordan, who supported me when I told him at the start of my second mission that I wanted to interview for a command post to challenge myself and hopefully get the necessary experience to become a 'good' supervisor and not one of the many bluffers you and I have worked for over the years.

As a result of Paul's support I achieved, through a structured interview and exercise assessment board, the Chief of Operations to the Specialised Police Units position, which I absolutely loved for over a year. I was responsible to a great Norwegian Supt, Lars Finstad and was in Command of 300 operators from all the specialised roles including the Specialised Policing Group (Team 6, Witness Protection Unit, Prisoner Escort, SPU coordinators office, PASU – Police Aviation Support Unit, K9 and Close Protection Unit).

And to your final question, did mission life change my attitude? I had been a copper for 13 years, had no MDP ambitions and was totally happy with my role and input, but those first two missions within Kosovo (and one since in Afghanistan 2008) changed my outlook completely. For me, being a supervisor means that I am predominantly a facilitator for my officers. I believe that I, and all other supervisors, should be first concerned for the welfare of team members and be slightly less concerned with results and trivia. From general feedback and what else I can gather, I believe that this approach has acquired me a healthy degree of respect, for which I am very grateful to the UN for... so 'YES' ... I think the UN Kosovo experience changed my outlook!'

ALASDAIR STEWART
Mission Dates:
December 2001 – June 2003

Out of all the positions held, including command positions, Alasdair (AJ) Stewart must surely have had the most exhilarating: Chief of the Police Air Support Unit (PASU).

Before becoming chief of PASU, AJ was a UN police observer, flying in a Bell 212 helicopter. Day-to-day work was meetings with UN Air Ops, Air Safety and Police Special Ops. Most flights were over Kosovo's cities carrying out reconnaissance, videoing and photographing demonstrations.

The unit also carried out surveillance of suspect properties, located in mountainous regions, reportedly to be safe houses for illegal paramilitary groups. Those surveillance operations allowed the PASU to then direct ground forces to targets.

The helicopter pilots were mainly British but all employed by Bristow Helicopters. AJ said:

> *'It was great job for an MDP RIB coxswain!!! Dunno how that came about. Scariest part was the helicopter rotor blade getting hit by lightning flying over Vushtrri. Not happy when even the pilot nearly wet himself!'*

ALLAN BARR
Mission Dates:
December 2002 - December 2003

I of course know Allan Barr from working at Coulport where he famously scaled a metal frame while being filmed by a pan, tilt and zoom camera. He was another copper who, in 1997, escaped Coulport and transferred to US Navy London, where he worked for three years before transferring again, on that occasion to Whitehall where he patrolled the Government Security Zone.

I would describe *wee Barrsy* as fragile but tough. I remember two occasions at Coulport when he fainted after jamming a finger in a metal gate and then sometime later crashed one of the police trail (motorcycle) bikes into the razor wire on the outside of Coulport's perimeter fence.

The tougher side to Allan was tested when he volunteered for his only UNMIK mission in December 2002. After just six months in mission and two months with the Pristina Regional Support Unit, Allan applied for the position, *Chief of Pristina Regional Support Unit.*

> 'When I went for the interview I was aware that the UN basically wanted a KPS specialist firearms unit, or SWAT team, ready and deployable as soon as possible. Some of the other applicants made assertions that they could manage this in 6 months. I told them 3 years.'

Allan's plan was based on UK police training standards and to train the KPS to the standard required as a Specialist Firearms Officer (SFO) its officers would have to do the same training as a UK police officer.

Allan's Plan, which he knew wouldn't be complete before his end of mission, was divided into three stages:

Stage one: Train the KPS to the standard of an Authorised Firearms Officer (AFO). This was achieved in three months and training included more time spent on the shooting range and on the firearm safety drills.

Stage two: Armed Response Vehicle (ARV) training. ARV training included driving techniques, hard stops, vehicle techniques and most importantly, MP5 (9mm submachine gun) training.

Stage three: The final stage of training was the SFO stage, which involved rope access techniques, helicopter deployments and amongst other specialist training sniper techniques.

When Allan finished outlining his plan he asked the interview board to consider a worrying point. He wished no offence to the other applicants but feared if only six months training was considered, KPS officers would be killed.

'The boys were willing but they weren't ready. It takes time to learn and practice the skills that management wanted and they had to be told that. As the guys reached certain standards they took over the role from the UN police specialist units.'

After his interview and outlining his much longer implementation plan and fears, Allan must have impressed and convinced his interview board. He was selected and appointed as the Chief of Pristina Regional Support Unit. His plan was up and running.

The support unit was kept busy and, between training and planned operations, was gaining valuable experience. In November 2003 it carried out simultaneous raids on three locations and apprehended a number of suspects wanted in relation to a multiple homicide. That was the first time the unit had used hard entry tactics to enter buildings. A TV crew followed the unit and filmed the operation for a local TV series, similar to the BBC's *Crimewatch*.

Unfortunately, and due to family reasons, Allan was to end his mission earlier than expected. The Support Unit was in stage two of training when Allan left for the UK. Eventually all its officers successfully completed all stages of training.

On writing the book Allan told me, 'The KPS now has fully trained SWAT and close protection officers. I still chat with some of the guys and a lot of them are now in command positions in these high risk units.'

The laid back DAVIE MCLEAN
Mission Dates:
June 2004 – June 2006
June 2007 – November 2008

'How do I introduce myself into a book that is a part of history and from being a boy growing up on the violent streets of Greenock (Scotland) to being a police constable who became a police commander, on two separate occasions, in a volatile country like Kosovo?

Growing up in Greenock and from an early age I learned how to move about the town and avoid getting involved in the violence that occurred on a regular basis. It wasn't until I arrived in Kosovo that I realised my upbringing would have such an impact on how I looked after myself and ultimately used my police training to effect in Kosovo.

I left school in 1979 and went straight into the Army as a boy soldier eventually joining the Royal Scots Dragoon Guards where I remained until 1990 and thereafter joined the Ministry of Defence Police in September 1991. After I completed my initial police training I was posted to RNAD Coulport, where I met John.

Having a young family to look after I did not apply to join the UN mission in Kosovo until 2004 when I sat down and completed, then submitted, an application form and CV. I deployed to Kosovo in June 2004 and on my arrival I could only describe Kosovo as like Berlin in World War Two.

My contingent was met by the Contingent Commander, Jim Chapman, who, after directing us to our temporary accommodation, instructed us to meet him the following morning at the UN training centre.

The contingent had to undertake an English test and I thought, "How crazy is this, me an English, oops Scottish speaker, how difficult could this be." As we all sat down in the class a Romanian officer came in and explained what the test was about. He would play a tape and we had to listen and then answer a few questions, how difficult could this be for us English-speaking nationals?

Well, when the tape started it was someone with an Asian accent speaking English and explaining a crime scene; you could have heard a pin drop in the room. For something that seemed straightforward was now a massive hurdle. Every one of us struggled to understand the poor English dialogue.

Needless to say most of us passed but I don't think it was a 100 per cent for the Scottish contingent. At the end of the induction course I was initially deployed to a region called Prizren, however, I was asked by a colleague to swap regions, from Prizren to Peja, as a number of his close colleagues, who worked with him at the same MOD establishments back home had been deployed to Prizren.

Regions made no difference to me; I was deployed to Peja Region which turned out to be a good choice. I was posted to Peja police station where I worked as a CIVPOL patrol officer. After several weeks of patrolling, I felt confident enough to apply for the position of Chief of Station Operations. During an interview I was asked how to create and implement an Operational Plan and luckily enough I had sufficient experience to answer this question which seemed to satisfy the interview board.

After a few days wait, I was selected for the post and became Chief of Operations for Peja police station. I worked alongside two KPS officers and one CIVPOL officer who was my deputy. During my first few days as Chief of Ops I sat down with my staff and asked what the main policing problem in the town is?

The KPS mentioned several issues that needed immediate attention and previous plans had not been successful, the CIVPOL officer agreed. After a lengthy discussion and offering advice, I gave the officers one week to draw up new plans and told them to bring the plans to my office when they were complete. The following week the KPS came back with new initiatives, however, to my disappointment the CIVPOL officer had nothing new to offer which didn't seem to bother him. The CIVPOL officer's poor attitude to his position was quite unacceptable and after one month of showing no improvement in his performance I recommended his redeployed from the operations department; the CIVPOL Station Commander agreed and he was redeployed as a patrol officer.

Within a matter of weeks three Ops plans had been implemented locally and success was achieved in controlling an on-going problem with traffic regulations, the prevention of street prostitution and assistance to KEK employees who were being threatened by local residents, as they turned off power supplies of electricity bill non-payers.

After just three months in mission I was asked to apply for a position as Peja Deputy Chief of Regional Operation which I happily accepted. I was now responsible for five districts in the Peja Region.

My first major Ops plan involved former Prime Minister of Kosovo Ramush Haradinaj who was to be extradited to the International Criminal Court in The Hague. I suggested drawing up an Ops plan that could assist Mr. Haradinaj and would not draw too much attention from the citizens of Kosovo as he was transported to Pristina airport. I advised Peja Regional Commander that we should speak to Ramush and his family, who are hardliners from the town of Decani which was an Albanian stronghold during the Kosovo conflict.

The Regional Commander and I approached the Haradinaj family *in Decani and talked with them. I came up with the idea of having a UN vehicle escort Ramush (in his vehicle) to Pristina airport in a very low profile approach; he agreed. My next hurdle was getting the UN Police Commissioner to agree. Initially the Commissioner wanted an escort of UN vehicles and KFOR, however, I said that would be overkill and may create problems rather than solve them. The Commissioner signed off on my Ops plan and was a bit skeptical that it would go without incident. Using the minimum amount of UN vehicles (and no KFOR) in a low profile escort worked perfectly and did not bring much attention from the citizens of Kosovo. Ramush arrived safely at the airport and was met by a number of well wishers who were waiting in a specially adapted area that I had organised with airport staff. The family was pleased with my planning and I got a pat on the back for good initiative.*

During 2005 my good work was recognised again when I was appointed Regional Police Commander of Peja Region (population around 170,000) and to put the position into perspective, I, a MOD police constable became responsible for approximately 300 International Police Officers, 1,200 KPS and over 200 local staff. I felt very proud of my achievement and would continue to thrive, assist and develop the KPS as it faced transition.

Even though I spent a lot of my time in my office and attending meetings, the conscientious police officer in me was never far away. One afternoon when I was out fuelling up my 4Runner a message was relayed over my police radio of an armed robbery which had just occurred at a nearby warehouse and KPS officers were in pursuit of three armed suspects who escaped the scene in a vehicle and were heading out of the city.

As I was only a few minutes away from the warehouse I transmitted a message that I would assist the KPS in the pursuit and asked for back up from the KPS Operational Support Unit. I also asked for checkpoints, roadblocks and outer cordons to be set up on the main highways out of the city.

Over the radio I heard messages of hand grenades being thrown at the pursuing KPS vehicle from the suspect's vehicle and shots being fired from an AK47.

I knew the area well and soon I was directly behind the pursuing

KPS vehicle. I could see the suspect's vehicle well ahead of the KPS and suddenly it stopped with all three suspects getting out and running off into an area of rough terrain. My Deputy, Big Mike Shanks, was now driving behind me and I could hear him on the radio shouting for me to slow down and not to get too close to the escaping suspects.

I stopped my vehicle when I reached the rough terrain and gave chase on foot, along with the KPS, Mike wasn't far behind us. As I ran, I contacted the police control room and gave the operator my location and instructed him to have the KPS support unit surround the area, but keep a fair distance. I was now within 300 yards of the three suspects and gaining ground. I was very aware my service pistol (Sig Sauer) was no match for an AK47; however, the suspect's intention was to keep on running in an attempt to escape.

I was now only 30 yards away from one suspect and drew my service pistol. I shouted "Stop armed police!" only to see a frantic suspect turn and take aim at me with a pistol. As he did I fired two shots, only to see the suspect lose his balance and fall, uninjured, to the ground. That gave me the chance to catch up and basically fall on top of him and disarm him. With my full weight on top of him I managed to put handcuffs on him and hand him over to Mike Shanks who had caught up with me.

I continued my pursuit of the next suspect; however, a KPS lieutenant on a pedal cycle was also giving chase. The Lieutenant managed to dive from his cycle and pull the suspect to the ground. Eventually KPS officers from the support unit arrived, however, by this time I had the situation under control. The third suspect was arrested later at a police check point. All in all three effective and successful arrests.

Later, investigations revealed the suspects were from a well known family Kurrbogi and I knew a KPS lieutenant with the same name worked with the KPS Operational Support Unit who, after arriving rather late on the scene, assisted me. I asked my CIVPOL operations officer to confirm who the support unit supervisor was on the day in question and could he supply me with his full report?

It came to light that Lieutenant Kurrbogi's unit was initially involved in the pursuit of the suspects, however, the KPS officers, who grew up in the area, got lost.

I still don't know if that KPS lieutenant was involved in the robbery *by providing an escape route for the suspects but whatever the plan was, the robbers did not count on the UN police and KPS being so well organised and determined.*

I was told that I would be given a reward for my courageous actions and when I was told I would be the only officer to be commended, I declined to accept any recognition for my actions. When I ended my mission and returned to the UK I received the MDP's Chief Constable's commendation for my actions that day, which I gave to my mum. I believe that without my other UN and KPS team members a successful apprehension of those suspects would not have happened.'

MITROVICA 2007

As you already know Davie returned to Kosovo in 2007 and became Regional Commander in the Mitrovica Region. Here is one story of how Davie created and implemented an operational plan which helped to de-escalate those violent outbursts during the 1244 March demonstrations in 2008.

'I spoke with the Police Commissioner and told him about an idea I had to stop or curtail the violent outbursts and persistent launching of dangerous projectiles during the 1244 demonstrations held at the main bridge. I worked all night on my plan and hoped it could be approved and implemented for the following day's demonstration. It was simple, yet I thought it could be a very effective plan.

I removed all CIVPOL and FPUs from the front line at the main bridge and sited them in a safer area, close to, but out of sight of, the bridge and still able to quickly respond if required. The UNMIK unit would be replaced by Serbian KPS who were, and let's be honest, supporters of the Serbian demonstrators. That ploy I hoped would stop the demonstrators from causing any more violence. Although it was a bit of a gamble I knew the demonstrators did not have a reason to attack their own people. When my plan was reviewed it was met with mixed opinions, however, only one opinion mattered to me, the Police Commissioners.

The plan was approved early the following morning and implemented immediately. Intelligence was passed on to the Bridge Watchers regarding the plan and that day's demonstration passed without incident. The plan stayed in position until the now peaceful demonstrations diminished. I can remember being approached by a few high ranking officers who thought my idea was a master plan. I was very chuffed indeed.'

* * * * *

I recently contacted my former Regional Crime colleague Jan Ravnholt and asked him, now that we were no longer in mission, did he have any thoughts or opinions on my position with the Mitrovica Regional Crime Unit in comparison to my position and rank with the MDP constable? Jan sent me this reply in an e-mail.

'Hi John

I had the pleasure of working together with your colleague David Mitchell for approximately three months before he had end-of-mission and I took over his job. From him I knew all about what kind of work you were doing at home; so your experience and qualifications in doing real police work were not completely unknown to me.

From my previous missions, I was fully aware of how the UN system works and how to achieve a position, but for me it has never been important to get a high position. It made no difference in salary or status; most of the time just more stress and trouble. I had enough of that already at my work at home so I had no intention of striving for that. If I had been able to read it on my paycheck, it would have been a completely different matter.

I never applied for the position you got in RIU, because the most important thing for me has always been just to be in a position where I, hopefully, could make use of my skills and work together with good people, both local and international. So I'm perhaps not the right person to ask about you being appointed instead of me.

Fortunately, I have been lucky working with nice people most of the times, but over time I have come across a few stupid people, who were given a position without any knowledge at all about management and who tried to compensate for their lack of qualifications by pulling rank and intimidating the staff in their unit. For me that kind of person is like a red rag to a bull.

To my pleasant surprise, you were not such a person. On the contrary, you were very easy to work with and as a whole a pleasant person to be with.

I vaguely remember one or two episodes where we did not quite agree on some things, but we had a good discussion about it and then no hard feelings afterwards – at least not on my part.

You will always be able to find things that might have been done in a different way, but in general you did a good job and especially your monitor reports were good, you're absolutely right in that.

Talking about monitor reports I do not believe they made a big difference to our counterpart. I believe the purpose was to document that we were doing something.

Take care my friend and stay in touch.'

I also asked a few of those colleagues if their rank as an MDP police constable was ever brought up or questioned when they achieved a senior position. I also asked if any of their 'subordinates' refused an order or if they were mistreated to any degree.

Davy Rodden said, 'No, but I had rank tell me they wouldn't do certain tasks as it was beneath them.'

Allan Barr: 'Only once did an officer object to my instruction. It only got as far as, "I am a captain in the Nigerian National Police". He still ended up doing traffic control at the intersection next to the University.'

Christian Linetty: 'My UK rank never came up in conversation with any of my UN colleagues and to be honest I deliberately never brought it up personally. This was not through ego; it was because once I became a supervisor I knew that my job could be considerably more difficult if it was openly known that I was merely a PC within the UK. This was in no way disrespectful to the "constable" rank; it was just that I had to consider team member perceptions when supervising two senior German ranks and one senior Italian rank within my team, not to mention, for a while, the Danish Contingent Commander who soon left the CPU for a more rank-fitting pasture.'

Pat Kearney: 'I remember my confidence took a little knock when an RUC (PSNI) Superintendent approached me at our end of mission party in the Kukri. John, do you recall we all wore white T shirts and people were writing good will messages etc on them? Well that Superintendent wrote on mine "Big Bluffer". I think it was an overall reference to me/us being MDP and therefore "not real cops" anyhow I soon forgot it and him.'

Well, if that Superintendent's remark was aimed at the MDP and/or its staff, here

is a list of several supervisory positions held (in Kosovo) by MDP constables, the
so called big bluffers:

Director of Personnel and Administration
Regional Commander
Regional Commander Liaison Officer
Deputy Regional Commander
Regional Operations Liaison Officer
Deputy Regional Commander Investigations Monitor
Chief of Operations
Deputy Chief of Operations
Chief of Operations Pristina Regional Traffic Unit
Regional Investigations Liaison Officer
Regional General Crime Investigations Liaison Officer
Deputy Chief of Investigations
Station Commander, Border and Boundary Police
Deputy Station Commander, Border and Boundary Police
Station Commander
Deputy Station Commander
Chief of Station Operations
KPS Station Commander Liaison Officer
KPS Operations Liaison Officer
Traffic Unit Liaison Officer
Chief of Special Support Unit
RMBS supervisor
Chief of Communications
Deputy Chief of Communications
Deputy Chief of Warrants
Chief of Police Air Support
Team Leader
Deputy Team Leader

I'm sure just about every supervisory position in a regional command chart,
from a Deputy Team Leader up to a Regional Commander, was held by a MDP
constable. Fantastic achievements for all concerned.

Looking Back

THESE LAST FEW words are my opinions and observations and have no bearing on any other person mentioned in this book. I just wanted to add a few more comments and give you a little bit more to talk and think about.

My life, and many others, has changed considerably since volunteering for that first UN mission in Kosovo. The whole experience of working in a foreign post-war territory really got a firm grip on me and I couldn't let go of Kosovo. Nearly fourteen years after my first mission in Pristina and after retiring from the Ministry of Defence Police in 2012, I now find myself living in Kosovo, in the small town of Zvecan, with my wife Vesela.

During and after being seconded to the UN mission in Kosovo several MDP police constables resigned from the force after securing contractual positions with the UN and other worldwide organisations. Other MDP constables pursued more UN seconded missions in Kosovo and thereafter in other parts of the world; and along the way took time out to successfully complete that MDP constable to sergeant promotion exam. I think one or two may now be police inspectors.

The whole experience of being, temporarily, part of UNMIK with its very disputable and controversial non-ranking policy is, in my opinion, a major talking point and certainly opened my eyes to that 'odd' system. Of all my supervisory positions 'brought about' by my three UNMIK secondments I was only ever formally interviewed for one: Deputy Regional Commander Investigations Monitor.

Without being interviewed, I became Deputy Chief of Communications because someone liked me. And although I was never tested on my suitability to become a CIVPOL monitor, I became supervisor to over eighty CIVPOL monitors because the Regional Commander ignored what was written in a UN operational (monitors) bulletin. And, of course, there was the mighty E-Force which I was, rightly or wrongly, talked into creating and leading, for a short time, before I was nudged off that precarious perch. And when I got bored with my next position I was offered and accepted a much better position, and became advisor to a KPS Lieutenant who was a Deputy Station Commander.

Looking at the UN system and 'my' particular circumstances; was it my fault higher ranked, more qualified, more experienced and more 'capable' police officers were overlooked (for managerial positions) in favour of me – John, the mod plod cop? Was it a case of the green-eyed monster strikes back? Was I just in the right place at the right (or wrong) time? Who knows?

Finally I'd just like to add one more point. The trend of MDP constables finding themselves in supervisory positions started during that first MDP (Kosovo) secondment in 2000 and continued until 2008 when UNMIK handed over the rule of law to the EU. I have no idea how many MDP PCs were fortunate enough to secure those senior positions, but I do know (and I include myself here) they would never have been trusted with so much responsibility had it not been for their training, professionalism, drive and determination, respect for race and diversity and also their leadership skills; qualities that were instilled in them through being a Ministry of Defence police officer.

John Duncanson